Teaching Essential Skills in the Early Classroom

Teaching and learning literacy in the early years can be a joyful, explorative and meaningful experience. This accessible book will give teachers and practitioners the practical and theoretical skills and knowledge they require to successfully and confidently teach reading, writing and oral skills in the early years classroom.

Foregrounding the ways in which literacy instruction can be made enjoyable and meaningful from the very beginning, *Teaching Essential Literacy Skills in the Early Years Classroom* explores the theory and practice of teaching various aspects of literacy and language, from phonological awareness, phonics and fluency, to vocabulary and comprehension. Chapters draw on the latest research to identify and showcase best practice in writing instruction, illustrate how language and literacy can be developed through play, and outline how a teacher might use the environment to enhance children's learning. Downloadable resources, examples of planning, classroom activities and vignettes can be quickly and easily adapted for use in any early years setting.

A rich and comprehensive source of information, ideas, activities and tips, this will be a key resource for pre- and in-service teachers and practitioners looking to adopt a cohesive, effective and meaningful approach to literacy teaching and learning.

Tara Concannon-Gibney is Assistant Professor of Literacy at Dublin City University, Ireland.

Teaching Essential Literacy Skills in the Early Years Classroom

A Guide for Students and Teachers

Tara Concannon-Gibney

Routledge
Taylor & Francis Group

LONDON AND NEW YORK

First published 2019
by Routledge
2 Park Square, Milton Park, Abingdon, Oxon OX14 4RN

and by Routledge
52 Vanderbilt Avenue, New York, NY 10017

Routledge is an imprint of the Taylor & Francis Group, an informa business

British Library Cataloguing in Publication Data
A catalogue record for this book is available from the British Library

Library of Congress Cataloging in Publication Data
A catalog record for this title has been requested

ISBN: 978-1-138-48104-6 (hbk)
ISBN: 978-1-138-48105-3 (pbk)
ISBN: 978-1-351-06119-3 (ebk)

Typeset in Melior
by Swales & Willis Ltd, Exeter, Devon, UK

Visit the eResources: www.routledge.com/9781138481053

To my husband Anthony and my sons James and John

Contents

Acknowledgements

Photographs (front cover and inside the text) are courtesy of Dave Conlon, Easton Road Photography.

These images were funded by a Dublin City University Book Publication grant.

Special thanks to James, Jack, Aoibheann, Aoife, Fintan, John, Mya, Ruby and Lucy for granting permission to use their images in this book.

Figures

Tables

Abbreviations

CALP	cognitive academic language proficiency
CVC	consonant/vowel/consonant (a three letter word such as 'cat')
ELL	English language learner
IRA	International Reading Association (now International Literacy Association)
IWB	interactive whiteboard
LEA	Language Experience Approach
NQT	newly qualified teacher
NRP	National Reading Panel
TPR	total physical response
UKLA	United Kingdom Literacy Association
ZPD	zone of proximal development

Preface

This book is based on my own classroom experiences and my attempts to teach literacy in meaningful and joyful ways. I worked in a very diverse school where the population spoke almost 50 different languages. Initially, I felt overwhelmed by the task of teaching these young children to read and write, but I found that by focusing on meaningful contexts, the children thrived. I wrote this book to share my experiences with other teachers who may have found themselves disillusioned or confused by the demands of literacy instruction, much like I did in the first vignette in Chapter 1. Becoming literate should be a delight for every young child, and teaching literacy should be an enjoyable experience for the teacher.

Literacy learning in meaningful contexts

GUIDING QUESTION FOR THIS CHAPTER

- What meaningful contexts can I use for literacy instruction in my classroom?

Introduction

Learning to read and write are key milestones for young children living in a literate society. It is widely recognised that a strong foundation in early literacy is critical for academic success as it allows a child to access the curriculum to their full potential. Literate adults benefit from a higher quality of life, financial security, positive self-image, and an ability to access knowledge and function in the workplace (Bialystok, 2001). It is crucial, then, that children develop a positive attitude towards literacy learning from the earliest stages. Teachers working in the early years classroom need to make literacy learning engaging, enjoyable and – most importantly – meaningful. Effective teaching in the early years should include the explicit teaching of early literacy skills, with frequent and extensive opportunities to apply this knowledge in meaningful contexts (Lewis & Ellis, 2006; UKLA, 2005). Ellis (2005) has also stressed meaning as a key element in learning an additional language. When English language learners (ELLs) encounter new language in context, they can access a range of contextual elements that support understanding (Lantolf & Becket, 2009). In this book, we will explore this notion of 'meaningful' literacy teaching in a variety of contexts. The next 10 chapters will explore the range of skills and strategies required by the emergent reader and writer, outlining instructional approaches that will engage and inspire young learners to become joyfully literate. This chapter introduces the meaningful contexts for literacy instruction that will be explored throughout this text.

Meaningful contexts for reading instruction

WHEN MEANING IS MISSING . . .

Tara, a newly qualified teacher (NQT), has been teaching a diverse class of 5- and 6-year-old pupils in a large suburban school for a few years. The curriculum and teaching approaches are quite rigidly controlled by the principal, and teachers in the junior classes are expected to teach long lists of sight words to the children to enable them to read three class readers by the end of the academic year. There are no other reading materials available. A phonics test and a sight word test are due to be administered by the principal at the end of each term, and students are expected to perform well. As a result, Tara spends a great deal of time drilling the children on the sight words and their letter sounds. Tara feels uncomfortable spending so much time drilling the children, sensing their lack of engagement, but as an NQT she lacks the confidence to explore alternative approaches. Then one day, towards the end of the second term, a stack of levelled readers is delivered to her classroom. Excited, she takes one of the easiest texts from the pile and sits with one of her pupils (named Daniel) who has achieved high marks in all reading tests so far this year. 'Let's read!' she says to Daniel. Daniel looks at the book and then says mournfully, 'What? but I can't read, teacher.' Tara stares at him (thinking of the hours spent drilling words and letter sounds, and his high scores on all the tests). 'Of course you can!' she says. 'No, I can't, teacher,' he says, and places his head on the desk. That is the day that Tara realises she needs to change the way she teaches literacy, so that the children in her class 'see' themselves as readers and writers.

The classroom vignette above outlines the central theme of this book: that literacy skills thrive when they are presented within meaningful contexts, and may wither when meaningful contexts are absent from instruction. Without meaning, children may fail to understand the 'point' of literacy instruction and may disengage at an early age. Therefore, children need to be introduced to the ultimate goal of reading – the generation of meaning – from the very beginning. It is important that from the first day at school, the child is encouraged to see books and reading materials as exciting, pleasurable and interesting. The early years classroom should be organised in a way that facilitates interaction between children and books, and develops their curiosity about print. The main contexts for teaching emergent reading skills include the creation of a print-rich classroom environment, regular shared reading of large-format books and poetry charts, the use of language experience charts, and frequent teacher read-alouds using high-quality children's literature.

A print-rich environment

Creating a print-rich environment involves more than a simple labelling of objects in the classroom. The regular use of job charts, weather charts and posters, for example, in which words, phrases or even sentences change very regularly, will help to focus children's attention on the written word, and they can be encouraged to respond appropriately. Environmental print borrowed from 'real life' can also be explored, as the addition of directories, newspapers, magazines, flyers and cookbooks to a play corner can encourage children to engage in play activities that resemble real reading activities.

An important element of the print-rich environment is the regular display of children's mark-making and writing, whether on the classroom walls or as items in the classroom library. As such, it can become part of children's reading material, and provide reading stimulation for the emergent reader and encouragement for the budding writer.

Figure 1.1 The reading corner

An attractive classroom library or reading corner is also essential in inspiring young children to read for pleasure from an early age (see Figure 1.1). The reading corner should be comfortable, with cushions, blankets and beanbags. The addition of a canopy held aloft by shelving can be very inviting. The books should be carefully organised according to theme, author and/or readability level. Children should be encouraged to read to each other and share book recommendations with classmates. While many children will simply 'read' the pictures, they should be encouraged to develop their own storylines or to spot words or letters that they know in the text. This practice will enhance their book-handling skills and their interest in learning to read.

Shared reading of large-format books

Don Holdaway (1979) was one of the first to promote shared reading back in the late 1970s. It is a social, enjoyable activity where children can acquire reading-like behaviours and develop essential reading skills (Strickland & Morrow, 2000). These reading skills include the 'five pillars' of reading instruction outlined by the National Reading Panel (NRP) – phonemic awareness, phonics, fluency, vocabulary and comprehension (NRP, 2000) – and also other important aspects of reading development such as developing concepts about print (Snow, Burns & Griffin, 1998). A big book engages children's attention and imagination: it draws them into the reading process. It is during these shared moments that the teacher can focus children's attention on the text to help them learn specific concepts, skills and/or strategies. Because they are learning key elements of the reading process (e.g. concepts about print, phonemes) through involvement with a book, they are both engaged at the moment and can also revisit these lessons later when they visit the book on their own. The use of these meaningful contexts encourages children to see the usefulness of learning these skills, as well as engaging them in the lesson. This allows the teacher to move away from isolated skill-and-drill activities while still being confident that his or her students are learning critical early literacy skills. Shared reading is an excellent way to engage learners with texts, particularly learners from diverse backgrounds (Allen, 2002; Koskinen et al., 1999; Meier, 2003), as English language learners (ELLs) learn more when new concepts are context-embedded (Cummins, 2003). Large-format books provide an excellent forum for the development of early literacy skills in shared reading lessons if they are chosen wisely. A high-quality big book should have an interesting storyline that promotes discussion, a large, clear font that is easy for children to see, appealing illustrations and thoughtful vocabulary. Ideally, it should also present possibilities for integration across the curriculum.

WHAT DOES A 'SHARED READING' LESSON LOOK LIKE?

- Children gather on the reading rug.

- A large-format book is placed on an easel.

- The teacher reads the text and models fluent reading.

- Pupils are encouraged to interact with the text.

- The book is used to teach early literacy skills in context – it is not just a storybook!

- It happens every day as part of a literacy teaching block.

Shared reading of poetry/rhyme charts

While poems and rhymes are an excellent method of enhancing phonological awareness, they can also be used to teach many of the other early literacy skills explored in this book. Simple poems, rhymes and songs can be written on sturdy chart paper or projected onto an interactive whiteboard (IWB) and used for shared reading lessons. Throughout this book, references will be made to this teaching resource.

Shared reading of digital texts

Shared reading lessons can be conducted using an IWB in the classroom. There are a number of websites that provide free texts that could be used for this purpose. For example, www.storyjumper.com allows the teacher and/or children to create their own stories on an online platform that can be printed out and shared as a library resource. Another useful website is www.starfall.com as it contains a selection of simple texts in a range of genres. Lastly, www.childrensbooksforever.com contains a variety of texts that can be shared in PDF format.

Language Experience Approach (LEA)

The Language Experience Approach (LEA) is an approach to teaching reading whereby children work together to create a communal text based on a shared experience. It allows children to see that written texts are someone's thoughts written down (the reading/writing connection). The use of this type of text has many advantages, ranging from motivational factors (the children are very interested and engaged as they contributed to the creation of the text) to logistical factors (the text is very accessible as it includes the children's current oral vocabulary store). It also allows for a seamless integration of the language arts: reading, writing, speaking and listening.

There are some disadvantages related to language experience texts. First, parents might have issues with the frequent use of language experience texts in the place of 'real' texts, which is what they might expect their children to be reading at school. Children may experience difficulties transitioning from language experience texts to a structured reader, and a language experience text is limited to the

WHAT DOES A LANGUAGE EXPERIENCE LESSON LOOK LIKE?

- The theme of the language experience text should be based on a shared experience (e.g. a class trip, a visitor to the classroom or a school event). It is advisable to use photographs or images to help young children remember the experience (particularly for ELLs who might need visual aids to support learning new vocabulary).

- The teacher leads the children in a discussion of the experience to get ideas flowing, to generate vocabulary, to sequence ideas and to eventually form a consensus to be written down.

- The children dictate while the teacher writes the story. The teacher should 'think aloud' while writing, discussing punctuation, spelling and other conventions of print.

- The chart is read. Generally, the teacher will read the entire chart first. Then he or she will encourage echo reading (teacher demonstrates, children 'echo' his or her reading) line by line. Then the teacher leads choral reading (the class reads together). Finally, the teacher may choose small groups (two or three students) or individuals to read sections of the text.

- A language experience chart is generally used over the course of a few days or a week (depending on chart length/student ability). When children return to the chart on the second and subsequent days, they will be engaged in a series of follow-up activities based on the early literacy skills, such as phonological awareness, sight vocabulary, phonics, fluency or concepts about print, discussed in Chapters 2, 3, 4 and 6 of this book. While traditionally language experience charts were created on chart paper, digital language experience texts created on an IWB are now very popular. Language experience texts are also often used in a one-on-one situation with English language learners.

children's vocabulary and may impact upon their vocabulary development. It may also be difficult to keep track of children's progress. However, these disadvantages tend to arise from a very frequent use of language experience texts. It may be advisable to use a language experience text as your meaningful context once or twice a month, and also use big books, poetry charts, levelled texts and regular storybooks to teach early literacy skills.

Guided reading

Guided reading involves teaching a small group reading lesson where children read texts that are at their instructional level (levelled texts). The approach is designed to enable the teacher to teach a wide range of literacy skills in the context of texts that are appropriate for each reader (Fountas & Pinnell, 1996). Guided reading is discussed in depth in Chapter 7. It is recommended that early literacy skills taught in the three contexts above (big books, language experience texts and poetry charts) be reinforced during guided reading sessions in order to maximise learning. Indeed, Knox and Amador-Watson (2002) recommend a shared to guided reading format for this reason.

Teacher read-alouds

Reading books aloud can enhance many of the early literacy skills discussed in this book (Fox, 2008). Indeed, reading aloud with children is known to be 'the single most important activity for building the knowledge and skills they will eventually require for learning to read' (Anderson, Hiebert, Scott & Wilkinson, 1985, p. 23). Children who love having books read to them today are children who tomorrow are engaged in lessons with books and who eventually become lifelong readers. Teacher read-alouds also help to develop a bond between a teacher and his or her pupils through the shared delight and wonder that a great book can bring, a bond that can prove essential in effective teaching (Routman, 2002). Indeed, according to Mem Fox (2008):

> The fire of literacy is created by the emotional sparks between a child, a book, and the person reading. It isn't achieved by the book alone, nor by the child alone, nor by the adult who's reading aloud—it's the relationship winding between all three, bringing them together in easy harmony.
>
> (p. 3)

Reading a range of genres aloud can develop children's vocabulary as they can be encouraged to think and talk about the different concepts and scenarios introduced in books (Beck, McKeown & Kucan, 2002). Reading aloud can also enhance young children's listening comprehension skills (Morrow & Gambrell, 2002), particularly if the book is read more than once. Hearing stories read aloud helps children tune into the sounds and syntax of the English language, which is important for reading fluency, and particularly important for English language learners (Chomsky, 1972). It is also apparent that reading aloud to children can increase their ability to recognise words (Stahl, 2003). Numerous book recommendations will be made in many of the chapters of this book. An additional list of recommended read-aloud books can be found in Appendix A.

When considering how read-alouds might fit into your classroom schedule, Teale (2003) suggests that teachers consider:

- the amount of read-aloud time;

- the choice of text for read-aloud activities;

- the method of reading aloud; and

- the fit of the read-aloud in the curriculum.

The amount of time that you choose to devote to read-alouds in your classroom may be dependent on your context. Children from high-poverty backgrounds and ELL children may need more exposure to teacher read-alouds than pupils from affluent areas. The texts that you choose must be of high quality, with an engaging storyline and attractive illustrations. They must also be culturally relevant to your pupils (Alanis, 2007). Books that offer numerous opportunities for the teacher to model fluent, expressive reading are recommended. Different genres may lend themselves to different teaching emphases. For example, rhyming books and poetry books can help children develop phonological awareness, while alphabet books can develop letter knowledge and counting books can encourage an interest in mathematics. Non-fiction books can develop background knowledge and an understanding of concepts relating to different curricular areas.

Teale (2003) describes several methods that make read-alouds effective. Reading the text in a lively, expressive manner, as well as using tone of voice and gesture, can help all children understand the story. Choose vocabulary words from the text to discuss with children in context or by using a child-friendly definition (Beck et al., 2002). A range of comprehension strategies can be taught using read-alouds. For example, children can be taught to predict what might happen throughout the story, to ask questions of the text, to draw inferences or to make connections between their own lives and the characters in the book. Read-alouds should be interactive in nature, with the children taking and thinking about the book before, during and after the teacher reads the story. Picture books are multimodal in nature as choices have been made by the author in terms of the choice of paper, size of the page, point of view, framing, arrangement, and the medium or media used (Sipe, 2001). Comprehension discussion can be enhanced by encouraging children to interrogate the book in a more critical manner (e.g. questioning the use of colour, line and shape to portray characters, events or emotions within the story). Lastly, the teacher should consider how well the text to be read aloud 'fits' within the curriculum. Reading books related to topics or themes under study can enhance children's learning and engagement across the curriculum.

The following reading skills and strategies can be taught in the meaningful contexts outlined above:

- phonological awareness;

- phonics;

- high-frequency words (sight words);

- concepts about print;

- vocabulary;

- fluency; and

- listening and reading comprehension.

These skills and strategies will be discussed in detail in the chapters that follow.

Meaningful contexts for writing instruction

Writing to enhance play

Writing should always be an enjoyable and meaningful experience for young children. Children should be encouraged to engage in mark-making as part of their play in the early years. Scribbles on a notepad may represent an 'order' taken by a waiter in a restaurant; later, as phonics skills develop, signs to indicate that the shop is 'clsd' (closed) can help develop play narratives. Birthday party invitations composed and delivered as part of 'playing house' sustain and expand the storyline. The need for writing in the real world is explored through 'signing in' when entering the doctor's surgery. Signs that indicate that the 'queue starts here' in the pretend 'bank' indicate the usefulness of environmental print. Research has demonstrated that the availability and encouragement to use literacy-related props and the existence of print-enriched environments during play enhance emergent literacy skills (Neuman & Roskos, 1990). Encouraging writing as part of play will be explored in more detail in Chapter 10.

Multisensory approach to handwriting and fine motor development

In order to progress from marks and scribbles (pre-communicative writing), children need a variety of supports. First, they need an adult who continuously models how to use writing for a wide variety of purposes across the school day. Young children also need lots of opportunities to develop their fine motor skills in meaningful and enjoyable ways so that they have the hand strength and dexterity to manipulate and control writing instruments as demands for writing increase. This includes both intrinsic motivation (children's desire to progress) and extrinsic motivation (relating to the demands of the curriculum). Children will also need to be taught letter formation in a multisensory manner, using tactile materials, kinaesthetic movements, songs and jingles. Handwriting is important as it is difficult for children to concentrate on their message and to share the meaning of their work if all of their energy is consumed with letter formation. Chapter 8 will outline how a teacher might incorporate a range of fine motor development activities in the classroom. It will also describe how to implement a multisensory approach to handwriting instruction.

The writers' workshop approach

Using writing skills for composition should begin as early as possible in a child's school career, so that children can see the potential inherent in letter formation exercises. The writers' workshop (Calkins, 1986; Graves, 1994) allows children to utilise their writing skills in a meaningful manner while developing both phonic and letter formation skills. The writers' workshop emphasises the need for children to take ownership of their work by choosing topics and exploring different genres that appeal to them. Writers' workshops are structured so as to enable the teacher to teach literacy skills in context throughout the lesson through modelling, scaffolding and celebrating children's efforts (in mini-lessons, conferences and share sessions). It is essential that children have the opportunity to engage in writing regularly (every day if possible) so that they can develop a writing 'rhythm'. While children generally work on texts individually, there is plenty of opportunities for children to talk about their writing within this lesson structure; indeed, the writers' workshop philosophy recognises the critical need to develop thought through language. Therefore, children discuss writing with the teacher and their peers throughout the lesson, learning from both the teacher and the other 'authors' in the room. The writers' workshop approach will be more thoroughly discussed in Chapter 9.

Play as a meaningful context for literacy development

Both Piaget (1962) and Vygotsky (1978) emphasised the cognitive connections between play and literacy. They drew attention to the transfer of symbolic transformations in play to similar cognitive activities in literacy (e.g. sound–symbol relationships in reading and writing). Thus, the ability to play in a symbolic manner – 'pretending' to be a doctor or 'pretending' that a coil of play dough is a snake – is highly significant in terms of the cognitive dexterity required for reading and writing. Therefore, it is beneficial for children to develop their ability to symbolise within play. This can be achieved through teacher modelling and scaffolding, and through the organisation of a 'play-rich' environment in which children have daily opportunities to interact with peers, playing in a variety of ways.

Play is an exceptional forum for the development of oral language skills as children are 'natural players' and are engaged and motivated to play. Careful planning, a cleverly organised environment and responsive teacher scaffolding can help children develop different language styles and registers, social conventions and complex vocabulary that is relevant and useful in play. Play requires communication, so listening to your peers and responding to requests appropriately are continuously practised. Play should be a cyclical process where children are encouraged to discuss their plans before playing, invest themselves deeply in play and then evaluate their play in a review session. Bookending play sessions in this manner encourages children to develop descriptive, elaborative and retelling skills. Children develop their oral language through talking about things that are meaningful, interesting and engaging for them. For an English language learner, it is crucial that they are afforded extended periods of 'language output' (Swain, 1996). As play encourages social interaction, it allows ELLs to develop confidence and motivation as they interact with other pupils. The contribution of play to literacy development will be discussed in detail in Chapter 10.

Key concepts for practice

- Literacy instruction should be embedded in meaningful contexts from the earliest possible juncture.

- Meaningful contexts for reading might include the creation of a print-rich environment, shared reading of large-format books and poetry charts, language experience charts, digital texts, guided reading and teacher read-alouds. All these approaches should be discussion-rich, enhancing oral language development.

- Meaningful contexts for writing might include writing during play, a writers' workshop, fine motor activities and a multisensory approach to handwriting. Children should always be encouraged to discuss their mark-making and writing to enable them to make their message clear to their intended audience.

■ Play can enhance literacy development through symbolism, oral communication and the use of reading and writing to enhance play narratives.

■ English language learners benefit from literacy instruction that is based on meaning-making as it is comprehensible and makes learning engaging for them.

REFLECTION: KEY QUESTIONS TO GUIDE THE READING OF THIS BOOK

■ What is your current approach to the teaching of literacy?

■ What are your strengths?

■ What are your weaknesses?

■ How do you hope to improve your practice?

For further exploration

Burns, M.S., Griffin, P. & Snow, C.E. (1999). *Starting out right: A guide to promoting children's reading success.* Washington, DC: National Academy Press.

National Early Literacy Panel (2008). Developing early literacy: The report of the National Early Literacy Panel. Washington, DC: National Institute for Literacy.

UKLA (United Kingdom Literacy Association) (2005). Submission to the review of best practice in the early teaching of reading. Royston: UKLA.

2 Developing phonological awareness

GUIDING QUESTIONS FOR THIS CHAPTER

As you read this chapter, use these questions to guide your study of phonological awareness:

■ What is phonological awareness?

■ How does phonological awareness differ from phonics?

■ Why is it necessary to teach phonological awareness skills in the early years?

■ What are the different levels of phonological awareness on the continuum, and how do they relate to each other?

■ How would you plan for instruction incorporating the different levels of phonological awareness?

Introduction

In this chapter, we will explore phonological awareness, a key early literacy skill. Phonological awareness refers to a sensitivity to the sounds of language that is crucial in order to be able to learn how to read and write. The chapter will begin by defining phonological awareness and its various components, namely rhyme and alliteration, syllabic awareness, words within a sentence sensitivity, knowledge of onset and rime, and phonemic awareness. The phonological awareness developmental continuum will be examined in terms of teaching and learning activities, and possibilities for assessment practices will also be considered. While phonological awareness skills are necessary to learn how to read and write, they must be applied in meaningful contexts that engage and inspire learners. Numerous examples of meaningful practices that can assist young children in acquiring phonological awareness will be explored in this chapter and discussed further in Chapter 6.

What is phonological awareness?

Phonological awareness is children's ability to manipulate the sounds that make up words, to combine or segment syllables, and to detect rhyme and alliteration. It is a conscious sensitivity to the sound structure of language. Learning to read requires that children have considerable awareness of the sound structure of spoken language. Phonological awareness is generally 'taught, not caught' (i.e. children do not tend to acquire this skill set spontaneously) (Invernizzi & Tortorelli, 2013). Hence, it should be part of regular instruction in the early years.

> The term phonological awareness refers to a general appreciation of the sounds of speech as distinct from their meaning. When that insight includes an understanding that words can he divided into a sequence of phonemes, this finer-grained sensitivity is termed phonemic awareness.
>
> (Snow et al., 1998, p. 51)

It is important to differentiate between the terms phonological awareness, phonemic awareness and phonics. Phonological awareness relates to the whole spectrum, from primitive awareness of speech sounds and rhythms to rhyme awareness and sound similarities, and, at the highest level, awareness of syllables, onset and rime, and eventually phonemes. Becoming phonologically aware (i.e. becoming attentive to the sound structure of language) is an aural and oral skill, unlike phonics, which concerns the relationship between letters and sounds in written words. Phonological awareness is an umbrella term that includes an awareness of words within a sentence, syllabic awareness, an understanding of onset and rime, and phonemic awareness (Bear, Invernizzi, Templeton & Johnston, 2012).

Why teach phonological awareness?

Phonological awareness supports children's ability to notice, think about and work with individual sounds in spoken language. Before children learn to read, they must have developed a sensitivity to the sounds of language. Sound awareness must precede and accompany symbol awareness so that children can learn to read with ease (Adams, 1990). There is a very strong consensus in the research that phonological awareness has a significant effect on reading achievement that 'persists throughout school and into adulthood' (Pufpaff, 2009, p. 679). While it has been acknowledged that phonological awareness has a reciprocal relationship with alphabetic knowledge, reading and spelling skills, it is generally agreed that phonological awareness plays a critical role in laying the foundations for reading and writing development (for a review of the research, see Pufpaff, 2009).

> If children are unable to break words down into their component phonemes, they will be quite unable to learn about the alphabetic code. A child who cannot work out that the word 'cat' can be broken down into three constituent sounds will be at sea with the alphabet.
>
> (Bryant, 1993, p. 86)

Phonological awareness enables children to:

- identify and create oral rhymes;

- identify and manipulate syllables;

- segment words into separate sounds;

- isolate and identify the first, middle and ending sounds in a spoken word;

- recognise which words in a set of words begin with the same sound;

- combine or blend separate sounds in a word to say the word; and

- understand that changing sounds in a word will change the meaning of the word.

The skill of phonological awareness is important because once children understand the concept of words when they are spoken, it is so much easier for them to grasp the concept of words when they are written. Engaging in phonological awareness activities is essential for learning to read and spell, because children will learn to understand the various sounds in words and how they all work together.

Phonological awareness involves both receptive and productive processing skills (Byrnes & Wasik, 2009). Receptive phonological abilities relate to hearing syllables in words, identifying onset and rime, recognising rhyme and alliteration, and demonstrating an ability to differentiate between phonemes in words.

Productive phonological abilities include the ability to produce rhyme and alliteration, and to combine syllables, onset rime and phonemes to form words. Both receptive and productive processing skills progress from larger to smaller units of speech; this is recognised as the continuum of phonological awareness (Ehri & Nunes, 2002). When children have reached the highest level where they can isolate and combine phonemes, they are deemed to have achieved phonological awareness (Snow et al., 1998).

Phonological awareness as a continuum

Phonological awareness develops sequentially, beginning with larger linguistic units, such as words within sentences and syllables, and eventually leading to the smallest sound unit, the phoneme (Pufpaff, 2009). Therefore, phonological awareness can be placed on a *developmental continuum*. This continuum is illustrated in Table 2.1, which demonstrates the expected progression of phonological skills. Along the continuum, phonological awareness skills such as rhyme and alliteration are deemed less complex, and are generally acquired earlier than more complex phonemic awareness skills.

Steps in the phonological awareness continuum

- *Listening*: The ability to listen carefully, accurately and actively. It is best developed through reading tasks (listening comprehension) and oral language games and activities.

- *Rhyme and alliteration*: The ability to detect and produce rhyme and alliteration. It is best developed through listening to, reciting and discussing songs, poems, rhymes and rhyming or alliterative books.

- *Sentence segmentation*: The ability to detect individual words within a sentence. It is the ability to identify that 'I like the cat' contains four words. This is best developed through a variety of listening activities and tasks involving counting the number of words within sentences.

- *Syllables*: The ability to identify the number of syllables in a word and to blend syllables together to form words.

Table 2.1 Phonological awareness continuum

Listening	Rhyme and alliteration	Sentence segmentation	Syllables	Onset and rime	Phonemic awareness

- *Onset and rime*: The onset is the word part within the syllable that precedes the vowel. The rime is the remainder of the syllable. For example, in 'cat', /c/ is the onset and 'at' is the rime.

- *Phonemic awareness*: This is the understanding that words are made up of sounds. It is also the ability to pick out and manipulate sounds in spoken words. A phoneme is the smallest unit of sound in a word. For example, the word 'boat' has four graphemes – 'b' 'o' 'a' 't' – but only three phonemes – /b/ /oa/ /t/. Phonemic awareness is the most complex level of phonological awareness, and can be difficult for some children to grasp (Adams, 1990). However, it is phonemic awareness that is most closely related to success in learning to read (Adams, 1990; Stanovich, 1986).

Planning for instruction

Having developed an understanding of phonological awareness and the different steps in the continuum, it is important to consider how to apply that knowledge in the classroom. Phonological awareness activities work best when they are included as part of a cohesive reading lesson or as part of classroom routines throughout the day. In this chapter, a wide range of activities that relate to phonological awareness will be explored. In Chapter 6, the integration of phonological awareness activities into reading lessons will be examined further.

Listening skills

In order for children to be able to understand rhyming and alliteration, and to be able to manipulate syllables, onset and rime, and phonemes, children first need to learn how to be active, responsive listeners. Their ears need to become 'finely tuned' to language in order to progress to more difficult levels of phonological awareness, and to eventually learn to read. Listening games can be easily incorporated into reading lessons and lessons in other curricular areas. Some of the games listed below might also work well when used for transitions and to enhance classroom routines. The following are some suggested games for teaching listening that will enhance children's phonological awareness:

- *Fruit bowl*: Children sit in a circle facing inwards. They are alternately labelled 'orange', 'apple' and 'lemon'. The teacher or a chosen child calls out 'oranges', 'apples', 'lemons' or 'fruit bowl'. Children in the named category change seats, and 'fruit bowl' requires that all children change their seats. This game can be altered to suit any theme. For example, when reading *Owl Babies* (Waddell, 1998), the labels could be 'Sarah', 'Percy', 'Bill' and 'Owl Mother', which are the names of the characters in the book. This would allow this listening activity to work well within a shared reading lesson.

■ *Telephone*: The object of the game is to successfully pass a 'secret message' around the circle by whispering it into each other's ears. To link this activity with shared reading, children could be encouraged to share messages relating to the story, perhaps their favourite part or a question that they would like answered about the plot or characters.

■ *Simon says*: This is a game where you try to copy a person only when they say 'Simon says'. One child is chosen to be 'Simon'. 'Simon' then orders all sorts of different things to be done, which must be obeyed only when the order begins with 'Simon says'. For instance, 'Simon says, thumbs up!' which, of course, all obey; then perhaps, 'Thumbs down!' which should not be obeyed because the order did not begin with 'Simon says'. This well-known activity could be integrated into a reading lesson by having the main character in the book give the commands. A puppet might be very useful here. For example, a snake puppet could give commands if the class were exploring the book *I Want My Mum* (Woody, 2000) in a shared reading lesson. The teacher might also incorporate the positional language contained in the book into the game, and say, 'Simon says, look under the table', 'Simon says, look behind the chair', 'Simon says, put your hands over your head', and so forth.

■ *Clapping commands*: The teacher tells the children that one clap means that they must stand, two claps indicate that they have to march on the spot, and three claps mean that they must sit. The teacher or a child stands in the centre and claps instructions. The children must listen very carefully to the clapped instructions each time so they follow them correctly. This activity can be linked to shared reading texts using ideas related to the characters or the storyline. For example, if using *Walking through the Jungle* (Lacome, 1995), which features a large number of jungle animals, the children could act like a lion when they hear one clap, an elephant when they hear two claps, and a crocodile when they hear three claps. Alternatively, the children can sit in an inwardly facing circle. The teacher claps a rhythm (e.g. clap . . . clap . . . clap/clap/clap), and the children either mimic the clap collectively or pass it around the circle and each child takes a turn. This phonological awareness activity works well as part of daily classroom transitions. For example, the students might engage in this activity before lining up to go outside to play or to encourage movement between lessons.

■ *Story roundabout*: The first child begins, 'I went to the shop and bought a carrot.' The next child adds an item, 'I went to the shop and bought a carrot and a cake.' You can align this to a letter that you are studying (e.g. /c/) or it can also be focused on rhyming items. Children can be encouraged to extend a story that they have just read. For example, in *A Squash and a Squeeze* (Donaldson, 2016), they could add other items that the old lady might have brought into her house.

- *Silly stories*: Say, 'I'm going to tell you a silly story. Every time you hear something silly, put up your hand.' Sample silly story: 'Once there was a man whose house was at the bottom of the sea. Every morning, he would dive downstairs to have a nice cup of seaweed for his breakfast. Afterwards, he would clean his teeth in the sink and then swim upstairs to put his clothes on', and so on. As part of a shared reading lesson, the teacher could give a 'silly summary' to the story that the class have just read to see if they can spot the errors.

- *Musical games*: The teacher gives children directions to be followed related to musical instruments (e.g. walk when you hear the drum, sit when you hear the triangle, jump when you hear the tambourine). This is an activity that might work well within the daily routine of the classroom. It might be a good way to start or end each day.

Rhyme and alliteration

This level of phonological awareness is best developed through a mixture of activities. Teaching and learning about rhyme and alliteration should be meaningful, active and fun. One of the best indicators of how well children will learn to read is their ability to recite nursery rhymes when they start school. Unfortunately, many children will come to school with little or no exposure to rhyme and alliteration, and thus the teacher must ensure that they are immersed in rhymes and alliteration in their early years at school.

- *Learning and reciting rhymes as part of classroom routines and transitions*: Children in the junior classes should be taught a wide variety of rhymes in order to develop their phonological awareness skills. An easy and effective method of incorporating a range of rhymes into the school day is to use different rhymes for classroom management, greetings, transitions and routines. Rhymes that include simple actions employ the total physical response (TPR) method, which involves using gestures and movements to develop understanding of the language chunks within the rhyme (see Figure 2.1). This is a recommended approach for English language learners. Table 2.2 provides some examples that could be used in the early years classroom. Further examples of rhymes that are suitable for classroom use can be found in Appendix B.

Figure 2.1 Children reciting an action rhyme

Table 2.2 Rhymes for the classroom

Greeting Rhyme
Hello everybody,
it's time to say,
it's time to start a brand
   new day.
So wake it up, shake it up,
give me five,
give me ten,
that's a wrap, let's begin.

Give Me Five
  (tune of Frère Jacques)
Eyes are watching,
ears are listening,
feet are still,
hands are quiet,
you should really try it,
listening well, listening well.

Circle Time
1, 2, 3, 4,
come and sit down on the floor.
5, 6, 7, 8,
hurry up and don't be late!

Clean-Up Song
Clean up, clean up,
everybody get some toys.
Clean up, clean up,
all the little girls and boys.
Clean up, clean up,
everybody do your share.
Clean up, clean up,
everybody, everywhere.

Lining Up
I will not push,
I will not shove,
I will not fall behind.
I will stand behind
   the rest,
I'll line up with
   my class.

For Story Time
Sometimes my hands are at my side.
Then behind my back they hide.
Sometimes I wiggle my fingers so.
Shake them fast, shake them slow.
Sometimes my hands go clap, clap, clap.
Then I rest them in my lap.
Now they're quiet as can be.

■ *Rhymes within lessons and as lessons*: Rhymes should also be used as part of lessons or as the focus on lessons across the curriculum. It is a good idea to try to use a rhyme that aligns with the theme of your current big book. For example, when using *We're Going on a Bear Hunt* (Rosen, 1996), the following rhyme could be used as it relates to the 'bear' theme in the book:

> Teddy bear, teddy bear,
>
> jump around.
>
> Teddy bear, teddy bear,
>
> touch the _____.
>
> Teddy bear, teddy bear,
>
> open the box.
>
> Teddy bear, teddy bear,
>
> pull out the _____.

When the children know the rhyme well, use it as 'oral cloze' (where the rhyming words are omitted and the children have to supply them as indicated in the 'blanks' in the rhyme above). Number and counting rhymes should be used regularly in math lessons as well. Well-loved rhymes such as 'Ten Green Bottles', 'Five Little Ducks' and 'Once I Caught a Fish Alive' are a great way to develop mathematical and phonological awareness together.

■ *Rhyming books*: Read rhyming books throughout the day as read-alouds and also as part of formal lessons. The box below contains some recommendations for rhyming books that would be suitable for young children:

> Alborough, J. (2009). Duck in a truck. New York: HarperCollins.
>
> Donaldson, J. (2016). The snail and the whale. London: Macmillan.
>
> Donaldson, J. (2016). The Gruffalo. London: Macmillan.
>
> Guarino, D. (1997). Is your mama a llama? New York: Scholastic.
>
> Mifong, H. (2000). Hush! A Thai lullaby. New York: Scholastic.
>
> Seuss, D. (2016). The cat in the hat. New York: HarperCollins (and any other Dr. Seuss books!).
>
> Shaw, N. (2016). Sheep in a jeep. Boston, MA: Houghton Mifflin Harcourt.

■ *Identifying rhyme*: Encourage children to identify whether pairs of words rhyme or not. It is very important to use images when asking children to identify rhyming words when they are unfamiliar with the task as it will make the task less cognitively taxing. Ideally, at least one of the words should emanate from the shared reading text. For example, if reading *Farmer Duck*

Figure 2.2 Identifying rhyme

(Wadell, 1996), this activity could be prompted by focusing on an illustration of the duck from the story. The teacher could present some word pairs, such as 'duck' and 'cook' and 'duck' and 'book', that rhyme, and others, such as 'duck' and 'cow', that don't rhyme, and ask the children to identify which pairs rhyme (see Figure 2.2).

Alternatively, rhyming words can simply be identified from hearing the text read aloud. For example, Dr. Seuss books are filled with enjoyable rhyming text. In *The Cat in the Hat*, the first page of the text reads, 'The sun did not shine. It was too wet to play. So we sat in the house, all that cold, cold, wet day.' The teacher could ask the children to identify the word that rhymes with 'play' in the text. The focus here is on finely tuning children's ears to hear the rhymes so that later they can successfully decode words for reading.

■ *Rhyme production*: In rhyme production, children must produce a rhyming partner for a word (make sure to use an image as a support). For example, if you had been reading *Rosie's Walk* (Hutchins, 2007) in a shared reading lesson, you might ask the children, 'What rhymes with hen?' The teacher can also use an oral cloze activity, such as 'Did you ever see a bear on a . . .?' 'Did you ever see a fox in a . . .?' 'Did you ever see a bat with a . . .?' Alternatively, use an illustration from the text you are using for your shared reading lesson as a starting point for a 'rhyming roundabout'. An illustration of the 'bear' from *We're Going on a Bear Hunt* (Rosen, 1996) could be used for discussing words that rhyme with 'bear'. Encourage the children to play 'rhyming I spy' using an illustration. For example, the illustration of the family wading through the river in *We're Going on a Bear Hunt* (Rosen, 1996) would be suitable for this activity as it contains lots of details. Having read the text in your shared reading lesson, the teacher could return to this page and ask the children to find something in the picture that rhymes with 'blue' (there is a 'shoe' in the illustration). The child who gives the correct answer can set the next rhyming riddle (e.g. 'I spy with my little eye, something that rhymes with "log"' – there is a dog in the illustration).

■ *Oddity task*: Present children with three different images that relate to the theme of the book. For example, if you were reading the large-format book *The Smartest Giant in Town* (Donaldson, 2003) in shared reading, you might use pictures of the 'giant', the 'boat' and the 'coat', and ask, 'Which one does not rhyme?'

■ *Oral rhyming snap*: Using words from a big book or read-aloud story, the children snap their fingers or say 'snap' when they hear two rhyming words. The words used below are taken from *We're Going on a Bear Hunt* (Rosen, 1996).

Teacher:	Grass and hunt
Children:	(The children do not respond.)
Teacher:	Bear and chair
Children:	Snap!
Teacher:	Cave and save
Children:	Snap
Teacher:	Door and bed
Children:	(The children do not respond.)

■ *Alliteration*: Children should be encouraged to discuss and identify alliteration in books. For example, in *We're Going on a Bear Hunt* (Rosen, 1996), there are lots of examples of alliteration throughout the story, such as 'Splash, splosh! Splash, splosh! Splash, splosh!' Using this book, the teacher might read the alliterative text to the children and ask them if they notice anything about the words. The teacher will guide their discovery that all the words begin with the same sounds. The teacher should discuss what sound all these words begin with. The children should engage in echo (teacher reads, then children copy) and choral reading (everyone reads together) of this section of the text. Then the teacher can turn to another page in the book that contains alliteration and ask the children if they can spot another example of alliteration.

Children's understanding and appreciation of alliteration could also be enhanced through the reading of alliterative books. A number of recommendations can be found in the box below. These could be read as a teacher read-aloud, during transitions or as part of lessons.

ALLITERATIVE BOOK RECOMMENDATIONS

Cole, J. & Calmenson, S. (1993). *Six sick sheep*. New York: HarperCollins.
Dragonwagon, C. Aruego, J. & Dewey, A. (1992). *Alligator arrived with apples: A potluck alphabet feast*. New York: Atheneun.
Edwards, P. & Cole, H. (2007). *Clara caterpillar*. New York: HarperCollins.
Geisel, T.S. (1963). *Dr Seuss' ABC*. New York: Random House.
Lester, J. (2014). *99 torturous, tricky, tough tongue twisters*. London: CreateSpace.

Children enjoy creating and reciting tongue-twisters. Well-known tongue-twisters can be recited by both the teacher and the children, such as 'Betty Botter' and 'Peter Piper'. When the children are very familiar with a tongue-twister, you can recite it and deliberately substitute one of the phonemes. Then ask the children if they can spot the error (e.g. 'Peter Piper liked a peck of tickled pepper'). Creating your own tongue-twisters based on the children's names is a popular classroom activity that promotes phonological awareness. For example:

- James wants jump on jelly and jam.

- Fiona found a fierce fairy in a field and it flew away.

- Leah loves licking lollipops.

IN THE CLASSROOM: EXPLORING ALLITERATION USING A MEANINGFUL CONTEXT

Fiona has been reading *Over in the Meadow* (Voce, 2000) with her class of 4- and 5-year-olds for the past three days. Today, she wants to include some phonological awareness work that focuses on alliteration. She decides to create a collaborative tongue-twister with the class focusing on the main character in the story – the frog. Holding a little frog puppet aloft, she has the 'frog' ask the children if they will help him make a tongue-twister as many of his friends already have tongue-twisters written about them. He mentions his friend spider, who has a great tongue-twister: 'Susie spider and her seven spider friends spent Sunday spinning webs'. Having modelled an example, the 'frog' explains to the children that a tongue-twister involves creating a sentence in which a lot of the words start with the same sound. Since he is a 'frog', they will need to think of words that start like 'frog' with an /f/ sound. The children begin sharing ideas, and through discussion and collaboration the class finally agrees on the frog's tongue twister: 'Five fat frogs fed on five fantastic flies'. Fiona writes down the tongue-twister on the chart paper. She models how to say it in different voices (high, low, sad, happy). Some children volunteer to say it solo. Fiona draws their attention to the number of syllables in 'frog' and 'fantastic' and leads a discussion on how the number of syllables influences the length of the word.

Source: Author experience in practice

Sentence segmentation

Many children will enter school with a good understanding that words form a sentence. A quick assessment (and a teaching method) to see if they have grasped the notion that our speech is composed of sentences and words within those sentences is an active sentence segmentation task, such as the 'words in a sentence' game. In this activity, the teacher says a sentence that relates to the shared reading text, such as 'This is the bear' from *This Is the Bear* (Hayes, 2003). Ask the children to count the words by placing counters in a cup as they say the sentence, one counter for each individual word. Sentence segmentation can also be easily integrated into all shared reading lessons by the teacher simply pointing to the words as they read them, as this demonstrates one-to-one correspondence and links phonological awareness to print awareness.

Syllables

If children have developed an understanding of syllable blending and segmenting, they will find it easier to break words down by onset and rime and into individual phonemes. Syllable blending requires children to bring together or 'blend' two or more syllables to form a word. In practice, the teacher might take several words from the big book currently being used in shared reading lessons, taking care to ensure that the words have a different number of syllables. For example, when using *The Pig in the Pond* (Waddell, 2006), the teacher might ask the children to blend words such as 'far . . . mer' and 'Nel . . . i . . . gan'. It can be helpful to use a puppet if one is available, as the puppet can say the syllables, and children find this very engaging.

Syllable segmentation requires children to break words into syllables. Here, the teacher might present them with words from the story and have them clap or count the syllables that are in the word (e.g. if they are given the word 'forest' and must break it into for/est). Syllable sorting boxes can be used to enhance this task.

In this activity, the teacher would choose several words from the big book. Nouns are ideal as they can be portrayed as images or concrete objects may be used. The teacher would present the children with three boxes, the first with the number '1' attached to it, another with the number '2' attached and the last with the number '3' attached. The children must break each word into syllables and place the object or picture in the box that has the corresponding number of syllables (1, 2 or 3). For example, if using *Monkey Puzzle* (Donaldson & Scheffler, 2002), words such as 'butterfly', 'monkey' and 'snake' could be used.

IN THE CLASSROOM: EXPLORING SYLLABLES IN A MEANINGFUL CONTEXT

Leah has a basket containing flash cards with the children's names written on them. The children are sitting in a circle. She lays out four hula hoops on the floor in the middle of the circle, labelled from '1' to '4'. She chooses the first name; it's 'Bernard'. She models how to clap the syllables in the name 'Bern/ard' and has the children echo clap while saying the name. She asks the children which hoop it belongs in. Nearly all the hands are raised, and one child answers, 'Number 2.' Leah agrees, 'Yes, there are two syllables in Bern/ard, so it goes in the hoop with number 2!' Leah models a few more names, taking care to ensure that the first few examples contain different amounts of syllables. She then encourages the children to figure out the syllable length themselves. She says the name of a classmate (e.g. 'Fiona') and asks the children to quietly clap the syllables to themselves. When they think they have figured out how many syllables are in the name, they should show their response by holding up that amount of fingers. On the first morning, they discuss approximately 12 names. This activity becomes part of their morning routine as it is an enjoyable way to welcome the children to the classroom.

Source: Author's experience in practice

Onset and rime

Onset is the part of the syllable that precedes the first vowel, while the rime is the remainder of the syllable. Table 2.3 demonstrates how words can be separated into their respective onsets and rimes. You will notice that not all words can be segmented.

Table 2.3 Onset and rime

Word	Onset	Rime
cat	c	at
stand	st	and
him	h	im
it	-	it

Two activities that support children's awareness of onset and rime are:

1   *Oral blending*: Listen to these word parts. Say the word as a whole. /b/. . ./ed/ – what's the word?
2   *Oral segmentation*: Listen to the word. Break it into onset and rime – 'dog', /d/. . ./og/.

Again, nouns from the shared reading text would be recommended, so that these activities can integrate into the reading lesson in a meaningful manner. If children are able to do this aurally and orally, they will be better able to spell and read the 500 primary-level words that can be derived from these 37 rimes featured in the box below.

-ack, -all, -ain, -ake, -ale, -ame, -an, -ank, -ap, -ash, -at, ate, -aw, -ay, -eat, -ell, -est, -ice, -ick, -ide, -ight, -ill, -in, -ine, -ing, -ink, -ip, -it, -ock, -oke, -op, -ore, -ot, -uck, -ug, -ump, -unk

Phonemes

Phonemic awareness is regarded as the most difficult element of phonological awareness and is critical to reading success (Cunningham & Cunningham, 2002; Ehri & Nunes, 2002; Yopp, 1995). Children who fail to develop phonemic awareness in the early grades tend to become poor readers in higher grades (Yeh & Connell, 2008). Phonemic awareness is the understanding that words are made up of sounds. The Snow et al. (1998) define phonemic awareness as:

> The insight that every spoken word can be conceived as a sequence of phonemes. Because phonemes are the units of sound that are represented by the letters of the alphabet, an awareness of phonemes is key to understanding the logic of the alphabetic principles and thus to the learnability of phonics and spelling.
>
> (p. 25)

There is often confusion between phonemic awareness and phonics as both involve the sounds that make up words. However, phonemic awareness refers to the sound structures of spoken words only, whereas phonics refers to the relationship between letters and sounds (Bear et al., 2012).

> Unless you have phonemic awareness…it is impossible to gain much from instruction in phonics.
>
> (Harrison, 2004, p. 41)

Phonemic awareness supports children's ability to pick out and manipulate sounds in spoken words. A phoneme is the smallest unit of sound in a word. For example, the word 'soap' has three phonemes – /s/ /oa/ /p/ – despite having four graphemes. A grapheme is the smallest unit of our writing system (a graphical sign). An individual grapheme may or may not carry meaning by itself, and may or may not correspond to a phoneme. It is important that children learn to distinguish between phonemes aurally and orally so that they are well prepared to blend and segment phonemes for reading. Most words have either the same amount of phonemes as graphemes or more graphemes than phonemes. For example, 'box' has three graphemes and three phonemes.

TEST YOURSELF!

How many phonemes in:

- 'dog';
- 'chop';
- 'soap';
- 'mouth';
- 'toy';
- 'brush';
- 'precious';
- 'straight'; and
- 'boil'?

The answers are at the end of the chapter!

Phonemic awareness is one of the best predictors of reading success (National Early Literacy Panel, 2008), and it does not develop naturally, so it must be taught explicitly to novice readers. A variety of activities can be used to develop and support children's phonemic awareness and manipulation. These include:

- *Phoneme categorisation*:

   Beginning consonants: Which two words begin with the same sound – man, moon, cup?

   Ending consonants: Which two words end with the same sound – man, cat, ten?

   Medial sounds (long/short vowels, consonants): Which two words have the same middle sound – top, cat, pan?

   When possible, it is recommended that you use nouns from the shared reading text to develop these activities. For example, if you were reading *This Is the Bear* (Hayes, 2003), then you might choose words such as 'bear', 'bin' and 'dump' for a beginning consonants activity. The use of visuals will also ease the cognitive load involved in these tasks and allow children to just focus on hearing the sounds.

- *Phoneme blending*: Using a puppet, ask the children, 'Can you guess what he's saying?' For example, when reading *The Pig in the Pond* (Waddell, 2006), the puppet might stretch the sounds in a word (e.g. /p/ /i/ /g/). The children can then tell the puppet what word it is saying.

   Another alternative activity is to hide an object or a picture in a bag and say the word phoneme by phoneme. For example, if reading *Farmer Duck* (Waddell, 1996), ask, 'What's in teacher's bag? It's a /d/ /u/ /ck/!' The children then blend the phonemes together, say the word, and the object is revealed!

- *Phoneme segmentation*: This skill can be taught using Elkonin boxes (Clay, 1993). This is a page that contains grids of different sizes to encourage children to identify how many sounds they hear. Usually, there is a grid with two boxes, three boxes and four boxes. Children must choose which grid corresponds to the number of sounds they hear in the word and place counters in the appropriate boxes. For example, if the word was 'cat', children would choose the grid with three boxes and place a counter in each of the three boxes.

- *Phonemic manipulation*: This task requires children to change or delete the initial, final or medial phoneme. For example:

   Initial phoneme: Change 'cat' to 'rat', or what is 'rat' without the /r/?

   Medial phoneme: Change 'bet' to 'bat'.

   Final phoneme: Change 'bag' to 'bat', or what is 'bat' without the /t/?

This task can be taught in a fun and meaningful way using a piece of rhythmic text from a big book or storybook. For example, in *Chicka Chicka Boom Boom* (Martin & Archambauld, 1995), the extract 'Dare double dare, you can't catch me' on the final page of the book can be manipulated as follows: 'Gare gouble gare, you can't catch me', or 'Ware wouble ware, you can't catch me', and so forth. There are also books that are specifically focused on phonemic manipulation, such as *The Hungry Thing* (Slepian & Seider, 2001) or *There's a Wocket in My Pocket* (Seuss, 1996). In *The Hungry Thing*, a monster comes to town seeking food. He mixes up his initial phonemes, causing confusion by asking for items such as 'flamburgers', which leads children to laugh when they realise he really wants 'hamburgers'. *There's a Wocket in My Pocket* is filled with ridiculous but pleasing phonemic manipulation. For example, on the first page, the author declares, 'Sometimes I feel quite certain, there's a jertain in the curtain.' Phonological awareness games can be developed based on these books; for example, children can be encouraged to develop their own sentences/words that demonstrate phonological manipulation (e.g. 'There's a fencil on my pencil'). A large cardboard cut-out of the 'hungry thing' can be created, and children can be encouraged to draw food that they think he will enjoy and then present it using phonemic manipulation (e.g. 'a panwich sandwich', and so forth). Phonemic manipulation aids spelling development as children grow older and begin to spell simple 'word family' words (words that contain the same rime but a different onset). For example, children with phonemic manipulation skills know that changing the /m/ in 'man' to /c/ will spell 'can'.

Assessing phonological awareness

Assessment in phonological awareness will take place informally during literacy lessons when the teacher notes how children respond to a task. For example, the teacher should note whether children can participate effectively in a listening activity, count the words in a sentence, clap the syllables in a word, isolate an onset or rime, or blend or segment phonemes.

At regular intervals, the teacher should assess each child more formally on the phonological awareness tasks that have been taught recently. This can be done orally, perhaps using a familiar book as a context. For example, the teacher may ask children to clap out the syllables in certain words or segment phonemes using a word from the book. A sample phonological awareness test is outlined below. It could be adapted to suit a particular context. This type of assessment could help the teacher to plan future instruction, as test results may indicate that certain tasks have been mastered while other areas still require development.

PHONOLOGICAL AWARENESS TEST (VISUALS COULD BE USED TO ASSIST ELLS)

1   Do these words rhyme?

   Men/cat _____

   Pig/wig _____

   Can/pan _____

   Fox/lip _____

2   Can you think of another word that rhymes with 'goat', 'coat', _____?

3   Which one does not rhyme?

   Dog, log, cake _____

   Hop, wing, mop _____

   Pen, dot, not _____

4   Say this word as a whole.

   Ri/ver _____

5   Say this word as a whole.

   h/at _____

6   Say this word as a whole.

   /m/ /a/ /n/

7   How many syllables in…?

   Dog _____

   Bicycle _____

   Pencil _____

8   What sounds do you hear in…?

   Sun _____

   Leaf _____

   Red _____

   Bat _____

   Hand _____

   Soap _____

9   Change the first sound in this word to /b/

Sad _____

Run _____

Cat _____

Phonological awareness and the English language learner

ELLs are learning how to speak and read English at the same time, which can be challenging. However, ELLs may have a 'bilingual advantage' in phonological awareness due to their heightened sensitivity to the nuances of spoken language, having been exposed to more than one language (Bialystok, Mujumder & Martin, 2003). Therefore, it is recommended that teachers highlight the transferability of phonological skills across languages. An example of this type of instruction is illustrated in the classroom vignette below.

IN THE CLASSROOM: USING CHILDREN'S HOME LANGUAGES TO ENHANCE INSTRUCTION

John teaches a diverse group of young children. Nearly all of the children in his class are ELLs, though their proficiency levels vary considerably. John tries to encourage the children to make connections to their home languages as much as possible to enhance their learning. This week, John's class have been reading *Farmer Duck* (Waddell, 1996), and today they are clapping the syllables in some of the keywords in the text. They clap 'far/mer'. John asks how many syllables they hear. Maria responds, 'Two.' John asks Maria how you would say 'farmer' in her home language (Polish). Maria responds, 'It is *rolnick*, teacher.' 'How many syllables are in *rolnick*?' asks John. Maria claps the syllables and smiles, 'Two, they are the same amount.'

Source: Author experience in practice

As languages can vary greatly in both sounds and structure, this may have a signifi-cant bearing on an ELL's ability to grasp certain phonemes. For example, phonemes such as /sh/ and /v/ are very common in English, but these sounds do not exist in other languages. Therefore, even though children might have very well-developed phono-logical awareness, they might struggle to identify an unfamiliar sound, and may need additional support not only in phonological awareness lessons, but also in phonics, spelling and reading situations (Helman, 2004). It is also important to remember that even simple nouns that are understood by native English speakers may be unfamiliar to ELLs, so visuals and props should be used to assist understanding. For example, asking an ELL pupil to identify the 'odd one out' when presented with 'cat', 'hat' and 'log' may prove too difficult if there are no visuals to help children understand the words and hold them in short-term memory long enough to decide which one does not belong.

ELLs need to work hard to keep up with the 'moving target' represented by their peers, so regular assessment in phonological awareness skills will assist focused, effective teaching. Whenever possible, it is recommended that children's phonological skills be assessed in both English and their home language to identify strengths and weaknesses (Pena & Halle, 2011).

Key concepts for practice

- Phonological awareness is a developmental continuum; therefore, attention should be paid to each step of the continuum, from the development of listening skills through to phonemic awareness.

- As children in the early years can vary considerably in relation to their phonological awareness levels, it may be appropriate to include a variety of phonological awareness activities in all your lessons (at different levels) or to use group work/station work so that all children are appropriately challenged.

- Any instruction in phonological awareness should have its roots in a meaningful, contextualised reading experience, such as a big book, a poetry chart, a language experience text or a digital text. These early literacy skills should form part of a literacy lesson and should not dominate reading instruction. Chapter 6 outlines how the activities discussed in this chapter might be incorporated into reading lessons that encourage children to identify the usefulness of these skills in learning to read.

- It is also important to bear in mind that phonological awareness is only one element in learning to read, and that devoting large amounts of time to phonological awareness instruction is not always helpful. Indeed, Armbruster, Lehr and Osbourne (2001) recommend that no more than 20 hours be dedicated to phonological awareness training within a school year. However, attention must be paid to the specific needs of the school population and the children's exposure to rhyme, alliteration, language play and books prior to entering school, as this would affect the optimal amount of phonological awareness training that a class or individual students may require to be able to successfully learn phonics.

- ELLs may have a 'bilingual advantage' in phonological awareness due to their sensitivity to different languages; however, teachers need to take care to encourage the transfer of skills across languages and take time to supply visuals/gestures/facial expressions to ensure understanding of new vocabulary.

REFLECTION: THINKING ABOUT YOUR PRACTICE

Having explored the topic of phonological awareness in this chapter, please consider the following questions:

- How does your school currently approach the development of phonological awareness?

- Does your current teaching recognise the developmental continuum?

- What resources do you currently use to teach phonological awareness?

For further exploration

Adams, M.J. (1997). *Phonemic awareness in young children: A classroom curriculum.* New York: Brookes.

Goswami, U. & Bryant, P. (1990). *Phonological skills and learning to read.* Hove: Erlbaum.

Juilebo, M. & Ericson, L. (1998). *The phonological awareness handbook for kindergarten and primary teachers.* Newark, DE: International Reading Association.

Yopp, H.K. (1992). Developing phonemic awareness in young children. *The Reading Teacher*, 45, 696–703.

Yopp, H.K. (1995). Read-aloud books for developing phonemic awareness: An annotated bibliography. *The Reading Teacher*, 48, 538–543.

TEST YOURSELF: ANSWERS

How many phonemes in . . .

- 'dog' (3)

- 'chop' (3)

- 'soap' (3)

- 'mouth' (3)

- 'toy' (2)

- 'brush' (4)

- 'precious' (6)

- 'straight' (5)

- 'boil' (3)

3 | Phonics

GUIDING QUESTIONS FOR THIS CHAPTER

As you read this chapter, use these questions to guide your study of phonics.

■ What is phonics?

■ What phonics should I teach?

■ How should I teach phonics?

■ How can I assess phonics?

■ What is the role of letter name knowledge?

■ What are the other cueing systems used in reading, and what is their relationship to phonics?

Introduction

Children's reading development is dependent on a thorough understanding of the alphabetic principle – the sound–symbol relationship also known as phonics. While phonological awareness developed children's knowledge of phonemes aurally, phonics introduces the corresponding symbols that will enable children to decode (read) and encode (write) words. Phonological awareness training and phonics are reciprocal, and while initial phonological awareness training may precede phonics, the two can also coexist in instruction and can be mutually beneficial as phonological awareness focuses on oral and aural skills, while phonics introduces the symbolic. The blend of these three elements are required by the beginning reader. This chapter explores the range of phonic knowledge that a young reader needs to effectively decode texts. While phonics instruction should be systematic and explicit (NRP, 2000), it must not be forgotten that instruction should always be focused on reading words, not learning rules (Snow et al., 1998). When learning about phonics, children need ample opportunities to apply their skills using texts that are rich in vocabulary and meaningful in content. Indeed, phonics instruction needs to exist within the realm of children's rich concepts about how print functions and the ultimate goal of reading – meaning. Phonics instruction is an important part of any reading programme, but it needs to be integrated into reading and writing instruction in a meaningful and enjoyable way. Based on the understanding that reading is a multilevel interactive process (Rumelhart, 1994), phonics should not dominate, but instead complement, children's developing reading skills and understandings of the reading process (Lewis & Ellis, 2006; Stahl, Stahl & McKenna, 1999; Strickland & Morrow, 2000). While the discussion on phonics in this chapter is closely related to the exploration of phonological awareness in Chapter 2, its application is further explored in Chapter 6 (in relation to planning) and Chapter 9 (in relation to invented spelling practice in writing instruction), as practice with invented spellings improves children's awareness of phonemes, which enhances their ability to decode and encode.

Defining phonics and its importance in reading

Phonics is the teaching of the orthographic code of language and the relations of spelling patterns to sound patterns. Effective phonics instruction needs to cover a large number of the phonemes (see Table 3.1), not just the 26 letters of the alphabet. In the sections that follow, this chapter will explore the range of material that needs to be taught to an emergent reader in relation to phonics instruction.

Phonics instruction is a crucial element in early reading instruction. The early ability to decode words successfully is a strong predictor of future reading achievement (Lundberg, 1984). Efficient decoding makes comprehension and enjoyment of the text more likely as attention can be devoted to the text meaning as decoding becomes more automatic (Beck & Juel, 1995; LaBerge & Samuels, 1974). Being a good decoder also increases one's reading speed, which leads to more extensive reading, which is also associated with reading growth (Juel, 1988). Children who are poor readers in the early years of schooling tend to continue to have difficulties as they progress through school. Stanovich (1986) coined this 'the Matthew effect', in which 'the rich get richer' (i.e. children who are strong decoders read more, and thus become better readers, whereas those who struggle to decode read less, and therefore fail to make significant progress). According to Chall (1967), all children, regardless of their background, can benefit from phonics instruction:

By learning phonics, students make faster progress in acquiring literary skills – reading and writing. By the age of six, most children already have about 6,000 words in their listening and speaking vocabularies. With phonics, they learn to read and write these and more words at a faster rate than they would without phonics.

(p. 67)

Children must gain control of the print-to-speech mapping system early if they are to become successful readers.

(Beck, 2006, p. 12)

While phonics instruction is important in learning to read, it is important to note that it is possible to overdo phonics instruction (Chall, 1996; Stanovich, 1993). Blevins (2006) notes that 'a little phonics instruction can go a long way' (p. 15).

Table 3.1 The phonemes in the English language

Consonant sounds	Vowel sounds
/b/ ball	/ā/ cake
/c/ cat, kite	/ē/ meet
/d/ dog	/ī/ bike
/f/ fish	/ō/ coat
/g/ gold	/yōō/ cube
/h/ hat	/a/ hat
/j/ jump	/e/ fed
/k/ kite	/i/ dish
/l/ lamp	/o/ sock
/m/ mop	/u/ duck
/n/ nest	/ā/ chair
/p/ pig	/û/ bird
/r/ roll	/ä/ car
/s/ sun	/ô/ ball
/t/ tall	/ou/house
/v/ vase	/ōō/ moon
/w/ wagon	/oo/ book
/y/ yogurt	
/z/ zebra	
/ch/ cheese	
/sh/ shark	
/zh/ treasure	
/th/ thumb	
/th/ the	
/hw/ wheel	
/ng/ ring	

While well-developed phonic knowledge is very useful in decoding text, it has a finite value. It has been described as a 'constrained skill' (Paris, 2005) (i.e. it 'has a narrow scope, is learned quickly, the trajectory of mastery is steep and the duration of acquisition is brief') (Paris, 2005, p. 188). Therefore, while phonics is useful, it is also limited in that it only represents one part of the 'reading puzzle', and must be complemented with the 'unconstrained skills' of comprehension and vocabulary development in authentic literacy tasks from the earliest juncture so as to create lifelong readers (Stahl et al., 1999). Hence, learning to read within a 'balanced literacy framework', where all aspects of reading development are recognised, is crucial. Indeed, according to the NRP (2000), phonics programmes that emphasise decoding exclusively and ignore the other processes involved in learning to read will 'not succeed in making every child a skilled reader' (p. 113). Waterland (1985) describes children who had mastered phonics but had learned how to decode in an isolated fashion. They did not enjoy reading and failed to see the 'big picture' of reading (i.e. the joy and understanding that it can bring a reader). For these children, reading was a task to be completed in school, and they had no inclination to read for pleasure. Indeed, according to Harrison (2004):

> Decoding skills may be the ladder to meaning, but as teachers we must also take responsibility for what children are going to encounter once they get to the top of that ladder. If children do not have positive experiences with books, then even if they have the ability, they won't want to make that climb.
>
> (p. 106)

Teacher knowledge for phonics instruction

The English language is a very complex language that contains many unreliable phonic generalisations. For example, some letters can represent different sounds (e.g. /ch/ makes different sounds in 'chip', 'choir', 'machine', 'character' and 'chasm'). Also, different letters can represent the same sound in different words, such as 'ai' in 'laid', 'ay' in 'bay' and [a]-[e] in 'take'. Therefore, it is critical that phonics be taught in a meaningful context, such as big books, and other forms of continuous text, such as poems, rhymes and environmental print, to ensure reliable decoding. Using texts also allows the teacher to develop comprehension skills alongside phonic skills. This is essential as phonics can be highly successful when intelligently combined with contextual information, but without contextual information phonics can be inconsistent and unreliable. It is important to highlight the goal of phonics instruction from the outset, that learning individual phonemes will eventually lead to the unassisted reading of continuous texts. While it is important that phonics be taught within a meaningful context, it is also crucial to teach sound–spelling relationships explicitly and systematically. Implicit instruction, where children are expected to 'discover' phonic rules for themselves, tends to be particularly ineffective with poorer readers (Snow et al., 1998).

Given that a teacher's knowledge of phonics has a strong effect on his or her ability to teach phonics effectively (Moats, 1995), a large portion of this chapter will be devoted to exploring the essential components of phonics instruction. In the following sections, we will explore the range of phonic knowledge that should be taught to children who are beginning to learn to read.

The phonemes in the English language can be divided into two major categories: consonants and vowels. A consonant sound is one in which the airflow is cut off either partially or completely when the sound is produced. A vowel sound is one in which the airflow is unobstructed when the sound is made.

Consonants

There are 26 letters in the alphabet, and 21 of these are considered consonants. These include 'b', 'c', 'd', 'f', 'g', 'h', 'j', 'k', 'l', 'm', 'n', 'p', 'q', 'r', 's', 't', 'v', 'w', 'x', 'y' and 'z'. The letters w and y also sometimes act as vowels. When teaching consonants, it is very important that one does not add the schwa sound (sounds like 'uh') after a consonant. For example, /f/ should sound like 'fffff' (air coming out of a tyre), and not 'fuh', and /s/ sounds like the hissing of a snake, 'sssss', not 'suh', and so forth. Consonants are generally easier for children to learn than vowels in relation to speech, writing and reading. Hence, this is where phonics instruction should begin. Start by teaching some consonants and one or two vowels. The first six or eight phonemes that you teach should be easily combined to form words that can be decoded (read) and encoded (written). They should also correspond with your handwriting plan and have some common directionality. For example, 'c', 'n', 'm', 'p', 'h', 'a' and 'o' could be a good place to start, as simple words such as nap, man, mop, hop, pan, can and cop could be decoded (read) and encoded (written). The letters 'c', 'o' and 'a' use the same directionality in forming their letter shapes; the same is true for 'n', 'm', 'h' and 'p'. So, this starting point would allow for synchronicity between phonics and handwriting instruction. Some commercial programmes such as Jolly Phonics recommend starting with the sequence 's', 'a', 'i', 't', 'p', 'n'. While these letters lend themselves to decoding and encoding of simple words, they do not correspond in terms of directionality in relation to letter formation.

Voiced and unvoiced consonants

All consonants may be classified as either voiced or unvoiced. In articulating a voiced consonant, the vocal cords vibrate (the vibration may easily be felt by gripping the larynx – the 'Adam's apple' – between the fingers and the thumb while articulating the consonant). In articulating an unvoiced consonant, the vocal cords do not vibrate.

English has several consonant pairs that are articulated alike except that one is voiced and the other is unvoiced. Some examples are the phoneme spelled 'b' in 'bat' (voiced) and the phoneme spelled 'p' in 'pat' (unvoiced), the phoneme spelled 'd' in 'dab' (voiced) and the phoneme spelled 't' in 'tab' (unvoiced), and the phoneme spelled 'th' in 'this' (voiced) and the phoneme spelled 'th' in 'thistle' (unvoiced).

Consonant blends

A consonant blend is when a combination of two or three consonant letters blend in such a way that each letter in the blend keeps its own identity. It can occur at the beginning of a word (initial blend), such as /bl/ in 'bland', or at the end of a word, such as /nd/ in 'bend'.

> *Initial blends*: bl, br, cl, cr, dr, fr, fl, gl, gr, pl, pr, sc, st, sk, sm, sw sn, tr, tw, vr, spr, spl, str
> *Final blends*: ct, ft, ld, lp, lt, pt, rd, rk, sk, sp, mp, nd, nk, nt, st

Consonant digraphs

A consonant digraph is a combination of two consonant letters representing one sound (phoneme) (e.g. /sh/ in 'shop'). When these two phonemes are combined, they create a new sound.

EXAMPLES OF CONSONANT DIGRAPHS

sh: fish, shop, ship, dish, wish, shed, brush, smash, shelf, shin, shut, rash, cash, shell
th (voiced): that, this, with, then, them, father, gather
th (unvoiced): then, three, cloth, thick, thank, tenth, think, thing, thorn, thrill
ph: alphabet, dolphin, orphan, elephant
ch: chin, chip, rich, chop, chat, much, punch, bench, lunch, chill, chick, chest
wh: when, wheel, whip, which, white, whisper, whisk
ng: ring, sing, wing, sting, bring, king, swing, strong, string, singing, hang, spring

Soft 'g' and hard 'g'/soft 'c' and hard 'c'

A soft 'g' sounds like /j/ (e.g. 'giraffe'), while a hard 'g' can be heard at the start of 'garden'. A soft 'c' sounds like /s/ (e.g. 'cyclone'), while a hard 'c' can be heard at the start of 'cat'.

Examine this list. Which words contain a soft 'g'?

- gang   gentle
- gum   germ
- gym   got
- geranium   gull
- giant   goal
- gypsy   gave

Soft 'g' sound: giant, geranium, gypsy, germ, gentle, gym

Examine this list. Which words contain a soft 'c'?

- cycle   candy
- city   cuff
- circle   contest
- copy   treacle

Soft 'c' sound: cycle, city, circle

Did you notice a pattern/rule for the soft 'g' and 'c'?

When 'c' or 'g' is followed by 'i' or 'e' (or 'y' using those vowel sounds), it is usually a soft 'c'/'g'. There are exceptions to this rule, though (e.g. 'give', 'get').

Vowels

The letters 'a', 'e', 'i', 'o' and 'u' are classified as vowels. Each vowel makes a large variety of sounds. For example, the letter 'o' has many different sounds ('old', 'on', 'horn', 'broom', 'book', 'word', 'lemon', 'shout', 'boil', 'Ouija', 'how', 'could'). The letters 'w' and 'y' often act as vowels (e.g. in words such as 'my' and 'show'). All the vowels, except 'a', can also act as consonants (e.g. the letter 'e' in 'azelea', the letter 'i' in 'nation', the letter 'o' in 'one' and the letter 'u' in 'measure'. Vowels can have a short or long sound, as illustrated below.

Short vowels:

- /a/ as in 'apple';
- /o/ as in 'octopus';
- /i/ as in 'Indian';
- /u/ as in 'umbrella'; and
- /e/ as in 'elephant'.

Long vowels sound like their letter name:

- /ā/ as in 'acorn';
- /ō/ as in 'oval';
- /ī/ as in 'ice';
- /ū/ as in 'unicorn'; and
- /ē/ as in 'eagle'.

Table 3.2 CVC words for instruction

Short 'a'	Short 'e'	Short 'i'	Short 'o'	Short 'u'
bad	bed	bib	box	bug
bag	bet	big	cot	bun
bat	fed	bit	dot	cut
can	get	did	fog	dug
cap	hen	dig	fox	fun
cat	jet	dip	got	gun
dad	led	fin	hog	hug
fan	leg	fit	hop	jug
fat	let	hid	hot	mug
had	men	him	job	nun
ham	met	hip	jog	nut
hat	net	hit	log	rug
jam	pen	kid	lot	run
lap	pet	kit	mom	rut
mad	red	lid	mop	sun
man	set	lit	not	tug
map	ten	pig	pop	
mat	vet	pin	pot	
nap	web	pit	rod	
pan	wet	rib	sob	
pat	yes	rip	top	
rag	yet	sit		
rat		six		
sad		tip		
sat		wig		
tap		win		
van		zip		

It is recommended to begin teaching the short vowels before the long vowels, as the short vowels are found in a large number of simple decodable words – known as consonant/vowel/consonant (CVC) words – that are found in children's books and beginning readers. CVC words are composed of a consonant, a vowel and a consonant (e.g. 'dog'). These are sometimes referred to as 'word families'. More examples can be found in Table 3.2.

Magic 'e' (CVCe words)

The final 'e' that changes the vowel sound from a short vowel to a long vowel is called the magic 'e' (and sometimes CVCe). For example, 'hid' (short 'i' sound like 'Indian') becomes 'hide' (long ' ' sound, sounds like letter name). This rule is reasonably consistent in the English language, and therefore it is useful to teach it to young readers. However, there are exceptions; not all final 'e's have the magic 'e' effect.

Find the magic 'e' exceptions on this list. Then compare your list with the answers below.

- cane
- pine
- note
- have
- cube
- give
- dive
- drive
- space
- love
- slide
- fine
- live
- hope

Exceptions: have, live (e.g. when it is used as 'I live in Dublin'), give, love

Vowel digraphs

A vowel digraph is when two vowels appear together and produce one vowel sound (e.g. 'maid', 'treat'). The rule is sometimes described as 'two vowels go walking, the first one does the talking', as the first vowel sound says its long vowel sound. For example, in 'maid', the long 'a' sound is pronounced and the 'i' is silent. Some examples are listed below.

- 'ay': day, hay, lay, pay, may, say, way, play, stay, pray, ray, clay, tray, away, crayon
- 'ee': bee, see, seed, need, feet, deep, queen, sleep, green, free, heel, beef, jeep, sheep
- 'oa': boat, goat, soap, road, toast, throat, moan, coal, goal, cloak, coat, toad, loaf, foam
- 'ie': tie, pie, lie, die
- 'ea': eat, meat, read, tea, sea, beach, leaf, beak, heat, clean, seat, peach, steal, teacher
- 'ai': rain, sail, pain, tail, rail, nail, train, snail, paint, aim, gain, fail, laid, vain, brain, chain

Vowel diphthongs

A vowel diphthong is when two vowels together produce a sound unlike that of either vowel (e.g. 'boil', 'toy') (technically, a diphthong is a kind of sound that, in the process of being made, requires a change in the mouth position). Some examples are listed below.

- /oi/: oil, coin, boil, coil, foil, soil, join, joint, point, noise
- /oy/: boy, joy, toy, annoy, joyful, destroy, enjoy, employ
- /ou/: couch, pouch, loud, cloud, proud, bounce, count, found, pound, round, ground, sound, our, hour, flour, house, mouse, out, shout, spout, mouth, south
- /ow/: bow, cow, how, now, brown, howl, growl, scowl, down, gown, town, clown, crown, drown, frown

R-controlled vowels: the bossy 'r'

When a vowel is followed by 'r', the vowel sound is different from either the long or short vowel sound. The /r/ sound tends to dominate, and hence it is called the bossy 'r'. Some examples are listed below:

- 'ar': arm, far, hard, jar, farm, barn, star, sharp, start, smart, bar, art, card, park, car, dart, ark

- 'or': or, for, torch, torn, horn, sport, storm, short, morning, pork, north, cork, fork, horse

- 'er': her, sister, herb, silver, litter, pepper, letter, slipper, winter, never, number, butter

- 'ir': bird, girl, dirt, stir, thirst, first, shirt, third, skirt, sir, birthday

- 'ur': turn, burn, fur, hurt, burnt, church, curl, nurse, purse, Saturday, purple, turkey

'Y' as a vowel

The letter 'y' often acts as a vowel within words.

Examine the list of words below. On a piece of paper, divide the words into two columns. On one side, write the words where 'y' sounds like /e/, and on the other side write the words that sound like /ī/.

fly, baby, cry, happy, bye, goofy, why, hairy, dye, try, scary, my, fairy, Mary

- Did you notice anything?

- Can you determine the rule?

In one-syllable words, 'y' usually sounds like 'i'. In two-syllable words, 'y' sounds like 'e'.

- Can you think of any exceptions to the above rule?

'Key' is one example.

TAKE THE PHONICS QUIZ!

no   toad   trace   planet   found   team
giraffe   girl   coma   annoy   this

Using the list of words above, can you identify:

1   A consonant blend _____

2   A hard 'g' _____

3 A soft 'g' _____

4 A consonant digraph _____

5 A hard 'c' _____

6 A soft 'c' _____

7 A vowel diphthong _____

8 A short vowel sound _____

9 A long vowel sound _____

10 A vowel digraph _____

Teaching phonics in meaningful contexts

Having examined the range of phonic skills that an emergent reader requires thus far in this chapter, the main principles of effective phonics teaching will now be explored in this section. Meaningful contexts, such as big books, and other forms of continuous text, such as poems, rhymes and environmental print, highlight the goal of phonics instruction from the outset, that learning individual phonemes will eventually lead to the unassisted reading of continuous texts. Using texts also allows the teacher to develop comprehension skills alongside phonic skills so that children learn to read for meaning from the outset. Effective phonics teaching should be multisensory in nature; therefore, lessons should include tactile, kinaesthetic, aural and visual elements so that all learners can be successful. Young children are active learners, so learning phonics should be playful and enjoyable. Children also need lots of practice to ensure mastery, so the teacher will need to use a range of activities.

Shared reading of large-format books

It is important that children understand why they are learning phonics from the very beginning. Therefore, it is helpful to begin your phonics lesson with a big book, a poetry chart, handmade books or environmental print. Try to match your phonics instruction with the shared reading texts that are available to you. Examine each text and identify phonemes that are prevalent within the book, and use this information in your planning. Different books will be suitable for teaching particular phonemes. For example, *Chicka Chicka Boom Boom* (Martin & Archambauld, 1995) might be a good book to use when introducing /ch/ as this phoneme is found frequently in the book and is central to the storyline. *The Smartest Giant in Town* (Donaldson, 2003) could be used to teach /ar/ as there are numerous words containing this phoneme in the book. This type of planning will be discussed further in Chapters 6 and 11. Large acetates (in A2 size) can be very useful as children can underline or circle the target phoneme in the book multiple times without marking the pages.

Poetry and rhyme charts

Poetry and rhyme charts can also be used as a starting point for phonics instruction. For example, the poem 'Baby in a High Chair' could be used as a forum to teach the consonant /b/, while the poem 'The Whale' could be used to teach the vowel digraph /ay/.

Baby in a High Chair (Jack Prelutsky)
Baby in a high chair,
baby in a bib,
baby in a buggy,
baby in a crib.
Baby with the giggles,
baby with a smile,
such a lovely baby,
happy all the while.

The Whale
Whale, whale go away!
This is not a place to stay.
Swim away, away, away,
The boats go out for whales today.
So do not stay in this bay.
Swim away, away, away.
This is not a place to stay!

Language experience charts

Language experience charts can also be used as a starting point to teach a new letter sound or to revise letter sounds previously learned. For example, the language experience chart featured below contains numerous words that begin with /f/, including 'farm', 'farmer', 'Friday' and 'fun'. This might represent an ideal opportunity for a teacher to introduce this letter sound to children within a meaningful context.

Our School Trip
On Friday, we went to a farm.
We saw the farmer.
He had lots of cows and sheep.
We got to hold baby chicks.
It was a lot of fun!
The farmer gave us a ride in his trailer.

A multisensory approach to teaching phonics

Effective phonics teaching should be multisensory in nature, so that all learners can be successful. Using a multisensory teaching technique means helping children to learn through more than one sense. Most teaching techniques involve using either sight or hearing (visual or auditory). The visual sense is activated when children are encouraged to look at letters, words, pictures, objects or texts. The hearing sense is used to listen to what the teacher says or to learn songs or jingles. Children's vision may be affected by difficulties with tracking or visual processing. Sometimes children's auditory processing may be weak. In order to ease these difficulties, the teacher should involve the use of more of children's senses, especially the use of touch (tactile) and movement (kinaesthetic). This will

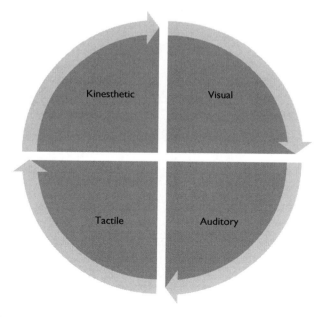

Figure 3.1 Multisensory approach to phonics

help children's brains to develop tactile and kinaesthetic memories in relation to phonics knowledge, as well as the auditory and visual ones. The following suggestions support a multisensory approach (see Figure 3.1).

Visual

It is helpful to associate a keyword and picture with each letter (Ehri, 1992). For example, if teaching the phoneme /b/, you might use the word 'ball' and have a corresponding picture of a ball. Children should be encouraged to identify the symbol in many different places, such as locating it in the big book, in environmental print, on the alphabet chart, the word wall (high-frequency words) and on a specific flash card. This letter should be highlighted, underlined and written many times.

Auditory

Children should hear/say the phoneme while looking at the symbol. Children should hear rhymes that relate to the letter sound and a verbal mnemonic that relates to writing the letter (e.g. 'around, up and down' for the letter 'a' – this is also visual). The songs from the Jolly Phonics programme could be helpful here (Lloyd & Jolly, 1995), or other songs and jingles related to the letter sound.

Tactile

Children should engage in a variety of tasks that are tactile in nature (e.g. tracing letters in a sand tray, creating letters on geoboards, making letters out of play dough, painting letters with fingers, using magnetic letters and feeling sandpaper letters). A feely bag filled with objects that begin with the target phoneme can be used (see Figure 3.2). Here, children must choose an object from the bag (with their eyes closed) and determine whether or not it begins with the target phoneme. For example, a feely bag for the phoneme /c/ might contain a carrot, a cat toy, a cup, a cake (plastic), a cloth, a comb, a toothbrush, a pencil and a book (it is important to include items that do not include the target phoneme).

Kinaesthetic

Children should use bodily movement to aid their learning. For example, when teaching a phoneme, a hand sign or action could be used. For example, when learning the phoneme /d/, children might be encouraged to pretend to beat a drum. Action songs or jingles that accompany phonemes are also helpful. These activities can involve physical movement to copy letter shapes and sounds, and manipulation of magnetic letters to build words (Rose, 2006).

Figure 3.2 Looking for objects beginning with 'c' in a feely bag

Games and activities for phonics instruction

Literacy lessons need to be active and social in nature. Incorporate different games, puzzles and activities into your lesson to maximise learning. The following suggestions introduce activity into children's learning.

Picture/letter sound sorts

Using picture cards, sort for either one letter sound or multiple letter sounds depending on the children's ability level. For example, if the target letter sound is /c/, then the activity might involve a mixture of picture cards of words that begin with /c/, such as 'cat', 'cow', 'cake', 'cup' and 'coconut', and words that do not begin with /c/, such as 'boat, 'dog' and 'elephant' (see Figure 3.3). The children have to identify whether or not the picture begins with /c/ and sort them accordingly. The activity can be expanded to focus on a number of letter sounds, such as /c/, /s/ and /t/, for example. In this activity, the children are presented with letter cards with /c/, /n/ and /t/ printed on them. They are given a mixture of pictures, such as 'cat', cow, 'cake', 'cup', 'nut', 'nose', 'nail', 'net', 'tennis', 'tap', 'turnip', 'taxi' and 'tiger'. This activity can be done as a whole class/large group first, and then children can try it with a small group/partner.

Figure 3.3 Picture sort activity

Letter puzzles

Children should have frequent opportunities to play with letter puzzles/jigsaws that involve matching upper- and lower-case letters or pictures to letters with a small group or a partner.

Bingo

A simple game of bingo can be played using the phonemes that the children have learned to date (see Figure 3.4). The teacher could create bingo cards using sturdy paper with a grid of 6 to 12 squares containing phonemes that the children have learned. Plastic counters can be used to cover any phonemes called by the teacher. The first child to cover all the phonemes can shout 'Bingo!'

Letter hunt

Children can hunt for the letter sound that they are studying in magazines and newspapers. Highlighter pens can enhance this activity, and children enjoy sharing what they found with the larger group. If there is a visualizer attached to the class interactive whiteboard (IWB), then it can be easy to share findings.

Sound muncher

This can be easily constructed out of a small wastepaper bin with a lid that opens and closes. Cut out a pair of eyes and stick them to the top of the bin – a 'sound

Figure 3.4 Letter bingo

muncher' is born. Then gather items/pictures of objects that begin with the target letter sound. Explain to the children that the sound muncher only 'eats' things that start with /?/ (the letter sound that the children are studying). Pictures of items or concrete items can be used. For example, if the children are studying /c/, the teacher might present the children with a picture of a 'cat' and ask them if the sound muncher will eat it. If the children agree that it can be 'eaten', then it is 'fed' to the sound muncher. Then the teacher might present a picture of a 'dog' and ask the same question. The activity can continue in this fashion.

Magnetic letters

These can be used for simple letter sorts (e.g. making a pile of all the 'c's) or to construct CVC words and then more complex words containing digraphs and diphthongs (see Figure 3.5).

Alphabet mat

An alphabet mat can be constructed out of a large piece of sturdy cardboard (3 ft by 3 ft). The teacher can draw a grid containing the letters of the alphabet or particular letter sounds under current study. The children are provided with a sack containing

Figure 3.5 Magnetic letters

items and pictures that relate to the phonemes. They must place the pictures/items on the correct phoneme. This can be conducted as a circle time activity with the whole class as a revision exercise, or pairs and small groups of children could partake in this activity during literacy stations.

Making words (Cunningham, 1998)

This activity is designed to encourage children to identify letters that can be used to build simple to complex words. The children receive the letters on small cards or on a grid that can be cut up by the children (see Figure 3.6). For example, the children might be each given a set of letters (e.g. 't', 'i', 'n', 'e', 'w', 'r'). The teacher begins by asking the children to make a few two-letter words, then some three-letter words, followed by some four-letter and five-letter words. They can only use the letters provided:

- Two-letter words: in, it

- Three-letter words: win, net, wet, nit, tin, ten

- Four-letter words: wine, twin

- Five-letter word: twine

Figure 3.6 'Making words' activity

Then the children are asked to create a 'secret word' using all six letters. In this example, the word is 'winter'. The words can then be sorted according to spelling patterns. When sorting the words, the teacher should encourage the children to encode new words (create the words from the letter tiles), as well as decode the words already discovered in the activity (read or 'sound out' the words).

Decoding (read)	in	it	net	wine	ten
	tin	nit	wet	twine	
	win				
	twin				
Encoding (write)	bin	hit	get	mine	men

A large selection of similar lessons is available in Cunningham (1998).

Reading-writing rhymes (Cunningham, 2004)

This is an activity where the children are given cards with various phonemes on them. They are then presented with a rime (e.g. 'ed'). They then have to decide whether or not their phonemes make 'real words' when combined with the rime.

The children can then place their phoneme beside 'ed' to see if it makes a 'real word'. This can be developed into a class chart:

-ed

sled   *dead

bed   *bread

red

shed

bled

led

wed

Words that sound like the rhyme but are spelled differently are added at the bottom of the chart.

The children are then challenged to create a 'rhyme' using some of the words from the chart:

A rhyme for '-ed'
Ted was in bed because he fell off his sled.
He bled and he bled so he stayed in bed.
His mum put the sled in the shed.

The teaching of phonics is only effective if children have regular opportunities to use their phonic knowledge in reading and writing. In addition to the activities listed above, phonic teaching should be reinforced in guided reading sessions, independent reading and the writers' workshop, as outlined in the chapters in this book.

Knowledge of letter names

Knowledge of letter sounds or phonemes helps children to decode words and can be used for invented spelling in writing. However, it is essential that children also learn the names of the letters of the alphabet, which will be essential for spelling as they grow older. Children should be taught the alphabet song while they are learning letter sounds. While many children arrive in school 'knowing' the alphabet, they tend to suffer from the 'elemno' problem (i.e. they don't tend to distinguish between letters, and often the letters are not pronounced correctly). Therefore, the teacher should teach the song using 'echo tracking' – the teacher sings a few letters using clear diction (e.g. 'a, b, c, d') while pointing to the letters on a large letter chart, and then the children 'echo' sing while pointing to the chart. When the teacher is satisfied that the letters are being pronounced correctly, the class can engage in choral singing while tracking the letters.

Teach the lower-case letters first as they are the letter forms most frequently encountered in text (Adams, 1990). Draw attention to the children's names and the initial letter they begin with. Attach flash cards with the children's names on them to the alphabet frieze. Encourage children to clap the syllables in their names and to distinguish between long and short vowel sounds at the beginning of names.

Alphabet books should also be read regularly to develop children's understanding of letter names and provoke discussion about the correspondence (or lack of) between the letter names and their sounds. These come in various different forms, from rhyming alphabets, such as *ABC: Alphabet Rhymes for You and Me* (Andreae, 2010), to stories about the alphabet, such as *Chicka Chicka Boom Boom* (Martin & Archambauld, 1995). When you have read a number of alphabet books during read-aloud sessions and the children are familiar with the genre, creating a class alphabet book can be an enjoyable and rewarding activity. The box below contains some recommendations for alphabet books that might be read during lessons or during teacher read-alouds. Alphabet books can be particularly helpful for English language learners as the pictures not only encourage knowledge of letter names and sounds, but they also provide an opportunity to learn a great deal of new vocabulary in a meaningful context that is 'comprehensible' to a child ELL.

ALPHABET BOOK RECOMMENDATIONS

Andreae, G. (2010). *ABC: Alphabet rhymes for you and me.* London: Orchard Books.
Blake, Q. (1989). *Quentin Blake's ABC.* London: Knopf.
Campbell, R. (2014). *ABC zoo.* London: Macmillan.
Carle, E. (2007). *Eric Carle's ABC.* New York: Grosset & Dunlap.
Deneux, X. (2016). *TouchThinkLearn: ABC.* New York: Chronicle Books.
Ehlert, L. (1996). *Eating the alphabet.* New York: Harcourt Brace.
Geisel, T.S. (1963). *Dr. Seuss' ABC.* New York: Random House.
Jeffers, O. (2017). *An alphabet fold-out A–Z.* London: HarperCollins.
Kerr, J. (2005). *Mog's amazing birthday caper.* London: HarperCollins.
Martin, B. & Archambauld, J. (1995). *Chicka chicka boom boom.* New York: Scholastic.
Segal, R. (2006). *ABC in NYC.* New York: Murray Hill Books.

Phonics as a cueing system

Language has three major cueing systems: grapho-phonic, semantic and syntactic (see Figure 3.7). To become skilled, fluent readers, children need to have a firm grasp of all three cueing systems in order to be able to figure out unfamiliar words and the meaning of sentences (Cunningham, 1990).

Grapho-phonic cues

Grapho-phonics refers to the teaching of the orthographic code of language and the relations of spelling patterns to sound patterns. Children use a knowledge of the sounds and letters and groups of letters and their skill at combining these sounds to interpret print. Eye movement studies have indicated that reading is a 'letter-mediated' rather than a 'whole-word-mediated' process, as skilled readers attend to almost every word within a sentence and process the letters that compose each word (McConkie & Zola, 1987). Poor readers who lack phonic knowledge tend not to fully analyse words and tend to rely on initial consonant cues, disregarding the rest of the word (Stanovich, 1992). Therefore, phonics instruction is required to ensure accurate decoding so that comprehension might be viable.

Semantic cues

The semantic system refers to the meaning of language – the words and parts of words that convey meaning. Children use semantic or meaning cues to predict the text (use knowledge and experience of the world to guess words). For example, if children read 'the baby started to . . .', they might 'guess' that the missing word might be 'cry' as that is a word that would make sense in the context

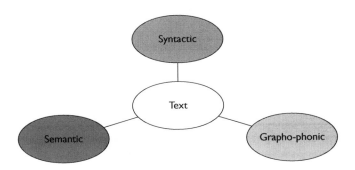

Figure 3.7 Cueing systems

of the sentence. Similarly, when reading 'There was a tear in my eye', children would 'sound out' 'tear' using a long e sound because semantically it makes sense. Whereas, if children read 'Don't tear the paper!', they might pronounce it with a short 'e' sound.

Syntactic cues

The syntax of a language is the way in which words are arranged in phrases and sentences. They are the underlying 'rules' that form the grammar of a language. Children's oral language gives them some understanding of the grammar and usage of language. For example, if children read 'John caught the . . .', they might 'guess' that the missing word is a noun as that would be grammatically correct.

Semantic and syntactic cues are important as they focus on the meaning within a text. However, over-reliance on either of these two cueing systems will result in flawed reading. Indeed, content words – those that carry most of the meaning within a text – are often the most difficult to predict. Children also need to have a firm knowledge of letter–sound relationships so that they can combine their decoding skills with semantic and syntactic cues (Stanovich, 1980). Therefore, literacy instruction needs to pay attention to all three of these cueing systems in order to produce confident and competent readers. While this chapter has been devoted to understanding phonics as a cueing system, semantic and syntactic cueing systems will be discussed further in Chapter 5 when we explore comprehension strategies.

Assessing phonic knowledge

Teacher observation and informal testing

Children's developing phonic knowledge should be assessed in a variety of ways. When teaching phonics, a teacher should use teacher observation and note-taking to keep track of children's progress. Some phonemes may be more difficult than others for young children to learn, and some children will need some additional small group or one-to-one instruction in order to master certain aspects of phonics instruction. The teacher should prepare a teacher-made test based on the phonemes taught and administer it at regular intervals (see Figure 3.8). This can consist of a list of individual phonemes and some words that would assess children's ability to blend phonemes together effectively. This type of test will help the teacher to plan appropriate instruction. The teacher may also wish to conduct a more holistic assessment, such as a running record.

Figure 3.8 Teacher-made test

Running records (Clay, 1993)

Running records can be used for a variety of reasons. They can be used to assess fluency, comprehension and decoding. They can also highlight children's ability to monitor their comprehension (through self-correction) and the use of semantic and syntactic cueing systems. Running records allow the teacher to determine children's instructional levels, and therefore appropriate texts can be selected for instruction. A miscue analysis of the errors made during the running record will also highlight areas of need that need to be targeted for instruction (e.g. consistent errors related to vowel digraphs would indicate that this might need to become the focus of phonics instruction within reading lessons). The running record and subsequent miscue analysis might also reveal information about children's reading behaviour, such as their tendency to over-rely on a particular cueing system, such as phonics, at the expense of meaning, or vice versa. This information would be very helpful in planning for balanced literacy instruction.

In order to conduct a running record, a text must first be chosen for the child to read. It is recommended that the text be one that is deemed to be relatively easy for the child to assure a positive assessment experience initially. Ideally, the text should be one that the child has not read before. A short extract of 100 to 200 words should be used for the assessment. The teacher should compose approximately 5 to 10 comprehension questions. Teachers beginning to use this assessment practice might find it useful to record the session so that they can listen back to it if required. The teacher would then introduce the text briefly to the child (e.g. 'This is a story about a little boy and his pet kitten'). The child is then asked to read the extract. The teacher records the errors made on the scoring sheet (see Figure 3.9). An example of a scoring sheet can be found in Appendix C. The reading can also be timed if information about reading rate is required, and the teacher can calculate the number of words read correctly per minute. The teacher tallies the number of errors made and the number of self-corrections made, and uses those figures to calculate the reading level (see the box below for information about reading levels). The teacher will need to continue testing (using either easier or more difficult texts) until the instructional level is reached.

DETERMINING READING LEVEL

- Independent level: 95–100% accuracy

- Instructional: 90–94% accuracy

- Frustration: <90% accuracy

To find accuracy: Divide the number of errors by the number of words in the text. Write it as a ratio. For example:

Words in the text: 150

Errors: 15

Self-corrections: 5

Accuracy level: 15 / 150 = 10

Ratio = 1:10

Accuracy: 90%

Level: frustration/instructional

Self-correction rate: 5 / 15 + 5 = 4

Ratio = 1:4

Note: If the self-correction rate is higher than 1:1, it indicates that the reader does not always read for meaning. The higher the ratio, the more significant the issue is. In the example given above, the reader only self-corrected one-quarter of all errors, which would indicate that more instruction related to reading for meaning and monitoring one's reading is required.

Figure 3.9 Teacher marks a running record

Having discovered the child's instructional level and his or her self-correction ratio, the teacher may also choose to conduct a miscue analysis of the child's errors. To do this, each of the errors must be analysed to determine what led the child to make the error. The teacher would use knowledge of the three cueing systems to guide his or her judgement in the matter:

- *Semantics/meaning*: Did the meaning of the text have an impact on the child's reading? Both pictures and information taken from them are considered meaning cues, as well as the 'gist' of the text.

- *Syntax*: Did the child read the sentence in a grammatical and linguistically reasonable manner? If there was a substitution, for example, did he or she substitute a proper part of speech?

- *Visual/grapho-phonic*: Did the child look at the word and make an attempt based on how it appears? Did he or she use a beginning or ending letter? A cluster of letters? What gaps in phonic knowledge are apparent? Is there a pattern of errors related to phonics?

For example, if the text next to a picture of a kitten reads 'I like my kitten' and the child reads 'I like my cat', it is likely that the child has used a picture cue to aid his or her reading (at the expense of grapho-phonic cues). This would be regarded as a meaning cue. As reading 'I like my cat' makes sense grammatically (both 'cat' and 'kitten' are nouns), it can also be regarded as a syntactic cue. However, since 'cat' and 'kitten' have no phonic correlation, the child is not making use of visual cues.

An example of a miscue analysis grid is given in Appendix C. The information gleaned from the analysis outlined above can be very helpful in planning for focused instruction. It can also aid the teacher in grouping children for guided reading instruction, which will be discussed in more detail in Chapter 7.

Phonics and the English language learner

ELL students, just like native speakers of English, need explicit phonics instruction in order to become efficient readers. It is important to realise that many of the words that we might use in teaching phonics might not be in an English language learner's spoken vocabulary. For example, when studying CVC words, examples such as 'cap' and 'rat' may need visuals so that the children can understand the word they have just read. Therefore, meaningful contexts such as books, poems and rhymes with pictures are particularly important in ensuring understanding. The use of kinaesthetic activities help all learners, but will be particularly beneficial to an ELL pupil, as they will often need to learn and remember new vocabulary, as well as letter sounds, when instructed, for example, to mime 'bouncing a ball' for the sound /b/. Some sounds may cause difficulties for English language learners if those sounds are not used in their home language. The use of small mirrors so that they can see the position of their teeth and tongue when making a sound has been found to be helpful in supporting phonics acquisition (Blevins, 2006).

It should also be noted that many ELLs come from homes where they are the only member of the family who can read English. This might mean that children would need additional support in school, and the teacher should be mindful of the content of any homework given. Some ELLs will have parents who are literate in English (often to a high standard), but the parents may have learned to read in a very different manner than the one outlined in this book. It is recommended that parents are informed through various forms of communication about the school's approach to reading so that they can support their children in an appropriate manner.

Key concepts for practice

- Phonics instruction needs to include the range of phonemes in the English language.

- Any instruction in either phonological awareness or phonics should have its roots in a meaningful, contextualised reading experience, such as a big book, poetry chart, language experience text or digital text.

- Phonics instruction should be multisensory, including visual, aural, tactile and kinaesthetic learning.

- Phonics games and enjoyable activities should be incorporated into instruction.

- Assessment should be ongoing and based on instruction.

- Phonics instruction should form part of literacy lessons and should not dominate reading instruction.

- English language learners may require visuals and kinaesthetic activities to help them learn phonics effectively.

REFLECTION: THINKING ABOUT YOUR PRACTICE

- To what extent do you currently use meaningful contexts such as big books, language experience charts and poetry charts as a starting point for phonics instruction?

- What sort of resources do you have available to you to teach in this manner? If there is a dearth of resources, how could you adapt the ideas described in this chapter to suit your context?

- Does phonics dominate your literacy instruction? How could your approach become more balanced (or meaningful)?

For further exploration

Chall, J. (1995). *Learning to read: The great debate.* Belmont: CA: Wadsworth.

Cunningham, P. (2012). *Phonics they use: Words for reading and writing.* London: Pearson.

Harrison, C. (2004). *Understanding reading development.* London: Sage.

Snow, C., Burns, S. & Griffin, P. (Eds.) (1998). *Preventing reading difficulties in young children.* Washington, DC: National Academy Press.

4 Other early reading skills

GUIDING QUESTIONS FOR THIS CHAPTER

- How would you plan, teach and assess children's concepts about print?

- How would you teach high-frequency sight words in a multisensory, meaningful manner?

- How would you scaffold children's fluency and vocabulary development using a range of approaches?

Introduction

We discussed the importance of phonological awareness and phonics in reading in the previous two chapters. In this chapter, we will broaden the lens to include other essential early literacy skills that can be taught in early reading lessons, including concepts about print, sight word knowledge, oral reading fluency and vocabulary development. These skills are best developed in a meaningful context, and hence numerous references will be made to the use of big books in shared reading lessons throughout the chapter. Other meaningful contexts also include language experience charts, poetry charts, guided reading and regular storybooks read aloud. When children are taught a literacy skill such as phonics or sight words in the context of a 'real' text, it allows them to understand why they need to learn these skills – that they will be able to read texts on their own one day. Using a 'real' text can also be very helpful in planning and teaching a range of literacy skills as it provides a starting point and a focus for your lessons. It allows the teacher to transition smoothly from teaching one literacy skill to another as they are all linked by a common text. In Chapter 6, you will be given an example of how a teacher could use one text to teach a wide range of literacy skills over several lessons.

Developing concepts about print

Concepts about print are elements of print that children need to understand in order to be a successful reader. These include the concepts of books/texts/reading materials, letters, words, sentences, print directionality, punctuation and other pre-reading skills. Developing concepts about print at an early age is an essential component of literacy development and has been regarded as a critical indicator in determining literacy achievement (Nichols, Rupley & Rickleman, 2004). 'When a child understands what to attend to, in what order, and a few things about the shapes and positions of letters and words, this opens other doors to literacy learning' (Clay, 2006, p. 40). Clay (1993) indicates that many children's reading difficulties stem from not knowing how and what to look at in a printed text. Hence, it is important to determine what children understand about how texts function, and teaching should focus on the concepts about print of which children are unsure. This may serve to reduce reading difficulties when children are exposed to formal reading instruction.

It is important that children's concepts about print and texts be developed in meaningful and enjoyable ways. The use of a big book provides a perfect forum for a discussion about the different aspects of a text. Instead of merely filling in a page of a workbook on full stops or capital letters, for example, children can be encouraged to locate them in the text and discuss how this type of punctuation affects how the teacher reads certain portions of the text. Seeing punctuation 'in action' in this manner can have a much more powerful effect on young children's understanding of how texts work. Concepts about print can also be explored in a guided reading context, and with language experience or poetry charts. These resources are meaningful to children as they illustrate how real texts work.

The following concepts about print should be taught to emergent readers:

- *How to hold a book*: This is the understanding that books have a front and a back and are read front to back in English. It also includes children's ability to notice if the book is upside down. Presenting children with an upside-down text or opening the text at the back page can be greeted with exuberant cries of, 'No, that's not how you do it', which illustrates an emerging knowledge of how texts function. When these actions are met with blank stares, then it may suggest that the children have had few opportunities to handle books prior to coming to school.

- *Left-to-right, top-to-bottom orientation*: This is the understanding that English language text is read from left to right and from top to bottom. Demonstrate this as you read a big book or a language experience chart by pointing to each word as you read it. Assess children's understanding by asking, 'Where should I start reading?' 'What will I read next?'

- *Title, author, illustrator, blurb*: Children should use and understand these terms from the earliest juncture. At first, simply explain, model their use and discuss each term, then elicit definitions/terminology from the children. When using poetry charts, the notion of the 'poet' should be introduced by drawing the children's attention to the poet's name at the bottom of the chart.

- *Table of contents, index, glossary*: These terms should be discussed when exploring non-fiction books with children.

- *Understanding the notion of a letter and a word*: Some children may come to school without the understanding that spoken words are strung together to form sentences (the most basic level of phonological awareness). The teacher should emphasise that each spoken word corresponds to a group of letters (a 'word') in the text by pointing to each word as he or she reads. There should also be some discussion on what a 'letter' is, and how it differs from a 'word', using concrete examples from a familiar big book or language experience chart. Cardboard 'windows' of different sizes attached to a pencil or a stick can be useful in helping children to highlight a 'letter' or a 'word'.

- *Capital letters and lower-case letters*: Children should be taught this terminology, and the teacher should lead a class discussion on how the letters differ from each other and when they are to be used.

- *Punctuation (full stops, commas, colons, semicolons, speech marks, exclamation marks, question marks, ellipses, parentheses)*: Children should be taught this terminology in a spiral approach as they progress through the junior classes. Generally, a discovery approach to learning works best. This can be followed by a class discussion on how and when the different types of punctuation should be used. For example, if the teacher is seeking to teach the children about the use of an exclamation mark, he or she may point to the exclamation mark on a page in a big book and say, 'Do you see this little mark on the page? It tells me how to read this part of the story. Listen carefully and tell me what you notice.' Then the teacher may reread the relevant portions of the text with great emphasis and excitement, and then elicit responses from the children. The teacher can then share with the children that the 'little mark' is called an exclamation mark, and invite the children to find other examples in the text. When creating a language experience text, the teacher can also lead a discussion on what punctuation is needed, depending on how the children said the sentences they wished to include in the chart. Punctuation is also very important when reading poems or rhymes, so it forms part of any lesson sequence based on a poetry chart.

- *Other print features (bold print, capitalised print, italics, speech bubbles)*: Certain print features may be quite prevalent in particular big books. For example, italics are used frequently in *Owl Babies* (Waddell, 1998) and speech bubbles are used on many pages of *This Is the Bear* (Hayes, 2003). Therefore, these texts might provide an ideal forum for the teaching of these skills.

Assessing concepts about print

In order to ensure that children understand the appropriate range of concepts about print for this age group, they should be assessed at regular intervals both to monitor their progress and to inform teaching. Both formal and informal assessments should be used. Informal assessment can be carried out using teacher observation. During lessons, the teacher should take notes in relation to student understanding of the concepts about print that he or she is currently teaching. A formal assessment, such as the one described below, will allow the teacher to benchmark children's progress. It may also alert the teacher to particular difficulties his or her students are having in relation to understanding how texts work.

Marie Clay created a 'concepts about print' assessment as part of reading recovery (Clay, 1993). Reading recovery is an early intervention for children who have made very little progress in reading and writing during their first year at school. It involves a daily one-to-one lesson with a highly trained teacher for a period of between 12 and 20 weeks. The aim of the programme is that these children will have caught up with their classmates and can read and write at a level within the average band for their age at the end of this time period. The purpose of the concepts about print assessment is to screen and diagnose children's procedural and conceptual knowledge about how printed language functions.

It attempts to ascertain whether children understand:

- that print contains a message;
- where the 'front' and the 'back' of the book are located;
- where to commence reading and where to continue when one reaches the end of the line;
- the return sweep to the left;
- word-by-word matching;
- the concept of what comes first and last;
- when there is a change in line order, word order and letter order;
- that the left page comes before the right;
- the meaning of full stops, commas, question marks and speech marks;

- the difference between lower-case and capital letters;

- the notion of a 'word'; and

- the notion of a 'letter'.

However, Marie Clay's assessment has been adapted and used in a wide variety of contexts as her original test requires the purchase of specific books, *Follow Me Moon* (Clay, 2015) and *No Shoes* (Clay, 2000). A similar test can be devised and used with any text, as can be seen in the box below.

CONCEPTS ABOUT PRINT ASSESSMENT (ADAPTED FROM CLAY, 1993)

You can use any simple picture book for this quick assessment. It should be administered on an individual basis.

1 Where would I start reading this book?

2 Can you show me a word?

3 Can you show me a letter?

4 Where does the story end?

5 Where would I find the title (name) of the story?

6 Show me how to hold the book.

7 Point to each word as I read this sentence (one-to-one correspondence).

8 Do you know what this is? (full stop/period). If children answer this question correctly, you could also ask them about other punctuation in the book to gauge the extent of their knowledge.

Developing a sight vocabulary (high-frequency words)

Sight vocabulary refers to high-frequency words that a young reader should be able to recognise automatically – 'on sight' without decoding. If children do not possess an adequate sight vocabulary, their reading fluency will be adversely affected. The Dolch list contains the sight vocabulary store required by a beginning reader. This list is made up of 220 of the most frequently occurring words in printed English, and 50 to 75 per cent of the words in children's books can be found on this list. Indeed, the first 100 make up 50 per cent of all printed material that any reader will encounter in books. If the beginning reader has a small store of sight words and a good grasp of some basic phonics, then he or she should be able to read simple sentences such as 'I like the dog' or 'This is my cat'. It would be recommended that children start by learning around 20 to 30 sight words. I have grouped the words according to frequency and also by their general usefulness in reading and writing. For example, although 'like' is not at the top of the list according to frequency, it is a very useful word in reading and writing contexts, and hence it is in the first listing. Sight vocabulary instruction should occur alongside phonics instruction as it allows children to read simple sentences with some degree of fluency, even in the early stages of reading instruction. Consider the following sentence, for example: 'I like the cat.' The first three words are sight vocabulary words and 'cat' is a consonant/vowel/consonant (CVC) word that is easily decoded. Children who have learned a handful of sight vocabulary words and can decode individual vowels and consonants would be well able to read sentences such as this.

Sight words for the first year of reading instruction

I	like	the	this	is	a	see	can	went	to
look	at	we	was	want	and	he	his	said	she
her	on	in	am	little	big	play	eat	me	my
if	of	here	going	are	it	has	they	but	with

Sight words for the second/third year of reading instruction

that	but	had	all	there	some	come	came	have	be	as	out
down	do	could	when	did	what	why	when	who	where	were	so
them	one	two	three	four	five	six	seven	eight	nine	ten	yellow
blue	green	red	black	white	orange	now	ask	very	nice	an	over
don't	your	from	up	not	will	yes	no	go	you	good	about
because		around	too	take	make	every	away	their	saw	call	called
after	brown	walk	or	before	again	never	today	try	myself	give	have
new	does	goes	always		once upon a time			soon	find	our	buy
open	those	use	say	found	live		together		thank	laugh	

Reading fluency can be developed through systematic phonics instruction (which was discussed in Chapter 3) and through acquiring a strong sight vocabulary of high-frequency words. The first 100 words on the Dolch list represent 50 per cent of all written material. Thus, if children are able to recall these words automatically, it will enhance their reading fluency. In the past, these high-frequency words were often taught through skill-and-drill activities, or 'death by flash card' (Harrison, 2004). However, meaningful contexts such as big books, language experience charts, poetry charts and guided reading can be used to teach children these essential words while also communicating their importance in the reading task. When considering which sight words to teach using a specific big book, it is important that there are many examples of the target words within the text. For example, in the text *Handa's Hen* (Browne, 2003), the words 'said', 'her', 'they', 'is' and 'see' (from the Dolch list) are repeated several times amid the text, so this will allow the children to locate the target word a number of times. Similarly, when choosing words for instruction from a language experience or poetry chart, consider those that are most frequent so that there are plenty of examples for children to locate and discuss.

Teaching sight words

In the beginning, children may need to see a sight word up to 100 or 200 times before it is memorised. As children's sight vocabulary grows, their learning rate will increase, but they will still need lots of practice. Therefore, sight word teaching needs to be multifaceted and multisensory (visual, aural, tactile and kinaesthetic in nature).

The following approaches can be used when teaching a sight word:

- Take the word from context. Show the children the word on a flash card, then find the word in the text many times (highlight it). Look for the word in environmental print around the classroom.

- Discuss the word's features (length, syllables, letters).

- Compare and contrast with similar words already on the word wall (see Figure 4.1). Words should only be added to the word wall when they are being taugh to the children –the word wall should be empty at the beginning of the school year!

- Compose oral sentences (e.g. if the target word is 'like', then model 'I like going to school'), and then encourage the children to compose similar sentences.

- Ask the children, 'How will we remember it?'

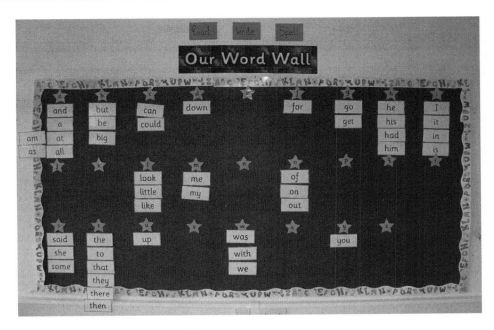

Figure 4.1 Alphabetised word wall

- Trace the word in the air. Trace the word using rainbow writing. Rainbow writing is when the target word is written in a large black font. The children then create a 'rainbow' by tracing around the word with different colour crayons while saying the word.

- Trace the word in sand trays. When using a sand tray, ensure that the surface underneath the sand is a bright colour and always have a flash card directly in front of children of the target word. Encourage children to say the word as they write it.

- Make the word out of play dough. Again, make sure that each child has a flash card to copy from, and that they say the word while they create it.

- Make the word out of magnetic letters. Make sure to limit the amount of letters so that the children have the letters that they need, and perhaps a few extra. If they have to sort the letters from a large pile, it might be a very time-consuming exercise that is not necessarily focused on the target word.

- Use games. This is an example of a game that can be used to teach sight words. Create a simple 'go fish' activity using coloured card cut in the shape of fish (with target sight words printed on them) and a pencil with a string attached (as a fishing rod). Tie or glue a magnet to the end of the string. Attach paper

Figure 4.2 'Go fish!' for sight words

clips or small magnets to each fish. Have children fish for words and say them aloud (see Figure 4.2).

■ Find the word in other contexts (big books, rhymes, handmade books, guided reading books and environmental print). Some sight words are quite abstract in nature, so it might be advisable to create resources that provide additional scaffolding. An example of this would be the word 'was'. On its own, it is difficult to define, but if it was combined with baby photographs of the children and used in the caption 'John *was* a baby', it becomes more memorable (see Figure 4.3). A large classroom display could then be used as a teaching resource and as a useful memory aid for a difficult word.

■ Word search. Create your own word search using target sight words. This focuses children's attention on the letter sequence or letter strings contained in the word.

■ Make sentences using a pocket chart. For example, if the children have learned 'I' and 'like' and 'see', numerous sentences could be created using the children's names, such as 'I like Mya' or 'I see James'. The use of the children's names in text makes this an engaging activity (see Figure 4.4).

■ Use computer games. Suitable games include:

  o Matching games: www.cookie.com/kids/games/sight-words.html

  o Memory games: www.dolchword.net/dolch-pre-primer-memory-game-1.html

Figure 4.3 Creating texts for sight words

- o Listening and responding games: www.fun4thebrain.com
- o Bingo: www.abcya.com

When teaching a new sight word, make sure that the text you use includes the target word several times. While big books are a wonderful resource, you can also use poetry/song charts.

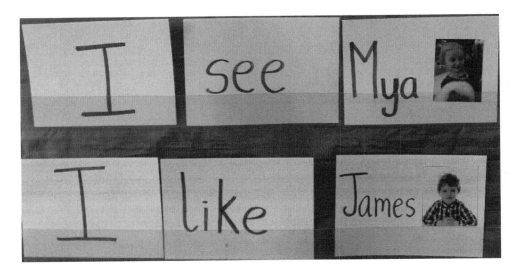

Figure 4.4 Pocket chart sentences

Examine the poem below by John Foster. It contains pleasing alliteration and interesting descriptions, but it would also be the perfect opportunity to teach the sight word 'like' as it appears numerous times in the poem.

I Like (John Foster)
I like sizzling sausages.
I like bubbling beans.
I like mashed potatoes
with gravy and greens.
I like cold ice cream.
I like chocolate cakes.
But most of all I like
the jellies my mum makes.

Consider this language experience text. What sight words would you teach using this text?

The Nurse
A nurse visited our classroom yesterday.
He was very nice. He was Alex's dad.
He works at the hospital.
He gives medicine to sick people.
He had a stethoscope.
He had hospital bracelets.
He had special gloves.
He let us look at his equipment.

Pick words that occur more than once in the text that haven't yet been taught. You will also revise any sight words previously taught. In this text, 'he' occurs numerous times, 'had' occurs three times and 'was' occurs twice. Any of these would work well as a focus word. Post-its can be used for sight word matching activities. Write the target word on a Post-it. Then have the children match the Post-it to the word in the text. This allows the children to find the word more than once. They can also use markers to underline or circle the target word in the text.

When you begin teaching sight words, focus on just two to three per week. As the children learn more words, you can increase this to three to five per week. Aim to teach 20 to 40 sight words in the first year children learn to read and an additional 40 to 80 sight words the second year. The first 100 words are the most important. The remainder can be taught at the end of the second year or in the third year. Of course, this will vary greatly depending on teaching context.

Fluency development (prosody)

Fluency is defined as the ability to read with speed, accuracy and proper expression (prosody). Children must be able to read fluently, either aloud or silently, in order to understand what they read. When reading aloud, fluent readers read in phrases and add intonation appropriately. Their reading sounds smooth and has expression. Children who have difficulty with reading fluency sound choppy and awkward. Some children may have difficulty with decoding skills or they may just need more practice with speed and smoothness in reading. Fluency is also important for motivation; children who find reading laborious tend not to want read! As readers progress through school towards the senior classes, fluency becomes increasingly important as it has a close connection to reading comprehension (Benjamin & Schwanenflugel, 2010). Therefore, it is important to lay a strong foundation in the junior classes.

The elements of oral reading fluency include (Padak & Rasinski, 2008):

- *Appropriate reading pace*: Children must read at a pace that is not too slow or too fast.

- *Expression (or prosody)*: Children must read with expression and correct intonation, adhering to any punctuation within the text to preserve meaning.

- *Accuracy*: Children need to read at least 90 per cent of the words correctly.

Children's oral reading fluency can be enhanced and developed in the following ways.

Teacher modelling, echo reading and choral reading

The first two factors (appropriate reading pace and expression) can be modelled by the teacher from the earliest stage through reading big books in shared reading, language experience texts, rhyme/poetry charts or digital texts by focusing the children's attention on various aspects of fluency. A discussion on various concepts about print (see p. 76) can open a discussion on 'how' to read certain sections of text (e.g. to pause when one reaches ellipsis, to speak louder when the author chooses to use bold print, and so forth). Having had a discussion on certain concepts about print, the teacher might invite the children to engage in choral reading (everyone together) or echo reading (the children echo the teacher, usually line by line or chunk by chunk) in order to emphasise and practise particular aspects of print that impact on fluency. In this way, the children use their print knowledge (e.g. how a full stop works) to aid their fluency (e.g. pausing when one reaches a full stop).

EXAMPLES OF CONCEPTS OF PRINT AND THEIR RELATIONSHIP TO READING FLUENCY

- *Full stop*: When you reach a full stop, you take a breath (pause).

- *Bold print or capitalised print*: This part of the text should be read in a loud, forceful voice.

- *Question marks*: When reading a sentence that ends in a question mark, your voice sounds like you are inquiring about something.

- *Exclamation marks*: When a sentence ends with an exclamation mark, your voice sounds excited/angry/emotional, depending on what has happened to the character.

- *Ellipses*: When you see an ellipsis, you pause dramatically.

- *Speech marks*: When you see speech marks, you change the tone of your voice to denote that a character is speaking.

Teacher modelling can also be used to demonstrate the 'rhythm' of the English language. Using echo reading, the teacher can demonstrate how a section of text should 'sound' when read with appropriate pace, phrasing and expression. This is particularly important when teaching English language learners who need to tune their ear to the sound and syntax of the English language. For example, the following extract from *Chicka Chicka Boom Boom* (Martin & Archambauld, 1995) works very well for echo and choral reading as it is rhythmic and has a consistent rhyming pattern.

Skit skat skoodle doot,
flip flop flee.
Everybody running to the coconut tree.
Mamas and papas
and uncles and aunts
hug their little dears,
then dust their pants.

(p. 9)

Buddy reading

Buddy reading involves children reading a text to each other. Extracts from a big book, a typed version of a language experience chart or a poem/rhyme text can serve as good texts for buddy reading. Generally, big books and language experience texts are used for lessons over a period of several days (see the lesson plans in Chapter 6). Towards the end of the week, the teacher will have modelled how to read the text at an appropriate pace with expression on several occasions. Suitable extracts can be chosen from the book or the entire chart (in the case of poetry or LEA) for buddy reading. When choosing a big book extract, it may be advisable to choose a section that contains many examples of a type of punctuation that the children have been learning about, such as exclamation marks, or a section that has a rhythmic or rhyming quality to it that would be enjoyable to read aloud. The teacher should also be mindful of the words and text complexity. An extract that contains simple sentences with decodable or high-frequency words is recommended. Sometimes it may be advisable to adapt the text to suit the readers in the class by simplifying it somewhat. The teacher should always model how to read the extract to a buddy as per the guidelines listed in the box.

HELPFUL GUIDELINES FOR BUDDY READING

1 Sit side by side with your buddy.

2 While the reader reads, the buddy listens carefully and follows along.

3 When the reader is finished, the buddy gives feedback using the 'star and wish' approach. This means that you tell your buddy something they did well first and then tell them about something they could improve. Buddies could use a holistic fluency chart that includes a Likert scale for smoothness, phrasing, pacing and expression (see Figure 4.5).

4 Change roles.

5 Report back to the larger group.

It is usually a good idea to derive 'buddies' from mixed-ability pairs. However, there should not be a very wide gap in ability between same-aged peers as this may lead to frustration. Buddies can also be derived from students of different ages, such as students from older grades reading with junior students. Because of the age difference, older students tend to enjoy 'helping' younger students (while improving their own fluency) and don't tend to be frustrated by students who are having difficulties. 'Buddy reading texts' can also be sent home, and parents can be encouraged to 'buddy read' with their children.

Story innovation

Story innovation involves the selection and adaptation of an extract from a text under study for focused instruction. It allows the teacher to change or alter wording, characters, setting or story plot to make a personalised version of the story. The extract is then read aloud to reinforce children's fluency skills with a now-familiar text. When using this approach in the junior classes, it would be advisable to use a short extract from the text that has a rhythmic quality. The example below is from *Chicka Chicka Boom Boom* (Martin & Archambauld, 1995). It allows the teacher to change the text by replacing the letter sound/name. This story innovation could be altered so that it reads 'Here comes (a child's name) up the coconut tree'.

> Chicka chicka
> boom boom!
> Will there be enough room?
> Here comes /p/ up the coconut tree. (Any phoneme can be added here; it is a good way to revise phonics previously studied while also working on fluency.)

Reader's theatre

A reader's theatre involves reading simple play scripts in order to develop fluency. It does not involve any memorising, props or costumes; instead, the focus is on expression. The steps in a reader's theatre lesson are listed in the box below.

STEPS IN A READER'S THEATRE LESSON FOR FLUENCY DEVELOPMENT

- Introduce the plot/storyline of the script.
- Pre-teach any difficult vocabulary/model phrasing.
- Divide the class into groups and distribute the scripts.
- Assign roles.
- Have the children rehearse in small groups. Circulate and 'listen in', giving feedback as appropriate.
- Have some/all groups perform for the class.
- Discuss vocabulary/phrasing as appropriate.

Simple stories can be converted into reader's theatre scripts. For example, the well-known tale of the Little Red Hen would make an appropriate script for beginning readers, as can be seen from the extract below:

Little Red Hen:	Who will help me plant the wheat?
Cat:	Not I . . .
Narrator:	. . . said the cat.
Pig:	Not I . . .
Narrator:	. . . said the pig.
Dog:	Not I . . .
Narrator:	. . . said the dog.
Little Red Hen:	Then I will plant it myself!

Teachers can create their own scripts or use the Internet as a resource. Some scripts appropriate for children in the junior classes can be found at:

- www.starfall.com

- www.timelessteacherstuff.com

- www.teachingheart.net

Poetry

Performance poetry can be a wonderful way to enhance reading fluency (Rasinski, 2003) as it can help develop children's confidence in reading aloud (Routman, 2000) and to encourage enjoyment of the genre. Poems such as 'The Hairy Toe' are fun to recite and are a delightful way to develop fluency through echo and choral reading (Rasinski, 2003).

The Hairy Toe (adapted from traditional American)
Once there was a woman went out to pick beans,
and she found a Hairy Toe.
She took the hairy toe home with her,
and that night, when she went to bed,
the wind began to moan and groan.
Away off in the distance
she seemed to hear a voice crying,
'Where is my hair-r-y to-o-oe? **Who's got my hair-r-y to-o-oe?**'
The voice had come nearer,
almost at the door now . . .
Then in an awful voice it said . . .
'Where is my hair-r-y to-o-oe? **Who's got my hair-r-y to-o-oe?**'
'YOU'VE GOT IT!'

The teacher can model reading the text with expression, adding body percussion such as handclapping, foot-stamping and finger-clicking when necessary. Fluency is often linked with concepts about print, so a discussion on the use of punctuation in the text, such as the use of commas, full stops, question marks and ellipses, could form part of the lesson. Poetry lends itself to practices such as echo, choral and buddy reading. So, while you might begin with echo reading of the poem, you could progress to buddy reading and choral reading.

RECOMMENDED POETRY BOOKS

Bruce, L. & Waterhouse, S. (2000). *Engines, engines: An Indian counting rhyme*. London: Bloomsbury Books.
Cookson, P. (1998). *Unzip your lips: 100 poems to read aloud*. London: Macmillan.
Cookson, P. (2000). *The works: Every poem you'll ever need for the literacy hour*. London: Macmillan.
Donaldson, J. (2013). *Poems to perform*. London: Macmillan.
Foster, J. (2007). *The poetry chest*. London: Oxford University Press.
Foster, J. (2016). *I can read! Poetry for five year olds*. Oxford: Oxford University Press.
Rosen, M. (2007). *Mustard, custard, grumble belly and gravy*. London: Bloomsbury.
Silverstein, S. (1974). *Where the sidewalk ends*. New York: HarperCollins.
Webb, K. (1987). *I like this poem*. London: Puffin Books.

Antiphonal reading

This is an adaptation of choral reading. In antiphonal reading, children are usually divided into groups. Each group reads an assigned part – sometimes alternately, sometimes in unison. The manner of reading is cued by the placement of the text on the page, which is placed left of centre, right of centre or in the middle of the page. Generally, the text is projected onto an interactive whiteboard (IWB) or written on chart paper. Ideally, the text might include target sight vocabulary, phonics and words for vocabulary development, so that several early literacy skills can be developed within the same lesson. Antiphonal reading calls for the repeated reading of a text in different ways (as rehearsal and performance), which has been found to benefit English language learners (Monobe, Bintz & McTeer, 2017). A wonderful series of books for antiphonal reading in the junior classes is *You Read to Me, I'll Read to You* (Hoberman, 2007). An extract from this book is given below:

(1st reader/group)	(2nd reader/group)
Who's that knocking at my door?	
Look, it's a dinosaur!	
	How do you do? How have you been?
	Long time no see. May I come in?

My goodness! How did you arrive?

I didn't think you were alive!

> They say I am extinct, I know;
>
> But here I am. Just call me Joe.
>
> (p. 10)

Self-selected reading

In the beginning, children may just 'read' the pictures and tell themselves the story, but as they progress, regular library reading can have a significant impact on reading fluency. Make sure your library has books that are 'readable' by your students. You may want to consider purchasing a levelled reading scheme different to that used in guided reading (such as Rigby Stars, Collins Songbirds or Story Worlds). It may be a good idea to organise the books in your library by difficulty so that children can be guided in book selection. This can be done using a colour-coded sticker system that is easy for young children to understand (e.g. the books with a blue sticker are the easiest books, and they should be returned to the blue basket). Alphabet books, counting books and nursery rhymes are also ideal for self-selected reading. The teacher should also have a basket of 'teacher's favourites' containing small versions of any big book read in shared reading and other storybooks that have been read aloud numerous times. As the children will be familiar with these texts, they will be able to 'read' or retell the story to themselves or a partner in a joyful manner. During literacy centres time, children should be encouraged to reread big books and poetry charts with a 'reading buddy'.

Assessing fluency

Reading fluency should be assessed using a range of approaches to encompass development in relation to accuracy, pace and expression. Informal teacher observation should be documented in careful notes taken during shared reading and guided reading sessions. More formal tools, such as running records, which were discussed in Chapter 3, should be used regularly to benchmark progress in reading accuracy, while simple assessments focused on reading can be used at regular intervals. Finally, children should be encouraged to partake in self-assessment using student-centred rubrics. Rubrics should be holistic in nature to ensure that reading pace and expression are valued as much as reading accuracy.

Figure 4.5 Fluency rubric

Fluency rubrics can be created collaboratively between teacher and children following a discussion. The number of indicators included in the rubric will depend on the age and ability of the children. The rubric can then be used during shared reading and guide reading sessions. The teacher can lead a discussion on fluency based on the rubric, perhaps by using the 'two stars and a wish' approach (two things you did well and one thing to work on). An example of a fluency rubric that could be used with beginning readers is shown in Figure 4.5.

The speed at which one reads will affect the ability to comprehend what is being read. Read too slow and it is difficult to remember the beginning of the sentence or paragraph by the time you reach the end. Read too fast and it is difficult to process the information. An appropriate reading speed allows for expression, accuracy and comprehension. As children get older, their reading speed should increase. A simple assessment, such as Rasinski's (2003) one-minute reading probe, allows a teacher to determine a child's reading rate. In this assessment, the teacher simply chooses a grade-level passage and times the child's reading to see how many words can be read correctly per minute. If the child makes errors while reading, these are tallied and deducted from the number of words read within the minute. According to Harris and Sipay (1990), by the end of first grade (approximately 7 years old), children should be able to read at a rate of 60 to 90 words per minute.

Vocabulary development

Vocabulary development plays an important role in learning to read. Research indicates that there is a strong correlation between vocabulary knowledge and reading comprehension (Snow et al., 1998). Comprehension improves when you know what the words mean. However, word learning can be slow. Children might have to encounter a word at least 12 times before they are capable of using it successfully, or to read it and comprehend what they have read (Beck et al., 2002).

Vocabulary instruction is an essential aspect of children's comprehension development, and shared reading can be an excellent way to enhance children's vocabulary acquisition (Fisher, Frey & Lapp, 2011), as explicitly teaching word meanings within the context of a big book can have a powerful effect on increasing children's word consciousness and interest in expanding their vocabulary. English language learners will need particular support in developing both the depth and the breadth of their vocabulary knowledge. Rereading the text several times over the course of a week can help in learning new vocabulary words, phrases and language chunks.

Vocabulary learning can be divided into three tiers (Beck et al., 2002), as demonstrated below. While children tend to acquire words from the first tier before coming to school (or in the case of ELL students, as a result of coming to school), vocabulary from the second and third tiers is learned as a result of wide reading, discussion, word study and direct instruction.

The three tiers are as follows:

- *Tier 1*: Basic words that most children know before entering school (e.g. boy, cup, table, dog).

- *Tier 2*: Words that appear frequently in texts and for which children already have some conceptual understanding (e.g. ancient, anxious, curious).

- *Tier 3*: Uncommon words that are typically associated with a specific domain/ subject area (e.g. mitochondria, lava, peninsula, cumulus).

Effective teaching involves providing numerous opportunities throughout the school day to help children activate and build their vocabularies. The following approaches can support vocabulary development.

Direct instruction of individual words

Use your big book and other teacher read-alouds to teach a range of new vocabulary. Select some words/phrases for discussion from each big book/read-aloud. This can be linked with the 'clarify' comprehension strategy that will be discussed in Chapter 5. The teacher may discuss certain words and/or phrases during an initial reading of the text or return to certain extracts later for a more in-depth discussion. The extract below, taken from *Chicka Chicka Boom Boom* (Martin & Archambauld, 1995) has some great opportunities for vocabulary development. For example, phrases such as 'patched-up', 'skinned-knee', 'stubbed toe' and 'out of breath' are all phrases worthy of discussion in an early years classroom. These phrases can be acted out to show meaning, which can really engage children's interest in learning. Young children learn best through kinaesthetic learning. Thus, it can be helpful to use bodily movements, facial expression and various actions to explain unfamiliar vocabulary. For example, it may be effective to physically stub one's toe as one reads 'stubbed toe E' in *Chicka Chicka Boom Boom* (Martin & Archambauld, 1995) to demonstrate the meaning of the phrase. The children can pretend to do likewise. This type of physical, kinaesthetic learning is more likely to be retained than a verbal definition:

> Next from the pile-up
> Skinned-knee D
> And stubbed toe E
> And patched up F
> Then comes G
> All out of breath.
> (p. 13)

Talk

Provide frequent opportunities throughout the day for pair work, group work and whole-class discussion in lessons and across subject areas. In relation to literacy lessons, talk should be maximised in all learning contexts. Whenever possible, children should discuss their reading and writing in pairs, small groups or with the whole class.

Wide reading

Include shared reading, guided reading, teacher read-aloud, independent reading and cross-curricular reading in your timetable every day. Make sure to include a wide range of topics and genres within your selections.

Word consciousness/word study

It is important that children develop a curiosity about how words work from an early age. Word web activities that involve synonyms work well in junior classes, particularly with language experience charts, where a simple word such as 'small' can become the subject of a class vocabulary brainstorm, where students attempt to provide synonyms for the focus word (e.g. 'tiny', 'little', 'petite', and so forth). Homonyms (words with multiple meanings, such as 'bat', 'fly' or 'saw') are frequently encountered in texts, and their various meanings should be discussed regularly. This is particularly important for ELLs, who may be confused by homonyms. Morphemic analysis consists of identifying prefixes, roots and suffixes found in derived words; it also consists of identifying meaningful parts in compound words and contractions. Morphemes differ from syllables

PREFIX SUFFIX BUILDERS: EXAMPLE OF AN ACTIVITY THAT DEVELOPS MORPHOLOGICAL SKILLS

In this activity, three different colours of card are used. The card is cut into approximately 30 rectangles (5 in. by 7 in.). On the first colour, a variety of prefixes are written (e.g. 'un'), on the second colour, root words are written (e.g. 'help'), and on the third colour, suffixes are written (e.g. 'ful'). The task involves assembling words using the root word and prefixes and/or suffixes (e.g. 'unhelpful'). The children might note down all the words that they manage to create and illustrate them (see Figure 4.6).

Figure 4.6 Word builder activity with prefixes, suffixes and root words

because morphemes are portions of meaning and syllables are portions of sound (see the box below for an example of an activity that develops children's morphemic awareness).

Early literacy skills and English language learners

For children who may have been read to in a language other than English before coming to school, they may have developed concepts about print that are markedly different from those used in English texts. In this situation, it might be helpful to conduct the assessment using a home language text first and then an English language text. A parent might be willing to help you with this task if you are not familiar with the language. This approach will reveal what textual features and knowledge might be transferable into English literacy learning. It will also empower children's prior knowledge. High-frequency words that might be firmly established in a native speaker's oral vocabulary may cause the English language learner difficulty as they are often quite abstract in nature. For example, words such as 'was', 'this' or 'here' can prove challenging, and it may be advisable to create further resources, such as home-made books, to demonstrate how these words are used in the English language. As ELLs may not be as 'tuned in' to the sounds of the English language as their native-speaking peers, they may also need additional fluency support. Teacher modelling and echo reading would be particularly helpful in becoming accustomed to the sound and syntax of the English language. It is also important to consider that ELLs are learning new vocabulary in every aspect of their literacy lessons, and not just when the focus in on vocabulary development. Therefore, the use of actions, facial expressions and visuals is recommended across all lessons to assist understanding. ELLs may also require more practice in learning literacy skills as the cognitive load involving both new vocabulary and another skill will be more taxing than just the skill alone.

Key concepts for practice

- Children need to develop a range of early literacy skills in order to become readers.

- Early literacy skills are best learned when they are explicitly taught within a meaningful context (such as a big book, a language experience text, poetry charts or guided reading).

- Developing children's concepts about print allows them to navigate texts with ease.

- A bank of high-frequency sight words enhances children's ability to read fluently. Sight words should be taught from context in a multisensory manner.

- Oral reading fluency includes prosody, accuracy and reading rate. Accuracy and rate can be developed through phonics and sight word instruction and attention to semantic and syntactic cueing systems. Prosody is best developed through teacher modelling, echo reading, choral reading, antiphonal reading, repeated reading and explicit teaching with regard to punctuation.

- Vocabulary instruction should be part of early years literacy instruction. Children should have frequent opportunities to talk during lessons and should be exposed to a wide range of genres. While direct instruction can be helpful, children should also be encouraged to become 'word conscious' and be eager to investigate word meanings in a variety of ways.

■ English language learners may need additional support in learning abstract high-frequency words due to their limited vocabulary and knowledge of English. Fluency activities can be particularly helpful in tuning their ears to the sounds and syntax of English.

REFLECTION: THINKING ABOUT YOUR PRACTICE

■ How have you taught the early literacy skills outlined in this chapter up to now?

■ What early literacy skills have you taught particularly well in the past?

■ What early literacy skills have you found difficult to teach?

■ How will you adapt what you have learned here for use in your context?

For further exploration

Beck, I., McKeown, M. & Kucan, L. (2002). *Bringing words to life: Robust vocabulary instruction*. New York: Guilford Press.

Clay, M. (2015). An observation survey of early literacy achievement. New York: Scholastic.

Rasinski, T. (2003). *The fluent reader*. Porstmouth, NH: Heinemann.

Smidt, S. (2007). Supporting multilingual learners in the early years: Many languages – many children. London: Routledge.

5 Listening and reading comprehension

Introduction

In the previous chapters, we examined a range of early literacy skills, including phonics, phonological awareness, concepts about print, sight words, fluency and vocabulary development. In this chapter, we will discuss the range of comprehension strategies that could be included in a literacy lesson in the early years. As the focus of this text is on the junior classes, comprehension is discussed in terms of both listening comprehension and reading comprehension. Listening comprehension occurs when children listen to a text read aloud, whereas reading comprehension occurs when children read a text on their own. All the comprehension strategies in this chapter are applicable in either situation, with the latter being more predominant in the early years and the former taking an increasing role as children learn to read and move into higher grades.

What is listening/reading comprehension?

Comprehension is the essence of reading. The International Reading Association (IRA) dictionary defines comprehension as the 'intentional thinking during which meaning is constructed through interactions between text and the reader' (Harris & Hodges, 1981). Thus, readers derive meaning from text when they engage in intentional, problem-solving thinking processes. Duke and Pearson (2002) added 'navigation' and 'critique' to the definition because they believed that readers actually move through text, finding their way, evaluating the accuracy of the text to see if it fits their background knowledge and personal agenda, and arriving finally at a self-selected location. Sweet and Snow (2002) contribute the notion of 'involvement with written language' (pp. 23–24) to the definition, highlighting the essential role of active engagement with text in comprehension. Most definitions take account of the complexity of reading comprehension, that it can no longer be thought of as a series of discrete skills to be mastered. Three levels of comprehension have been identified: literal, inferential and metacognitive. Literal comprehension involves extracting the details of the text and recognizing the author's purpose. Inferential comprehension requires the reader to 'read between the lines' and interpret the text using their background knowledge and the explicit knowledge within the text. The strategies discussed in this chapter take account of these two levels. A step beyond inferential comprehension is metacognition, which is the awareness of one's thinking and the self-regulation and self-monitoring of a learner's thoughts. In comprehension strategy, instruction thus involves choosing from a range of strategies depending on one's reading purpose. Initially, strategies may be taught individually, but the goal of instruction is to teach children how to orchestrate the range of strategies taught. Thus, effective comprehension instruction should include the development of all three levels of comprehension to produce a competent reader.

A reading strategy is an action (or series of actions) that is used in order to construct meaning. Reading comprehension strategies provide a language around comprehension processes, giving the reader a vehicle to express their thinking and monitor their thinking. Readers who know what strategies are, and how and when to use them, are strategic readers. The competent reader is a strategic reader. Focusing on comprehension strategies (in both listening and reading situations) in the early years can have a powerful effect on reading achievement as children move into older classes.

The importance of comprehension instruction

The goal of reading is to understand text, whether listening to a story read aloud or reading on one's own. While the contributions of decoding, vocabulary knowledge and engagement are acknowledged, without the activation of the cognitive processes that enable comprehension, the reading act remains futile. Research has highlighted that younger and weaker students often do not expect a text to make sense and do not seek meaning when reading. It is not uncommon for younger and weaker readers to define the reading task in terms of a decoding act rather than the construction of meaning. This is significant as students who view reading as a decoding act are unlikely to progress to become lifelong readers.

The 'fourth grade slump'

Therefore, as weaker readers do not tend to monitor their comprehension, they must be taught how to do so; comprehension needs to be 'taught, not caught' (Dole, Duffy, Roehler & Pearson, 1991), as many young readers do not tend to comprehend simply by osmosis. Without adequate comprehension instruction in the junior classes, weaker readers can be prone to the 'fourth grade slump' (Pearson, 1985), an educational phenomenon where weaker students can no longer keep up with their counterparts in the reading stakes and begin to struggle in reading class. This usually tends to occur around third or fourth grade, when the emphasis changes from learning to read to reading to learn. This phenomenon has often been linked to poor instruction (Pearson, 1985), and can often lead to reading failure.

The 'Matthew effect'

Without effective comprehension instruction, the gap between weaker readers and their more competent peers widens. This can lead to a 'Matthew effect' (Stanovich, 1986). This theory suggests that better readers tend to have more positive experiences with reading, especially when they see comprehension and meaning-making as the ultimate goal. When a reader comprehends text successfully, this inspires the learner to read more, thereby increasing reading ability. At the same time, the weaker reader who reads books for the purpose of decoding derives little pleasure from this act. Therefore, the learner reads less and their reading ability gradually deteriorates, leading to the aforementioned 'fourth grade slump' (Pearson, 1985). According to Stanovich (1986), the 'Matthew effect' suggests that students with more reading skill and knowledge experience a powerful 'bootstrapping of further vocabulary, knowledge and cognitive structures' (p. 151), creating even wider gaps in reading achievement between pupils. The explicit teaching of comprehension strategies can help all readers to see the purpose of reading through more active engagement and meaningful reading experiences.

How to teach comprehension strategies in the early years classroom

While traditional teaching often tended to assess comprehension rather than teach it, the current view is that comprehension should be taught in a very explicit manner. The research has shown that young children are capable of complex thought, and thus explicit comprehension instruction should be an integral part of early literacy instruction (Block & Pressley, 2002). Large-format books provide an excellent forum for the development of listening comprehension (as do regular storybooks). Strategies taught in shared reading lessons can be further developed in guided reading situations. Regular self-selected reading can allow for independent practice. In order to teach comprehension strategies effectively, it is recommended that teachers use the 'gradual release of responsibility' model described below.

Comprehension strategies should be taught in an explicit, systematic manner using quality literature and a range of genres. Based on Vygotskian principles, Pearson and Gallagher (1983) recommended a 'gradual release of responsibility' model for teaching comprehension strategies, whereby student learning is carefully scaffolded by the teacher, building from teacher-directed learning towards independent use of the strategy. This methodology was further developed by Duke and Pearson (2002), and they included the following teaching steps (see Figure 5.1):

- *Explain the strategy*: Name it and tell the children what it does and why it helps you as a reader/listener.

- *Demonstrate*: The teacher 'thinks aloud', demonstrating how they use the strategy while reading. Though this is usually oral in nature, it can progress to a written format as the children grow more confident. In that situation, the teacher may 'think aloud' while adding to a chart/grid that contains their thinking process.

- *Guided practice*: The children attempt to use the strategy with guidance from the teacher. This can be oral or written.

- *Reflection*: The children and teacher discuss their strategy use.

- *Independent practice*: The children are given opportunities to use the strategy independently. This step generally occurs in the context of self-selected reading (library reading). In this situation, the children's use of strategies can be monitored through teacher–student conferences (i.e. the teacher discussing the children's strategy use with them).

The method outlined above would be regarded as a direct approach to teaching comprehension strategies. This approach has proven successful in the research field (e.g. Duffy, 2002). Generally, strategies are taught one at a time, and each strategy is added to the children's repertoire, so that eventually the children can pick and choose which strategy to use at different points in the text (metacognition).

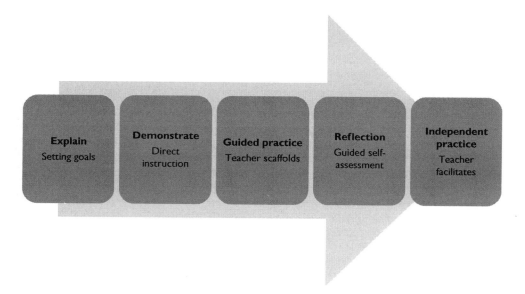

Figure 5.1 The 'gradual release of responsibility' model

Source: Duke and Pearson (2002), adapted by the author

What comprehension strategies should I teach in the early years?

The comprehension strategies that we will focus on in this chapter are:

- predicting;

- retelling;

- questioning;

- inferring;

- visualising; and

- making connections.

Comprehension instruction should begin in the early years with listening comprehension and progress in complexity and depth through to the higher grades. Early years teachers should concentrate on the first three or four strategies initially. The remaining strategies should be taught when children are deemed ready for that type of instruction (this may be dependent on ability/language level). It should also be noted that much of the comprehension instruction in the early years is oral in nature. As children grow older, they should be able to construct effective written responses that demonstrate strategy use. We will explore each strategy in turn as we progress through the chapter. The overall aim of your instruction will be that children can orchestrate a range of comprehension strategies and that they will be able to select the appropriate strategy from their repertoire in order to extract meaning from texts (metacognition). In order to facilitate this end goal, the following recommendations should be borne in mind:

- When beginning strategy instruction, focus on one strategy initially. Spend at least a few weeks on this strategy until you are sure that the children are confident in using this strategy.

- Then add to the children's strategy repertoire by introducing a second strategy. While the focus of the lesson might be on this second strategy, ensure that you also include the first strategy.

- Continue in this manner.

- When the children have a store of about three or four strategies, you can create a 'strategy spinner' (see Figure 5.2). This tool encourages metacognition as it visually demonstrates changing from one strategy to another according to the demands of the text.

- Add to your spinner (see the second spinner in Figure 5.2) as you teach a new strategy. You can adapt the terminology in this chapter if you wish. The most important thing is to use consistent terminology, not just in your class, but in your school.

Predicting

Learning how to make predictions is important, as in order to predict, readers must activate their prior knowledge and use it to think about what they are going to read. In this way, predicting enables readers (or those listening to a story) to connect what they are reading/hearing with what they already know, and bring this prior knowledge to the text in order to get meaning from it. According to Kintsch (1994), knowledge becomes 'encapsulated' if readers form text bases without connecting the information to prior knowledge, and the information read remains context-bound and specific to the situation where it was read. With this limited understanding, it can be difficult to engage with the text and it can significantly affect recall of what has been read. Research has shown that many children do not activate their prior knowledge automatically, that they need instruction in how to do so (Block & Pressley, 2002). Before and during reading, children can be shown how to use their prior knowledge to generate predictions about the possible content of the text through teacher modelling ('thinking aloud') and scaffolded guided practice. Effective comprehenders monitor their predictions as they read.

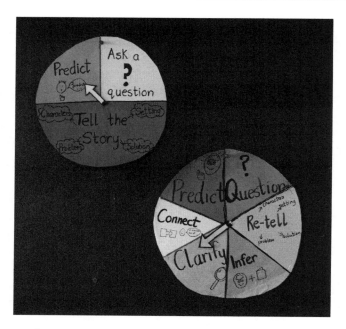

Figure 5.2 Comprehension strategy spinners

The background knowledge used for predicting comes not only from the reader's previous experience, but also from meaning that is constructed during reading. So, children should be shown how to recognise when their predictions are incorrect and revise their thinking. Hence, it is important to teach children to make predictions throughout the story, not just at the beginning of the book.

Prediction can be taught using the 'gradual release of responsibility' model as follows:

■ *Explain*: The teacher might say, 'Today we are going to learn how to make predictions. When you make a prediction, it is like making a good guess about what might happen in the story. Predictions help you to get your brain ready to understand what is happening in the story.'

■ *Demonstrate*: The teacher 'thinks aloud'. It is essential that the teacher supports their predictions and describes their thinking clearly. For example, in the book *Room on the Broom* (Donaldson, 2003), the teacher might say, 'I see a witch on the cover, and I predict that this witch might cast some spells because I have heard that that is what witches like to do.' Here, the teacher uses both the illustration and his or her world knowledge to make a prediction.

■ There are other ways to model/demonstrate prediction:
   o Predict using personal experience (using something that happened to you to predict).

- o Predict using world knowledge (using something you read or saw on TV to predict).

- o Predict using genre knowledge (using the format of the genre to make a prediction).

- o Predict using illustrations (parts of the picture might give you an idea for a prediction).

- o Predict using cover features.

- o Predict using knowledge about characters/settings (from earlier in the text).

- o Predict using text features (in non-fiction books, bold print, italics, captions and so forth might help you make a prediction).

- *Guided practice*: Encourage the children to 'think aloud' and make predictions. Having modelled how to make predictions several times, invite the children to make predictions throughout the story. It can be helpful to teach the children to indicate that they wish to make a prediction by making a 'P' shape with their fingers (see the hand signs for comprehension strategies in Appendix D). As the children progress, the teacher may feel that it is appropriate that children create written responses during the guided practice section of the lesson (see Figure 5.3). In this situation, the teacher would demonstrate how to create the written response. Class charts can be created in a similar fashion. Non-writers can use drawings with labels to show their thinking.

- *Reflection*: The teacher can ask questions such as: What does it mean to predict? How do we predict? Why is it helpful to make predictions? When the story is complete, lead the children in a discussion regarding the usefulness of predictions in understanding the story.

- *Independent practice*: The children should be encouraged to make predictions during independent reading time. Younger students who are not yet reading can achieve this by 'reading' the pictures in books (or wordless picture books). Those who have begun reading can attempt strategy use using simple texts or levelled readers.

Retelling

Retelling a story involves the ability to identify and recall a story's structure. This is a skill that needs to be taught in the junior classes as it aids children's understanding and recall of story elements. In order to become proficient at retelling, children need to be exposed to a wide variety of narratives that are read aloud by the teacher and read individually in guided reading situations:

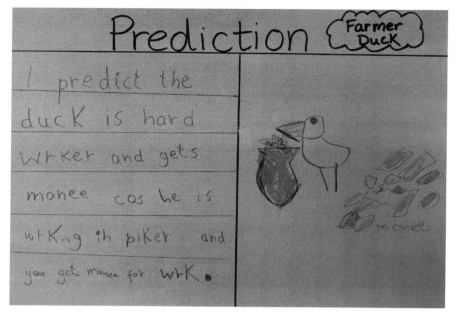

Figure 5.3 Prediction T-chart

■ *Explain*: The teacher might say, 'Today we are going to learn how to retell a story. While we are reading the story and when we finish reading it, we are going to talk about the characters (the people in the story), the setting (where it happened), the problem and the solution (how they fixed the problem).'

■ *Demonstrate*: Use the props mentioned below to illustrate your demonstration. It is advisable to discuss the notion of 'characters', 'setting' and 'problem' while reading the story, instead of waiting until the story has ended. For example, having read the first page of *Owl Babies* (Waddell, 1998), the teacher might comment, 'So, Sarah, Percy, Bill and Owl Mother are the characters in this story so far.'

■ *Guided practice*: Prompt cards can be a very useful tool during the guided practice stage. Visual props can be very useful for the youngest pupils and English language learners (ELLs), such as the one pictured in Figure 5.4.

Concrete props can also work well, particularly with ELLs. For example, if attempting to retell the story of 'The Three Little Pigs', the teacher could use puppets, straws, blocks and pieces of wood to enhance understanding and vocabulary development. Children also enjoy using larger 'life-size' props. Consider the text *We're Going on a Bear Hunt* (Rosen, 1996). If a large space is available, the creative use of coloured paper and large cardboard boxes could create the various scenes in the book, such as the river (large blue

Figure 5.4 Retelling prompt card

paper placed on the floor), the snowstorm (white paper) and the meadow (green paper). A cave could be constructed from large cardboard boxes, and the bed from which the characters declare that they are 'not going on a bear hunt again' could be created using large blankets. Pictorial props can also be useful. There are some wonderful images available at www.sparklebox. co.uk for a wide range of large-format books.

■ *Reflection*: The teacher might ask: What does it mean to retell a story? Was it easy or hard to do? What do you need more help with?

■ *Independent practice*: Encourage children to utilise the strategy during independent reading. Include a retelling activity during literacy centre time (for further details on literacy centres, see Chapter 7).

RECOMMENDED BOOKS FOR RETELLING

When choosing books for retelling lessons, it is essential that the story has a clear structure. The texts below can be described as 'problem resolution tales'.

Allen, J. (2000). *The bear who wouldn't share*. London: Pearson.

Donaldson, J. (2000). *The Gruffalo*. London: Macmillan.

Donaldson, J. (2007). *A squash and a squeeze*. London: Macmillan.

Waddell, M. (1996). *Farmer Duck*. London: Walker Books.

Questioning

There are two main types of questions that may be asked or answered when reading a text:

- 'book' questions; and

- 'brain and book' questions.

The answers to 'book questions' can be found directly in the text (literal questions), whereas 'brain and book' questions require higher-order thinking (inferential questions). A 'book question' will elicit the basic facts of a story (e.g. if the teacher asks, 'How many bears were in the story?' in *Goldilocks and the Three Bears*). If the teacher asks, 'Why do you think that Goldilocks thought it was a good idea to go into someone else's house?' then the children are required to use both the 'book' and their 'brain' to think of an answer to this inferential question. Inferential questions promote classroom discussion as there may be several plausible answers to the question, whereas literal questions can be 'conversation stoppers' as there is only one correct answer to be found directly in the text. When children are generally asked literal questions, this is what they will focus on subsequent reading. If pupils are constantly asked to search for trivial information, they will not have the cognitive capacity left to attend to more crucial elements such as plots, events and sequences. Hence, it is vital that teachers ask higher-order questions reflecting the different levels of comprehension and show children how to find the answer. This can be done by discussing the different types of questions that exist, and using this information to locate the answer.

REFLECTION

Keeping the previous section on questioning in mind, complete the following exercise.

Read this passage carefully. Then answer the questions below.

Yesterday I saw the palgish flester gollining begrunt the bruck. He seemed very chandrebrill, so I did not jorter him, just deapled to him quistly. Perhaps later he will besand cander, and I will be able to rangle him.

1   What was the flester doing?
2   What sort of flester was he?
3   Why did the writer decide not to jorter him?
4   How did she deaple?

Answers:

(1) He was golilning begrrunt the bruck (2) He was a palgish flester (3) He seemed very chanderhill. (4) She deapled him quistly.

Source: Ur (1996)

■ What have you learned or confirmed about simply answering book questions?

■ *You can answer the questions even if you have no idea what you are reading about!*

■ Therefore, effective comprehension instruction must include higher-order questions as well as literal questions!

Question generation

Asking and answering questions have traditionally been major aspects of school life. However, it is now acknowledged that simply answering questions is more of an assessment of comprehension rather than the teaching of comprehension processes. Indeed, research has found that simply practising answering questions does not lead to improved student performance in reading. This strategy was deemed ineffective as the technique is extremely teacher-centred and offers little explicit explanation with regard to how children can find the answer to a question (McEwan, 2004). It is also apparent that the nature of questions children become accustomed to can shape their understanding and recall. When teachers ask questions, the emphasis is on the product of comprehension. When children are shown how to generate questions as they read, they become active comprehenders and the focus is on the processes involved in comprehension (Trabasso & Bouchard, 2002). Therefore, children need direct, explicit instruction regarding various types of questions combined with regular opportunities to see the teacher model the processes involved in self-questioning, and further opportunities to self-question as they read texts independently. Self-questioning requires greater cognitive effort, which results in enhanced recall and retention of information due to a deeper interaction with the text. It also heightens children's metacognitive awareness and aids comprehension monitoring. Training in question generation has been found to be effective in familiarizing children with the cognitive and linguistic demands of question answering as it allows the reader to probe the relationship between questions and answers (Raphael, Highfield & Au, 2006). Explicitly teaching children how to self-question while reading or listening to a text leads to significant improvement in comprehension performance. Question generation is an important comprehension strategy as it places the locus of control firmly with the reader. It engages children in deep processing of text material, thus improving comprehension ability. Indeed, according to Zimmerman and Hutchins (2003), 'If you ask questions as you read, you are awake. You are thinking. You are interacting with words' (p. 73). Therefore, self-questioning has an important role to play in active comprehension of text.

Generating 'book questions'

In this section, we will examine how to teach children to ask questions as they read using the 'gradual release of responsibility' model. 'Book questions' are easier to start with and will provide a good basis for children developing the ability to ask questions:

- *Explain*: The teacher might say, 'Today we are going to be working on asking questions as we read. The type of questions that we are going to ask are called book questions. They are called book questions because the answers can be found in the book. These questions start with words like what, who, where, when, how and why. Asking and answering questions helps us keep track of what's happening in the story.'

- *Demonstrate*: At different points in the story, the teacher might pause and announce, 'I'm going to ask a book question. It's a 'what' question. What . . .?' And so forth.

- *Guided practice*: The children should be instructed to sit 'knee to knee' with their reading buddy and ask a question, then share the questions with the class. Have other children answer the questions.

- *Reflection*: The teacher might ask: Did you like asking questions? Was it easy or difficult? Why is it a good idea to ask questions about a book?

- *Independent practice*: Encourage the children to ask themselves questions during independent reading. It might be a good idea to encourage the children to read library books in pairs (buddy reading) and then ask each other questions.

Generating 'brain and book' questions/'wonders'

When teaching 'brain and book' questions, the teacher could follow a similar lesson plan. However, generally, 'brain and book' questions tend to begin with 'Why do you think . . .?' and have many different possible answers. An answer is viable as long as it is supported by the text.

Sometimes children can find posing inferential questions challenging, and the notion of encouraging 'wonders' about the text might be more accessible to the children. Introducing 'I wonder' questions is an effective way of helping them grasp the concept of reading between the lines and thinking beyond the written text. It also draws on their predicting skills. The following outline draws on the 'gradual release of responsibility' model to introduce and develop their use:

■ *Explain*: The teacher might say, 'Today we are going to learn how to "wonder" as we read. Wondering is important because it makes our brains think harder about what is going on in the story.'

■ *Demonstrate*: The teacher demonstrates 'I wonder' questions while reading. For example, in *Room on the Broom* (Donaldson, 2003), the teacher could say: I wonder if the witch is good or evil? I wonder if she was lonely before she met the animals? I wonder what her name is? I wonder if they are on earth or in a magical land? And so forth.

■ *Guided practice*: The teacher encourages the children to demonstrate their 'wonders'.

When the children have become confident in developing 'wonders' about the text, record their thinking (and your modelled thinking) using large Post-its on a chart. Figure 5.6 illustrates a wonders chart for *Gorilla* (Brown, 2000). Demonstrate how to brainstorm possible explanations for a 'wonder' (see Figures 5.5 and 5.6). Put the children into pairs and have them complete a brainstorm grid. If your children are not writing yet, this can simply be done as a whole-class activity (see Figures 5.5 and 5.6).

■ *Reflection*: The teacher might ask: What does it mean to 'wonder' about a story? Why do we wonder? Did you find it easy or hard to wonder? Why?

■ *Independent practice*: Encourage children to 'wonder' as they read library books. Perhaps they could write down their 'wonders' in a notebook and share with the larger group at the end of independent reading time.

Using a dramatic response to promote higher-order questioning

Higher-order questioning can also be developed through hot-seating. The following example uses *Farmer Duck* (Waddell, 1996) as the text:

■ *Explain*: The teacher might say, 'Today we are going to focus our questioning on a particular character in the book. We're going to put him in the hot seat and ask him about what happened to him in the story. I will pretend to be one of the hens first and ___ will be the duck.'

■ *Demonstrate*: Use an illustration in the story that shows the main character at a crucial point of the story, such as the image from *Farmer Duck* that depicts the duck in a distressed state. The duck is described as 'sleepy, weepy and tired' after spending day after day tending to the farmer's demands. Three hens gather around him sympathetically. One of the children can take the role of the duck and the teacher can take the role of one of the hens, and asks the duck

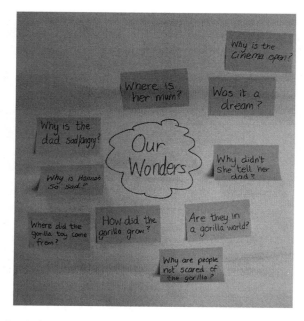

Figure 5.5 'Wonders' chart

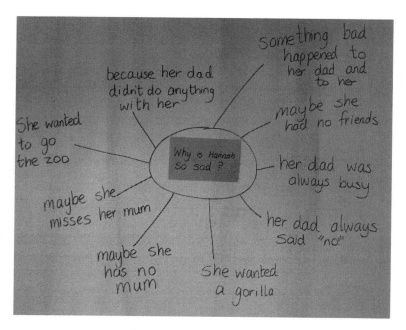

Figure 5.6 Our biggest wonder

about his experiences. For example: Why are you so tired? Why didn't the farmer do this work? What will you do to change your situation?

- *Guided practice*: When the children are more confident, they can take the role of both the duck and the hens. The children can also work in small groups if they are able, and perform for the larger group.

- *Reflection*: The teacher might say: Did you enjoy asking questions? What sort of questions did you ask? Was it easy or hard? What do you need help with?

- *Independent practice*: The children act out similar scenes during literacy centres (see Chapter 7).

Inferring

An inference can be defined as information that is activated during reading yet not explicitly stated in the text. It is the ability to 'read between the lines' using personal prior knowledge to understand the text. According to Oakhill, Cain and Yuill (1998), 'a fully explicit text would not only be very long and boring, but it would destroy the reader's pleasure in imposing meaning on the text- making it their own' (p. 347). Indeed, it is the reader's own personal interpretation of a text that makes reading enjoyable. If one reads without pleasure, then one will not choose to read, and thus reading achievement will suffer.

Inferring is one of the most essential cognitive strategies that skilled readers use. However, many weak readers fail to develop this strategy, often claiming that they 'read it but don't get it'. Because not all information is explicit in the text, it is imperative that teachers encourage children to reflect on information and infer meaning using background knowledge. Although children have the mental capacity to infer, some do not do so automatically without teacher direction. Inferential comprehension can be taught effectively using the 'gradual release of responsibility' model, which can make the readers (or listeners) consciously aware that clues hidden in the text can become meaningful when considered alongside the appropriate prior knowledge by observing the teacher thinking aloud.

Inferring can be introduced to young children by demonstrating how we can 'infer' what characters in a story may be thinking or could be saying by using what we've read in the story combined with our brain/imagination. For example, a thought bubble can be drawn onto a blank sheet of paper and attached to a page in the big book. Then the thought that the character might have at that particular point in the story can be recorded in the thought bubble. The example given below uses *Gorilla* (Browne, 2000), and follows the steps in the 'gradual release of responsibility' model when teaching children how to use the strategy:

■ *Explain*: The teacher might say, 'Today we are going to learn about inferring. Inferring means that we use the information in the book and our own brains to infer what a character might be thinking or saying at different points in the story.'

■ *Demonstrate*: Picking a point in the story that is suitable for this activity, the teacher draws a speech/thought bubble and says, 'What would Hannah be thinking right now? Well, I'm going to imagine I'm Hannah. I think I would say, "I feel so lonely" because the story told us that she is on her own and that her dad wouldn't play with her, and I'd feel lonely if I was her.' The teacher would continue in this manner, giving a few more examples.

■ *Guided practice*: The teacher might have the children turn to their 'buddy' and brainstorm some ideas for the thought bubble. The children might share their ideas with the group. Their ideas can be added to the thought bubble. This process can be repeated several times during the rading of the text, if appropriate. The children could complete an individual worksheet that contains an illustration from the book and a blank thought bubble.

■ *Reflection*: The teacher might ask: What does it mean to infer? Was it easy or hard? How could I help you with inferring?

■ *Independent practice*: Encourage the children to infer during self-selected reading time, particularly if they are attempting to read well-known stories that have been read aloud numerous times.

Poetry is naturally ambiguous, and thus lends itself very well to inferring. A simple yet effective way to develop the notion of drawing inferences from text using poetry is to select a descriptive poem, such as 'What Is an Alien?' (Collett, in Cookson, 1998, p. 153), and remove the title:

■ *Explain*: The teacher might say, 'We have been working on inferring meaning from texts, but today we are going to work on inferring meaning from poetry. Remember, inferring means finding clues in a text and using your brain to figure out what the author is trying to say. Today we are going to look for clues in some poems because their titles are missing, and we are going to use the clues and our brains to figure out what the titles could be.'

■ *Demonstrate*: The teacher thinks aloud, demonstrating how to find clues and make sense of the poem. For example, in the poem in Figure 5.7, the teacher might say, 'The creaking of the door at night-time makes me think of the monsters from that movie *Monsters Inc.* sneaking into bedrooms, so I'll write that inference here.'

■ *Guided practice*: When your demonstration is finished, display a similar poem, such as *Count Dracula* (Foster, in Cookson, 2000, p. 253), for the children to annotate with a partner. As a class, attempt to infer what the poem could be

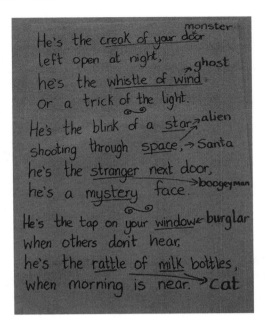

He's the creak of your door *monster*
left open at night, *^ghost*
he's the whistle of wind.
Or a trick of the light.
He's the blink of a star, *alien*
shooting through space, *→ Santa*
he's the stranger next door,
he's a mystery face. *→boogeyman*

He's the tap on your window *←burglar*
when others don't hear,
he's the rattle of milk bottles,
when morning is near. *→cat*

Figure 5.7 Inferring the subject matter of a poem

about. Make sure to emphasise that each inference must be supported in the text. Write down the children's thinking in a chart similar to the one shown in Figure 5.7. Share the findings with the entire group.

- *Reflection*: The teacher might say: What does it mean to infer? Was it easy or hard? How can I help you with inferring in the future?

- *Independent practice*: Provide similar activities during literacy centres (see Chapter 7).

Visualising

The ability to visualise is a critical aspect of good comprehension. It is a central factor differentiating good and poor readers. Decades of research have proven that getting children to create visual images before, during and after reading is a viable way of enhancing comprehension, and research has demonstrated that this skill can be taught (Gambrell & Bales, 1986). Visual structures, whether purely in the mind or transferred onto paper, are powerful tools for comprehension instruction because they offer concrete, memorable representations of abstract thinking processes. Visual representations of text can enhance both short-term and long-term memory for text, which can then provide a template for more sophisticated comprehension strategies (Gambrell & Koskinen, 2001). The process of creating images can help children when they are monitoring their comprehension, essentially increasing their awareness of whether the text is being understood. The construction of mental imagery also encourages the use of prior knowledge, and enhances a reader's ability to construct inferences on a text, make predictions and remember what has been read.

The rationale behind the inducing of mental imagery is firmly rooted in Paivio's (1971) dual coding theory. This theory suggests that the mind contains two mental subsystems: verbal and non-verbal (visual image). Each system is both independent and interconnected. Learning is enhanced when both systems are activated. For example, when children are learning language, they need the 'mental peg' or the visual image in the non-verbal system to understand the verbal component. The word 'cat' means nothing to children who have never seen a cat; however, when children are given a visual image connected to the word, it can then be processed.

Visualising is connected to children's prior knowledge. When a reader visualises something (e.g. 'a dog'), they generally visualise a dog that is already in their memory (perhaps a pet they once owned). Rosenblatt's (1994) transactional theory of reading highlights the role played by mental imagery in allowing the reader that 'lived through' experience with text, which enhances the personal, unique interpretation of the reader. This means that no two readers (or listeners) visualise a text in exactly the same way, as each person brings their personal prior knowledge to the text and uses it to create the visualisation. This phenomenon can create a rich discussion in the classroom during visualisation lessons.

Many children will not automatically use mental imagery; to do this, they will require direct instruction from the teacher. Bell (1997) recommends a progression in teaching visualisation, from the creation of mental images from observed concrete objects, to word imaging, to visualising paragraph by paragraph. Although visualisation, like all other comprehension strategies, would be taught using the Duke and Pearson (2002) model, the integration of artistic and dramatic response to text has been found to aid visualisation instruction (Wilhelm, 2001). As poems are generally highly descriptive, they are an ideal genre to begin teaching visualisation. In the example given below, the children are taught how to visualise poetry through sketching (and labelling):

- ■ *Explain*: The teacher might say, 'Today we are going to learn how to visualise when we read. It is important to visualise while you are reading or listening to a story or poem as when you imagine what is happening in your mind, and you can see the characters and what they are doing, you will remember all the parts of the poem much better. Today we are going to visualise some poems.'

- ■ *Demonstrate*: The teacher 'thinks aloud' while sketching the first eight lines of the poem 'My Neighbour's Dog Is Purple' (Jack Prelutsky). In her 'at first . . .' sketch, the teacher adds the 'large green eyes', the 'endless tail', the 'wicked smile' and, of course, the colour purple and a terrified onlooker. Then the teacher reveals the last two lines of the poem and completes an 'and then . . .' sketch in which the dog has become a crocodile (see Figure 5.8).

My Neighbour's Dog Is Purple (Prelutsky)
My neighbour's dog is purple,
Its eyes are large and green.
Its tail is almost endless,
The longest I have seen.
My neighbour's dog is quiet,
It does not bark one bit
But when my neighbour's dog is near
I feel afraid of it.
My neighbour's dog looks nasty,
It has a wicked smile.
Before my neighbour painted it,
It was a CROCODILE!

■ *Guided practice*: The teacher presents the first verse of the poem 'A Chubby Little Snowman' (see box below). The children sketch their 'at first . . .' visualisation as the teacher reads the poem. Then the teacher reveals the second verse, reading it several times as the children complete their 'and then . . .' visualisations. The teacher reminds the children to add labels and as many details as possible. Older students could read the poem with a partner.

■ *Reflection*: The teacher might say: What does it mean to visualise a poem? Was it easy or hard? Why? How can I help you visualise in the future?

■ *Independent practice*: The teacher could provide a similar activity during literacy centres (see Chapter 7).

Making connections

The comprehension strategy of 'making connections' entails activating one's prior knowledge and making a personal connection to the text. When this personal connection is made, the reader (or listener) links old knowledge (their prior knowledge) with new knowledge (the text). This linkage helps the reader retain, recall and engage with the text, thereby promoting comprehension and motivation to keep reading. There are three types of 'connections' that children can make to a text:

■ *Text-to-self connection*: This is when a book might be compared to personal experiences. For example, when reading *Leonardo and the Flying Boy* (Anholt, 2016) to children, the teacher might model a connection between Zoro and Salai's desire to see inside the secret workshop and waiting to open a surprise present.

■ *Text-to-text connection*: This is when a book might be compared to another book that has the same author, theme or genre. For example, when reading

Figure 5.8 Visualisation of 'My Neighbour's Dog'

A CHUBBY LITTLE SNOWMAN

A chubby little snowman,
Had a carrot nose.
Along came a bunny,
And what do you suppose?
Hungry little bunny,
Looking for his lunch.
Ate the snowman's carrot nose,
Nibble, nibble, CRUNCH!

RECOMMENDED BOOKS FOR VISUALISING WITH YOUNG CHILDREN

Frost, R. (2001). *Stopping by woods on a snowy evening*. San Bernadino, CA: Clearway Logistics.
Lewis, P. (2012). *The National Geographic book of animal poetry*. Los Angeles, CA: National Geographic.
Perry, S. (2006). *If…* Los Angeles, CA: Getty.
Prelutsky, J. (1991). *New kid on the block*. Dubois, PA: Mammoth.
Worth, V. (1994). *All the small poems and fourteen more*. New York: Squarefish.
Yolen, J. (2000). *Color me a rhyme*. Midletown, DE: Birdsong.
Yolen, J. (2007). *Here's a little poem*. London: Candlewick Press.

The Huge Big Bag of Worries (Ironside, 2011), the teacher or the children might make a connection to *Little Mouse's Big Book of Fears* (Gravett, 2007) as it has as similar theme.

- *Text-to-world connection*: This is when a book is compared to real-world events. For example, if the class were reading *One Big Family: Sharing Life in an African Village* (Onyefulu, 1996), the teacher or the children might make a connection to a programme on TV that portrayed family life in Africa.

The following demonstration outlines how 'text-to-self' connections might be taught using the book *The Pain and the Great One* (Blume, 2014). In general, stories that focus on family, special occasions, friends or school work well for connections lessons as the children will relate to the topic. This book focuses on the relationship between a brother and sister, which children might identify with in different ways:

- *Explain*: The teacher might say, 'Whenever we read something in a story that reminds us of something, we can call it a connection. We make connections so that we can understand the storyline or the characters better. When we make a connection, we can make a "c" sign with our hand' (see Appendix D).

- *Demonstrate*: The teacher demonstrates how to make connections by thinking aloud. For example, the teacher might say, 'I can make a connection here because my sister always got the most attention in our house. I used to feel irritated just like the girl in this book.'

- *Guided practice*: The children are encouraged to join in and 'think aloud'. The children may be encouraged to record their connections on a simple T-chart (see Figure 5.9). When the children are younger, an oral discussion with pictorial recording will work well. As the children progress, encourage them to record their thinking with words and images.

- *Reflection*: The teacher might say: What does it mean to make a connection? Why do we make connections? Was this strategy easy or hard to learn? Why?

- *Independent practice*: The children are encouraged to make connections when they read library books. The teacher might provide an activity based on making connections to a familiar book during literacy centre time (see Chapter 7).

RECOMMENDED BOOKS FOR MAKING CONNECTIONS

Keats, E. (1993). *The snowy day*. New York: Scholastic.
Pfister, M. (2007). *The rainbow fish*. London: North South Books.
Waddell, M. (1998). *Owl babies*. London: Walker Books.

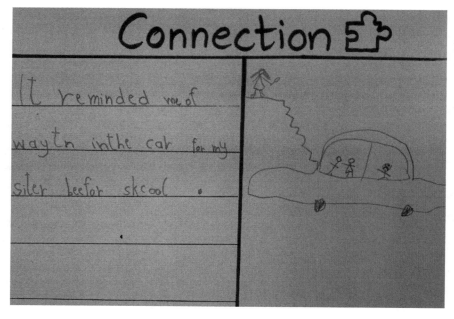

Figure 5.9 Recording connections

Monitor/clarify

The strategy of 'monitor/clarify' is based on the understanding that the competent reader is aware of when they need to exert more effort to understand the text and of when their comprehension breaks down and needs to be repaired. Comprehension monitoring is defined as a metacognitive process that is affected by person, strategy and task variables. It is executive in nature, controlling the use of all other strategies. It is an essential component for reading as it directs the reader's cognitive processes as they attempt to make sense of a text. Clarifying is how readers repair comprehension when it breaks down. It consists of drawing on different language/cueing systems: grapho-phonic, semantic, pragmatic and syntactic. When the competent reader experiences a breakdown in understanding, the monitoring function decides which clarifying strategy best suits their purpose. If clarification needs to take place at the word level, the reader may use structural analysis of the word (grapho-phonic cues), they may read on to discover further clues in the text (semantic cue), use prior knowledge to infer possible meaning (pragmatic) or analyse sentence structure (syntactic cue). Monitoring and clarifying function together. Monitoring is evaluative; clarifying is regulatory. Therefore, instruction should reflect this relationship.

Clarifying involves monitoring one's reading comprehension and recognising when meaning breaks down. You can clarify a word or an idea. It is sometimes referred to as 'fixing up my mix-up' or 'clicking or clunking'. When you model this strategy, choose a book that has some challenging vocabulary or concepts. A good example is the large-format book *The Great Chase* (MacCaughrean, 2007). The teaching steps for clarifying are outlined below:

- *Explain*: The teacher might say, 'Today we are going to learn about clarifying. When you are reading a text or listening to me read, sometimes you might come across a word or an idea that you don't understand. When this happens, you should clarify the word. Here are some things that you could do:
    - sound out the word;
    - break it into parts you know;
    - reread the sentence;
    - look at the picture (picture clues);
    - ask yourself, "What would make sense here?" (context clues);
    - think of what you know (prior knowledge);
    - read on (a sentence or two and then come back); or
    - ask someone.'

- *Demonstrate*: When you want to clarify something, make the hand sign for clarify (holding up your hands as if you are putting on glasses, see Appendix D). The teacher reads the text and models how to clarify various words.

- *Guided practice*: Now encourage the children to clarify words on their own using the steps with the teacher's guidance.

- *Reflection*: The teacher might ask: What does it mean to clarify? What was difficult about this strategy? What was easy? Why?

- *Independent practice*: Encourage the children to clarify during self-selected reading. Create an activity based on this strategy during literacy centres (see Chapter 7).

Since poetry is generally shorter and less text-dense than prose while still being linguistically diverse, it can provide a very suitable forum for vocabulary instruction using the 'clarify' strategy (Chall, Jacobs & Baldwin, 1990; Elster & Hanauer, 2002). 'Stormy Weather' (Gosselin, in Chanko, 2014) is an example of a poem that could be used in this manner in the junior classroom. Using context, the teacher could model how to clarify words such as 'pane', 'frown', 'mope', 'splatter' and 'spirits start to soar'. The children could be encouraged to use gesture and mime to act out the rain on the window pane, moping and frowning over bad weather, and joyfully putting on their boots and jumping in puddles.

Stormy Weather
When I hear a pitter-pat
Against my window pane,
I do not frown or mope about,
For I just love the rain!
I rush to put my boots on,
My spirits start to soar.
I grab my red umbrella
And go running out the door.
I find a great big puddle
And I jump in with a splatter.
It's muddy and it's very wet.
To me it doesn't matter!

Assessing comprehension

Comprehension development should be assessed both informally through teacher observation and formally through teacher-designed tasks, running records and standardised tests. The 'gradual release of responsibility' model (Duke & Pearson, 2002) includes many opportunities for assessment through teacher observation and careful note-taking. During the guided practice stage, the teacher should note who participates and whether children's comments demonstrate strategy use. This will help determine future instruction. Perhaps a teacher will decide to spend longer on a particular strategy, to work with small groups or to consider the literature used more carefully. The reflection stage of the 'gradual release of responsibility' model is also designed to inform the teacher how the children are doing in relation to strategy use. The reflection step encourages self-assessment among the children, which helps them to become more metacognitive (thinking about their own thinking). Throughout this chapter, numerous references were made to pictorial or written responses as part of guided practice. These samples can also be used in the assessment process. Outside of the 'gradual release of responsibility' model, comprehension can also be assessed more formally as part of running records (discussed in Chapter 3), and of course in standardised tests.

Listening/reading comprehension and the English language learner

Research has identified reading comprehension as a particular challenge for English language learners (Cummins, 2003). Therefore, it is critical that comprehension instruction begins in the early years in order to develop the cognitive skills that will be required as children move into the older grades. Explicit instruction in comprehension strategies has been proven successful in raising ELLs' comprehension (Chamot & O'Malley, 1994; Fung, Wilkinson & Moore, 2003). Comprehension strategy instruction is discussion based, which is important for the ELL who needs to make active use of the target language (Krashen, 1985). Learning comprehension strategies in either home languages or English can increase comprehension achievement across languages, and the strategies learnt can be transferred to other languages or areas of learning (Muniz-Swicegood, 1994). It is highly important that ELLs are taught reading comprehension strategies explicitly as it will enable them to catch up with the 'moving target' of grade-level standards more efficiently. Indeed, the work of Moll (2000) and Au (1997) have also highlighted the importance of focusing on meaning construction in an English language learner's reading instruction in order to provide 'culturally responsive' learning situations that can enhance achievement.

Key concepts for practice

- Listening and reading comprehension needs to be explicitly taught in the early years so that children read for meaning from the very beginning. This is particularly important for English language learners as it makes learning 'comprehensible' to them (Krashen, 1985).

- The 'gradual release of responsibility' model (Duke & Pearson, 2002) is recommended for comprehension strategy instruction.

- Young children should be taught a range of comprehension strategies, including predicting, retelling, questioning, inferring, visualising and making connections.

- High-quality children's literature and poetry should be used to teach comprehension strategies.

REFLECTION: THINKING ABOUT YOUR PRACTICE

As you read the following extract, think about the following questions:

- Were you taught how to comprehend text when you were in school? If so, how were you taught?

(continued)

(continued)

■ Have you taught comprehension like Mrs. Silver? How can you further your ability to teach comprehension strategies? What sort of changes would you like to make to your current approach to comprehension instruction?

Our teacher, Mrs. Silver, asked us a question about a story we had just read. I was puzzled by the question because I didn't remember reading the answer. So I went back into the text to find several paragraphs where I though the answer might be located. I read those paragraphs carefully, and then I read them over again. But I didn't find the answer to Mrs. Silver's question. Another child answered the question and Mrs. Silver responded, "Yes, good," I was incredulous.

I had read the story carefully and had read one specific part twice, and I knew the answer was not there. So I raised my hand and asked, "Where did he get his answer? It's not in the story." Mrs. Silver responded to me, "No, it's not. You have to read between the lines."

"Hmmm," I said to myself, "That is a very odd answer." I learned a lesson that day in Mrs. Silver's classroom. I learned not to ask Mrs. Silver questions because she wasn't going to help me get any answers.

Source: Dole (2003)

For further exploration

Block, C.C. & Pressley, M. (2002). Comprehension instruction: Research-based best practices. New York: Guilford Press.

Harvey, S. & Goudvis, A. (2000). Strategies that work: Teaching comprehension to enhance understanding. Portsmouth, NH: Stenhouse.

Keene, E. & Zimmerman, S. (1997). *Mosaic of thought*. Portsmouth, NH: Heinemann.

Miller, D. (2002). *Reading with meaning*. Portsmouth, NH: Heinemann.

6 Planning instruction using a meaningful context

┌───┐
│
│ **GUIDING QUESTIONS FOR THIS CHAPTER**
│
│ ■ How do you usually plan for literacy instruction?
│
│ ■ To what extent do you use big books, language experience charts or poetry
│   charts in your instruction?
│
│ ■ How can you teach a variety of early literacy skills within one lesson in a
│   meaningful way?
└───┘

Introduction

This chapter will bring together all of the reading skills discussed so far in this text and will develop the central theme of the book, which relates to literacy development through meaningful experiences. In this chapter, the author will illustrate how a range of reading skills can be taught in a cohesive manner using connected text. Connected texts can consist of large-format books, language experience charts, and poetry or rhyme charts. According to a study conducted by UKLA (2005), exemplary teachers of literacy used pedagogic practices that involved the integration of literacy skills in context, carefully balancing skills instruction within contextual learning opportunities. A critical aspect of this approach was that 'children need to see the rewards to be gained from the effort expended' (Lewis & Ellis, 2006). The UKLA (2005) study also identified the benefits of 'instructional density' (i.e. where several aspects of literacy learning are carefully orchestrated within and across lessons), as can be demonstrated from the planning grids found in this chapter.

Planning using big books

Fiction

Ideally, a big book would be used in a shared reading context over the course of a week. Every day, the book would be used in a slightly different manner, depending on what skills the teacher wishes to develop. When planning a series of lessons based on a big book, it would be advisable to start the process with a brainstorming grid, such as the one featured in Table 6.1. This grid is based on the book *Owl Babies* (Waddell, 1998). The brainstorming grid reveals that the teacher will focus on a review of the author, illustrator and blurb in relation to developing the children's concepts about print this week, while also exploring new concepts about print such as the author's use of capitalised print (e.g. 'their Owl Mother was GONE.'), exclamation marks (e.g. 'I want my mummy!') and question marks (e.g. 'Where's Mummy?'). The teacher might say, for example: Why does the author use large writing? What should we do to our voice when we are reading? As concepts about print are often closely related to fluency, the extracts that the teacher chooses for echo reading and choral reading should include these punctuation marks in order to maximise learning. The introduction of speech marks will enable the children to participate in a simple version of a reader's theatre where they might take the roles of Sarah, Percy and Bill, while the teacher plays the part of the narrator, in the extract below:

One night they woke up and their Owl Mother was GONE.

'Where's Mummy?', asked Sarah.

'Oh my goodness!', said Percy.

'I want my mummy!', said Bill.

(Waddell, 1998, p. 3)

The approach taken to developing fluency skills during the week mirrors the children's emerging knowledge of concepts about print. As the teacher introduces capitalised print, exclamation marks and question marks, the children partake in echo reading. As their confidence grows, they proceed to choral reading, where the text is read in unison. The introduction of speech marks allows for a reader's theatre towards the end of the week.

A number of vocabulary words are chosen for instruction from the text. Tier 1 (T1) words are chosen with English language learners in mind. The words 'owl', 'tree', 'gone' and 'woods' are essential in order to develop a basic understanding of the storyline, and might need to be taught to children who have very low levels of English. Tier 2 (T2) words such as 'swooped' are selected for instruction as they

Table 6.1 Planning grid using a fiction big book

Early literacy skill	Monday	Tuesday	Wednesday	Thursday	Friday
Concepts about print	Author Illustrator Blurb (review)	Capitalised print Exclamation marks	Capitalised print Exclamation marks Question marks		Capitalised print Exclamation marks Question marks Speech marks
Fluency		Echo reading	Echo reading	Choral reading	Choral reading Reader's theatre
Vocabulary	T1: owl, tree, gone, woods T2: hunting, ivy, brave, swooped, silent, fuss	T1: owl, tree, gone, woods T2: hunting, ivy, brave, swooped, silent, fuss		T1: owl, tree, gone, woods T2: hunting, ivy, brave, swooped, silent, fuss	
Sight words	'they'	'they'	'they' 'my'	'they' 'my'	'they' 'my'
Phonics	Revise previous work	'ow' (as in 'owl')	'ow' (as in 'owl')	'ow' (as in 'snow')	'ow' (as in 'owl') 'ow' (as in 'snow')
Phonological awareness	Clapping syllables in new vocabulary words	'Owls Fly' listening game	Sentence segmentation	Counting phonemes	Alliteration name game
Comprehension	Predictions Retelling	Retelling		Inferring	Inferring

are words not generally found in the spoken vocabulary of young children, but are words that will assist comprehension of the text.

Three high-frequency sight words are chosen for instruction. These words are chosen due to their frequent occurance in the text, taking into account the children's prior and future learning in relation to this skill. The teacher begins the week by teaching the sight word 'they', and then adds 'my' on Wednesday and 'for' on Friday. The children hunt for the words using the 'word swatter' pictured in Figure 6.1. They echo-read the sentences in which they occur. The teacher models oral sentences containing the target word and encourages the children to contribute oral sentences of their own. They discuss each word's features (length, syllables, number of letters, phonemes) and then compare them with other words beginning with the same letter on the word wall. The teacher will also review previously learned sight words during shared reading lessons.

In relation to phonics, the teacher introduces the sound 'ow' (as in 'owl') on Tuesday. This phonics focus has been chosen due to the central theme of the books so that phonics instruction can seemlessly integrate into the shared reading lesson. Later in the week, the teacher explores the alternative sound for 'ow' (as in 'snow'). On Monday, the teacher also revises other phonics material previously taught.

In Chapter 2, the different levels of phonological awareness were examined. This weekly plan includes activities at various different levels to account for the varying stages of development within the class group. On Monday, phonological awareness is integrated with vocabulary instruction as the children are encouraged to clap and

Figure 6.1 Finding sight words in a big book

count the syllables in the new vocabulary they encounter in the text. On Tuesday, the children play a version of the well-known 'fruit bowl' game, renamed 'Owls Fly' to fit with the theme of the book. This game is designed to develop listening skills. It is also a nice active way to begin or end the shared reading lesson. Here, the children sit in a circle and each child is assigned a character's name from the story – Sarah, Percy, Bill and Owl Mother. When the teacher calls one of the names, the children who have been assigned that character must change seats with another child who has also been assigned that character. If the teacher calls 'Owls Fly', then all children must change seats. On Wednesday, the teacher includes a sentence segmentation task as part of the shared reading lesson. The teacher chooses sentences from the text and askes the children to count the number of words within the sentence (e.g. 'I want my mummy', 'Where's Mummy?', 'Oh my goodness!' and so forth). On Thursday, the phonological awareness task involves hearing phonemes in words. The children are asked to identify the phonemes that they hear in 'Sarah', 'Percy', 'Bill' and 'Mother'. The final phonological awareness activity also emanates from the characters' names. In the alliteration name game, the children are encouraged to add an adjective to each of the characters' names (e.g. 'Super Sarah', 'Perfect Percy', 'Brilliant Bill' and so forth). Having played with various suggestions, the children then attempt to do the same with their own names.

The planning grid assumes that the children have already had considerable experience in using the predicting, questioning and retelling strategies. The new strategy being introduced is the 'inferring' strategy. The teacher adopts the 'gradual release of responsibility' model (Duke & Pearson, 2002) to teach all comprehension strategies, as described in Chapter 5. The teacher plans to use 'thought bubbles' throughout the story to help the children draw inferences (outlined in Chapter 5).

When the brainstorming web is complete, it is time to consider dividing the material into five lessons. Many aspects of the brainstorming grid will feature in several lessons as young children need numerous exposures to new learning material. Thursday's lesson is outlined in the box below.

THURSDAY'S LESSON: *OWL BABIES* (WADDELL, 1998)

Before reading:

■ The teacher reviews the tier 1 vocabulary prior to reading the story in a manner that engages the whole class (focus in on ELLs). 'This story is about … (shows a puppet and one of the target children says "owls") and they lived in a … (points to illustration to aid another target child, who answers "tree"). Lots of trees together

(continued)

(continued)

(point to visual) is called a ... (another child answers "wood"). Who can remember the characters' names?'

■ As the children answer, the teacher instructs them to 'sound out' the names orally to 'hear' the phonemes.

During reading:

■ As the teacher reads the text, she encourages the children to engage in choral reading for the repetitive, predictable parts that they echo-read for the past two days.

■ They also review the tier 2 words that they discussed earlier in the week.

When the teacher gets to the point in the story where all three owl babies are sitting on the branch with their eyes closed, she introduces the 'inferring' strategy:

■ *Explain*: The teacher says, 'Today we are going to learn about inferring. Inferring means that we use the information in the book and our own brains to infer what a character might be thinking or saying at different points in the story. Making an inference helps us to understand what is happening in a story better.'

■ *Demonstrate*: Picking a point in the story that is suitable for this activity, the teacher draws a speech/thought bubble and says, 'What would Bill be thinking right now? Well, I'm going to imagine I'm Bill. I think I would say, "I'm so scared! ... I wish Mammy would come back quickly! ... It's so late, I should be in bed."' The teacher writes these thoughts into the thought bubble.

■ *Guided practice*: The teacher now places a blank thought bubble above Sarah's head and encourages the children to think of what Sarah might be thinking at this point in the story. These ideas are recorded by the teacher on a chart. Then the same is done for Bill's character.

■ *Independent practice*: At the end of the story, the teacher asks the children to discuss what Owl Mother might be thinking in pairs. They record their thinking by writing their ideas into a speech bubble using invented spelling. They share their responses.

After reading:

■ The teacher asks the children to reflect on the strategy of inferring, asking: What does it mean to infer? What sort of inferences did we make? How does drawing inferences help our understanding of the story?

- The teacher then reviews the sight words 'they' and 'my', asking the children for oral sentences and asking them to locate them in the text.

- The teacher reviews the chart they created yesterday containing words that have the sound 'ow' (as in 'owl'). Today, she tells them how this phoneme can also be pronounced 'ow' (as in 'snow'). She writes several words containing this sound on the chart for the children to decode. To ensure that her English language learners can comprehend the words, she includes a visual after each word has been sounded out. The children are encouraged to encode (write) some words containing the new sound on mini-whiteboards.

- Using the list of 'ow' words, the teacher encourages the children to help her write a 'silly rhyme' using some of the words containing the new sound.

- Next week, the children will be taught a picture/word matching game focused on the 'ow' sound.

Please note that an additional lesson plan exemplar is available in Appendix E.

Non-fiction

It is essential that children have opportunities to learn and develop their early literacy skills across different genres. While there may be a tendency to focus on fiction texts in the junior class, there are many high-quality non-fiction titles available in large format, such as the big book *Big Blue Whale* (Davies, 1997) featured in Table 6.2.

In this planning grid, the teacher explores several concepts about print across the three days. The teacher begins on Monday by introducing the book and talking about the author, the illustrator and the blurb. On Tuesday, the teacher begins the lesson by reviewing the pages they read together yesterday. This time, she draws the children's attention to the different sizes of font that the author uses to emphasise certain information. The teacher links the concept about print to fluency instruction by encouraging the children to echo-read the text that is affected by this concept about print, focusing on pitch, tone and volume while reading. On Wednesday, after reviewing the part of the book read so far, the teacher draws the children's attention to the use of dashes in the text. They discuss how dashes are used and echo-read the sentences in the text containing dashes.

In relation to vocabulary development, the planning grid demonstrates that the teacher plans to teach tier 1 vocabulary to her English language learners who have a low level of English in order to keep them engaged in the lesson and tier 2 and tier

Table 6.2 Planning grid using a non-fiction big book

Early literacy skill	Monday	Tuesday	Wednesday
Concepts about print	Author Illustrator Blurb	Size of font	Dashes Index
Fluency		Echo reading	Echo reading
Vocabulary	T1: whale, bigger, earth, touch, eye, ears, breathes, mouth T2/3: creature, blowhole, mammal, surface, stale, krill, jaw	T1: tongue, eating, summer, winter T2/3: gulp, blubber, shoals, vast, equator	T1: baby, milk, hum T2: calm, slithers, nudges, vastness
Sight words	'blue' 'as'		'all' 'will'
Phonics	Revision	Magic 'e' (whale)	Magic 'e'
Phonological awareness	Clapping syllables in new vocabulary words	Clapping phonemes in new vocabulary words	Phonemic manipulation
Comprehension	KWL	KWL	KWL

3 vocabulary to the rest of the class (though the former group might benefit from this instruction as well). The teacher uses actions, gestures and visuals for the keywords in the planning grid to ensure that the ELLs have a basic understanding of the text. The addition of a few additional visuals, such as a seasons chart and a picture of milk, will enhance understanding. When they encounter the target tier 2 and tier 3 words in the text, they discuss the meaning of new vocabulary words in context. On Monday, they clap the syllables in these words, and on Tuesday they stretch the phonemes so as to heighten phonological awareness and as an 'aide-memoire' to remember the words.

While phonological awareness activities are integrated on the first two days of instruction, on Wednesday the children are encouraged to manipulate phonemes related to the central theme of the book. The teacher begins the lesson by playing a phonemic manipulation game with the word 'whale'. She models how to change the initial phoneme of the word (e.g. 'male', 'pale', 'zale', 'jale', 'lale', 'tale') to create real or 'made-up' words. She then encourages the children to try this for themselves.

The teacher plans to teach four new sight words while using this text, as well as revising familiar words. On Monday, the teacher will present the children with the new sight words 'blue' and 'as', and on Wednesday they will learn 'all' and 'will'. The children hunt for the word in the texts and cover it with a Post-it of the word each time it occurs. They echo-read the sentences in which they occur. The teacher models oral sentences containing the target word and encourages the children to contribute oral sentences of their own. They discuss each word's features (length, syllables, number of letters, phonemes) and then compare them with other words beginning with 'b', 'w' and 'a' on the word wall.

Phonics instruction on Monday consists of a review of phonics sounds they have learned so far. The teacher encourages the children to give the sound for each phoneme, and then they sound out some of the words in the book that contain phonemes that are familiar to them (e.g. 'big', 'out', 'egg', 'wet', 'soap', 'deep', 'get'). On Tuesday, the teacher introduces the magic 'e' rule by writing the word 'whale' on the chart paper. She demonstrates how the vowel sound would change to a short vowel if the magic 'e' was not at the end of the word. She leads the children to find more words containing magic 'e' in the text and adds them to the list (e.g. 'place', 'hole', 'time', 'stale', 'plates'). They might even find exceptions to the rule, such as 'come'. On Wednesday, the teacher reviews magic 'e' and adds more examples from the final section of the book to the list. The children are encouraged to write (encode) some magic 'e' words on their whiteboards. The use of magic 'e' words in their writing during the writing workshop is discussed later in the day (see Chapter 9). Following a whole-class demonstration, the children have the opportunity to engage in a magic 'e' word-to-picture matching game during literacy centres time the following week (see Chapter 7).

Comprehension instruction in this planning grid is focused on the introduction of a KWL chart. This strategy is useful for non-fiction texts as it encourages the children to activate their prior knowledge, ask questions of the text and to determine the important points made in the text. In junior classes, this activity is usually completed as a whole-class activity, and may include visuals and drawings to enhance understanding. The activity is extended over three days as the class navigates their way through the text. On Monday, the teacher introduces the KWL chart to the class. The chart has three columns, labelled 'K', 'W' and 'L'. She explains that the 'K' stands for 'what I already know about whales'. She models one fact that she knows about whales (e.g. 'they can swim') and then invites the children to share their prior knowledge. She records all the ideas on the chart. Next, she points to the 'W' section, and explains that this stands for 'what I want to learn about whales'. She models how to locate key facts (e.g. 'How long do they live?') and invites the children to share their ideas, recording them on the chart. The teacher begins to read the text, reminding the children to look out for the answers to their questions as they navigate the text. After reading the first page of the text, the teacher introduces the 'L' part of the chart, which stands for 'what I learned'. She models the facts that have been gleaned from this page and writes them on the chart. Then she continues reading. After the next page, she invites the students to contribute new knowledge to the chart. When they have read approximately one-third of the book together, they review the chart. The next day, they review the KWL chart from the previous day and the teacher continues to read the next part of the book, pausing frequently to add to the chart. Similar to the day before, they continue to read the last section of the text, pausing frequently to add to the KWL chart. On completing the book in Wednesday's lesson, they review the KWL chart. Then children are then given a fact from the 'L' section of the chart on a strip of paper and illustrate the new knowledge with a partner for a class book about whales.

In this example, the book *Big Blue Whale* (Davies, 1997) was used over three days. Wednesday's lesson on day 3 is described in more detail in the box below.

WEDNESDAY'S LESSON: *BIG BLUE WHALE* (DAVIES, 1997)

Before reading:

■ The teacher begins the lesson by playing a phonemic manipulation game with the word 'whale'. She models how to change the initial phoneme of the word (e.g. 'male', 'pale', 'zale', 'jale', 'lale', 'tale') to create real or 'made-up' words. She then encourages the children to try this for themselves.

■ The teacher then reviews magic 'e' and adds more examples from the final section of the book to the list for the children to decode. The children are encouraged to write (encode) some magic 'e' words on their whiteboards.

During reading:

■ Similar to the day before, they continue to read the last section of the text, pausing frequently to add to the KWL chart. They discuss the meaning of new vocabulary words in context. On completing the book, they review the KWL chart.

After reading:

■ Next, the teacher draws the children's attention to the use of dashes in the text. They discuss how dashes are used, and the teacher models how it affects her tone of voice. Then the children echo-read the sentences in the text containing dashes.

■ The teacher reviews the sight words learned on Monday and presents the new sight words 'all' and 'will'. The children hunt for the word in the texts and cover it with a Post-it of the word each time it occurs. They echo-read the sentences in which they occur. The teacher models oral sentences containing the target word and encourages the children to contribute oral sentences of their own. They discuss each word's features (length, syllables, number of letters, phonemes) and then compare them with other words beginning with 'w' and 'a' on the word wall.

■ Then children are given a fact from the 'L' section of the chart on a strip of paper and illustrate the new knowledge with a partner for a class book about whales.

Planning using the Language Experience Approach (LEA)

Language experience charts (outlined in Chapter 1) can also provide a meaningful context for the instruction of a range of early literacy skills. They have the advantage of being inexpensive (only chart paper and a marker are required) and they are based on the children's language and experiences. An example of language experience text is given in Figure 6.2, and a related planning grid is given in Table 6.3.

Figure 6.2 Language experience text

Table 6.3 Planning using a language experience text

Early literacy skill	Tuesday	Wednesday	Thursday
Concepts about print	Title Left-to-right orientation Return sweep Full stops and capital letters		
Fluency	Echo reading	Echo reading	Choral reading
Vocabulary		Words to describe the 'dog'	
Sight words	Revise 'a', 'her', 'and'	'She'	'was'
Phonics/handwriting	/v/	/v/	
Phonological awareness	Clapping syllables in words		Rhyming words for 'vet', 'dog', 'cat'
Comprehension		Question generation	Visualising

The visit from the vet took place on Monday. On Tuesday, the majority of the lesson is focused on the creation of the text. The lesson begins by introducing the topic – the vet. The topic was chosen because a vet visited the classroom on the previous day. The children are encouraged to discuss the vet's visit with a partner and then share ideas to the whole class. The teacher displays some photographs of the visit on the interactive whiteboard (IWB) to aid the children's memory and to add depth to the discussion. Photographs can also be helpful to reinforce key vocabulary for English language learners. After some discussion, the teacher lifts the pen and asks the children to help her create a text about the visit. The children contribute their ideas and these are written on the chart. The teacher asks the children: 'Where will I start writing?' (left-to-right, top-to-bottom orientation), 'Where will I continue to write?' (return sweep at the end of a line). As the teacher writes, she 'thinks aloud' in relation to spelling words, capital letters, finger spaces and full stops. In this way, the teacher demonstrates and teaches numerous concepts about print through writing the chart, thinking aloud and encouraging children's contributions. When the text is complete, the teacher invites the children to echo-read the text. They play a clapping game where the children are invited to clap the syllables in a variety of words and count them (e.g. 'yesterday', 'Fiona', 'dog', 'hamster'). The teacher ensures that she chooses words containing different amounts of syllables to maximise the teaching of phonological awareness. The sound /v/ is introduced as the word 'vet' begins with this sound. The teacher displays the symbol and the children find it in the text. They discuss other words that begin with /v/. They sing a song about /v/. Then they return to their seats and create the letter /v/ out of playdough using a paper template as support.

The next day, they begin the lesson by echo reading the text. The teacher models how to ask a question about the text. She encourages the children to ask their partner a question about the text. These questions (and answers) are shared with the class. The teacher presents the children with a photograph of the vet's dog that she brought into the classroom on Monday and asks them to think of words to describe the dog. The children discuss this with a partner and then share their ideas with the class. The teacher models some tier 2 vocabulary, referring to the dog as having a 'sleek coat' that was 'jet black'. Both the teacher's and children's contributions are recorded on a word web with 'dog' at the centre. The teacher presents a new sight word, 'she'. The children hunt for the word in the text and match it with a Post-it of the word each time it occurs. They echo-read the sentences in which it occurs. The teacher models an oral sentence containing the target word and encourages the children to contribute oral sentences of their own. They discuss the word's features (length, syllables, number of letters, phonemes) and then compare it with other words beginning with 's' on the word wall. Then the teacher focuses the children's attention on the new letter sound that they learned yesterday. They locate the letter 'v' in the text and discuss other words that contain the letter. The children sing a song about the letter and 'skywrite' it. They then attempt to write the letter in their copybooks with teacher guidance. When the letters are complete, they are encouraged to draw the 'vet' at the top of the page and to label the picture.

On Wednesday, the teacher begins the lesson with a 'round-robin rhyming game'. First, she models a number of words that rhyme with 'vet'. Then she repeats the word 'vet' and asks the children to contribute words that rhyme with 'vet'. As this is a task designed to develop phonological awareness, the words do not have to be 'real words', which can add to the children's enjoyment. The same task is carried out with other words from the text, such as 'dog' and 'cat'. Then the teacher leads a choral reading of the text. The children find the sight word 'she' in the text and highlight it. The teacher displays a new sight word – 'was'. The children highlight the word in the text and the sentences containing the word are read orally. The teacher models an oral sentence for the target word and encourages the children to share their own sentences. The last activity is focused on the comprehension strategy of visualising. The children are given blank pieces of paper to sketch their visualisation. The teacher reads the text line by line and encourages the children to add each detail to their drawing. She challenges some children to add labels if they are able to. The children are encouraged to share their visualisation with a partner and then with the whole class.

Planning using poetry charts

Poetry charts can provide an interesting context for the teaching of early literacy skills. A simple poem can be written on large chart paper or projected onto a screen for use in lessons. If you are trying to adhere to a particular theme in your planning, then poetry can be a good choice for shared reading lessons, as once you have found a suitable poem either online or in an anthology, you can begin planning for instruction (see Appendix B for some recommended poetry sources). A planning grid in Table 6.4 for the poem featured in Figure 6.3 ('The Monkey') demonstrates how a range of early literacy skills can be taught in this meaningful context.

As poems are shorter than books, the teacher might only spend a day or two on a poem rather than an entire week, as was the case with the big book discussed earlier in this chapter. In the lesson outlined in the planning grid in Table 6.4, the teacher begins the lesson by rereading other poems previously taught and engaging

Figure 6.3 'The Monkey' poem

Table 6.4 Planning using a poem

Early literacy skill	Teaching possibilities
Concepts about print	Full stops and capital letters
Fluency	Echo reading, choral reading
Vocabulary	'ripe' 'treat'
	Words to describe the monkey
Sight words	'in'
Phonics	'ee' 'ea'
Phonological awareness	Clapping syllables in words
	Identifying rhyming words
Comprehension	Visualising

the children in a discussion about sight words and phonics that they learned in those contexts as a 'warm-up' to the new reading material. It is a good idea to write all poems on large pieces of sturdy card so that they can be used again and again in different ways.

Then the teacher presents the children with the poem; she starts the lesson by reading the poem to the class, modelling appropriate prosody. She leads a discussion on the use of commas, full stops and exclamation marks in the poem, and how the punctuation affects her reading in order to develop the children's concepts about print. Then she encourages the children to engage in echo reading of the poem for fluency practice. This might be followed by a discussion on vocabulary words such as 'ripe' and 'treat'. They echo-read the poem again, this time adding actions as they read. The kinaesthetic learning is enjoyable and also helps English language learners learn key vocabulary. The teacher asks them to identify the rhyming words within the poem, such as 'tree' and 'free', to develop phonological awareness. The teacher introduces the new sight word 'in' at this point. She displays it on a flash card and the children highlight the word in the text and the sentences containing the word are read orally. The teacher models an oral sentence for the target word and encourages the children to share their own sentences. They discuss the word's features (length, syllables, number of letters, phonemes) and then compare it with other words beginning with 'i' on the word wall. They may also locate other familiar sight words within the text (such as 'a' and 'to'). Next, the teacher focuses the children's attention on the sound 'ee'. She presents a flash card containing the sound and has the children say the sound. She encourages them to locate words within the text containing this sound. The words are written on a list on one side of chart paper. The teacher asks the children if they had noticed any other words that contain the long 'e' sound but are spelled differently. The children respond that 'ea' is an alternative spelling for the long 'e' sound. Words containing 'ea' are identified in the poem and added to a new list on the other side of the chart paper. The children read the words and the teacher adds some additional words containing 'ee' and 'ea' for decoding. She also prompts the children to encode some words containing these phonemes by writing them on mini-whiteboards. Finally, the class echo-reads the poem again using actions. Then the children attempt to read it chorally. When they return to their seats, the poem remains on display and the teacher reads it again as the children draw a visualisation of the poem (sketch with labels). The children share their drawings with a partner and with the whole class.

Key concepts for practice

- Planning needs to take account of all the early literacy skills.

- Not every early literacy skill may be taught in every reading lesson, but the use of planning grids ensures that all skills are addressed across the week on different days in different ways.

- A variety of reading materials, such as big books (fiction and non-fiction), language experience charts, poetry, and interactive e-books/Internet resources would be recommended to ensure depth and engagement in reading lessons.

- It is important to differentiate your teaching to take account of varying levels of English competency and literacy skills.

REFLECTION: THINKING ABOUT YOUR PRACTICE

■ To what extent could you implement the planning approach outlined in this chapter?

■ Given your current teaching situation, can you identify any challenges in teaching literacy using the methodologies outlined so far in this text?

■ How might you adapt this teaching approach to make it appropriate to your teaching context?

For further exploration

Cunningham, P.M., Moore, S., Cunningham, J. & Moore, D. (2004). *Reading and writing in elementary classrooms.* Boston, MA: Pearson.

Routman. R. (2018). *Literacy essentials.* Portsmouth, NH: Heinemann.

Strickland, D. (2010). *Essential readings on early literacy.* Newark DE: International Reading Association.

Strickland, D. & Morrow, L. (2000). *Beginning reading and writing.* Newark DE: International Reading Association.

7 Guided reading and literacy centres

GUIDING QUESTIONS FOR THIS CHAPTER

■ Can you explain how a guided reading lesson is structured?

■ What skills and strategies might be taught during a guided reading lesson?

■ How would you organise literacy centres to complement your guided reading lessons?

■ How would you assess guided reading and literacy centres?

Introduction

So far, this book has focused on whole-class or large group instruction. However, children also need opportunities to develop their literacy skills in small group settings reading books that correspond to their current level of reading development. Therefore, shared reading practices need to be complemented with a more individualised approach. Guided reading is a suitable method. It is a component of a balanced literacy programme where the children are taught reading skills and strategies in small groups according to their instructional level (Fountas & Pinnell, 1996). The approach is designed to enable the teacher to teach a wide range of literacy skills in the context of texts that are appropriate for each reader. Multiple copies of levelled texts are used for a guided reading lesson, and as the children's skills develop they move on to more difficult texts when assessment data illustrate that they have increased their reading level. Guided reading allows for individualised instruction that is focused on the learners' needs. It also emphasises the need to teach literacy skills within a meaningful context and to have children apply their learning using engaging and enjoyable texts in a social manner (Fountas & Pinnell,

1996; Knox & Amador-Watson, 2002). This explicit, contextual instruction is particularly important for English language learners (ELLs), but their experience can be further enhanced if certain modifications are made (Avalos, Plasencia, Chavez & Rascón, 2007) in relation to vocabulary, text structure and cultural relevance. While the teacher is working with a small group of students in a guided reading session, high-quality literacy centres will enable the other children in the class to work independently while practising essential literacy skills in a social context. This chapter will begin by defining and describing how to organise guided reading sessions in your early years classroom. It will also outline the modifications that can be made to guided reading sessions to maximise English language learners' learning. Finally, it will describe how to set up, manage and assess literacy centres in the classroom.

What is guided reading?

Guided comprehension is a social constructivist model of reading instruction where children are gathered together in small groups to read and discuss levelled texts. It fits well within the balanced literacy framework as it provides opportunities for children to interact with authentic texts in an enjoyable manner that promotes cognitive development (Pearson, 2001). During a guided reading session, the teacher provides support for small groups of readers as they learn to use various reading skills and strategies. Generally, the teacher would begin with groups of three or four children in the first year of school. This group size may then gradually increase to five or six (if necessary due to class size or support available) by the second or third year at school. The children read books at their instructional level and are grouped accordingly (Fountas & Pinnell, 1996) – see below for further details on instructional level. Each child in the group will read the same levelled text during a guided reading session. An instructional-level text provides the opportunity for children to experience both success and some degree of challenge within the one reading session.

A guided reading session generally lasts between 8 and 15 minutes. The time is dependent on the age and ability of your students as the children who are not in your guided reading group will be working independently during this time. When children first begin reading, a small group could be expected to stay on task for approximately 8 to 12 minutes, whereas older children should be able to work independently for up to 15 minutes. With this advice in mind, the teacher should decide on an appropriate time frame for their students.

Organising groups for instruction

Running records, which we discussed in Chapter 3, can help determine each child's instructional level. An instructional-level text is a book that a child can read with 90 to 95 per cent accuracy (i.e. out of 100 words, they need assistance with less than 10 words). Books at instructional level are used in guided reading as they provide the appropriate amount of challenge in a supportive setting. Children will be able to read the text successfully under the guidance of the teacher. A frustration-level text is one that a child reads with less than 90 per cent accuracy. This type of text is too hard as the child would struggle with more than 10 words in every 100. Children should not be encouraged to read texts at this level as comprehension will be adversely affected. An independent-level text is one that a child can read with more than 95 per cent accuracy. This means that a child has some difficulty with less than 5 words per 100 in the text. This text is suitable for self-selected reading.

Structure of a guided reading lesson

A guided reading lesson should generally follow these steps:

- Introduce the book. Encourage the children to examine the front cover and to read the blurb. They might like to make predictions about what is going to happen in the story. You may need to pre-teach difficult vocabulary/new sight words. You may encourage the children to do a 'picture walk' through the book. Phonological awareness activities relevant to the book might be included in this section. It might be appropriate to discuss certain concepts about print at this stage.

- The children begin 'whisper reading' the book simultaneously. When the teacher leans in towards a particular child (or sits beside them, depending on the seating arrangement), the child 'turns up the volume' so that they can be heard by the teacher. In this way, all the children get to read the book instead of simply listening to others read (or struggle to read).

- When the children have finished reading, discuss the book. Perhaps have the children retell the story or ask each other questions. You could use the comprehension strategy spinner we discussed in Chapter 5.

- Review the new vocabulary/sight words. It might be appropriate to do some fluency work at this stage.

- Word work. You can take this opportunity to do some word work or phonics based on the text that you have just read.

Note: Aim to take each reading group at least every second day so that they have two sessions a week at a minimum. Try to take weaker groups more often if possible.

Skills and strategies that can be taught during guided reading

In our previous chapters, we discussed many skills and strategies that the emergent reader requires in becoming literate. Let's review some of these strategies and explore how they might fit into your guided reading lesson:

- *Phonological awareness*: In the early stages of guided reading, it would be particularly appropriate to include some phonological awareness activities as part of your guided reading lesson, such as clapping syllables in words, phonemic manipulation, discussion of rhyming words, and so forth (see Chapter 2).

- *Phonics*: Draw the children's attention to any example of phonemes that you have studied recently. Encourage students to use their phonic knowledge to 'sound out' words (see Chapter 3).

- *Word study*: Encourage students to break an unknown word into parts (to 'clarify') (see Chapter 5). Discuss prefixes, suffixes, compound words, synonyms and homonyms as appropriate.

- *Comprehension*: Include the comprehension strategies mentioned in Chapter 5, such as predicting, retelling, visualising, connecting, inferring, questioning and clarifying where appropriate.

- *Sight words*: Highlight or have the children find particular sight words before, during or after reading (see Chapter 4).

- *Concepts about print*: Discuss left-to-right orientation, word-to-word matching, the front and the back of the book, and punctuation marks (see Chapter 4).

- *Fluency*: Choose an extract of the book, discuss the phrasing and punctuation, and have the children echo-read the text to develop their expression (see Chapter 4).

- *Vocabulary*: Choose some words from the text that are challenging in meaning and discuss them as part of the lesson (see Chapter 4).

GUIDED READING EXAMPLE 1: EARLY READING LEVEL

'I want a car,' said Mr Marvel. 'I can help you,' said Squeak. 'ABRACADABRA!' said Squeak. 'We want a car.' 'Here is a car,' said Mr Marvel. 'But it is too little.' 'No, it is not too little,' said Squeak. 'I like it.' 'I can't go in this car,' said Mr Marvel. 'I am too big.' 'ABRACADABRA!' said Mr Marvel. 'I want a big car.' 'Here is a car,' said Squeak. 'But is it too big?' 'No, it is not too big,' said Mr Marvel.

The teacher would choose a few early literacy skills to focus on during each guided reading session. Below is a list of suggestions for the book mentioned above; we are not suggesting that a teacher attempt to teach all of these aspects in one guided reading session:

- *Phonological awareness*: Clap out the syllables in unfamiliar words (e.g. 'ABRACADABRA') and the names of characters (e.g. 'Squeak' and 'Mr Marvel') and keywords in the story such as 'car', 'big' and 'little'. Discuss words that rhyme with 'car'.

- *Phonics*: Discuss the r-controlled vowel sound found in 'car' – /ar/ – and look at other examples.

- *Comprehension*: Have the children predict the storyline using a 'picture walk'. Have children retell the story using the vocabulary of 'character/setting/ problem/solution'. Discuss other magic tricks that Mr Marvel might perform.

- *Sight words*: The words 'want', 'you' and 'we' are found frequently in early readers. It might also be useful to discuss the contraction 'can't' and its origin.

- *Concepts about print*: It may be appropriate to discuss the author's use of speech marks and exclamation marks, and link this to fluency instruction.

- *Fluency*: The children could take on the roles of the characters and the narrator and read extracts aloud, paying attention to punctuation (especially speech marks).

- *Vocabulary*: Synonyms for 'big' and 'little' could enhance the children's vocabulary development.

Source: Mitton and Doyle (1998)

GUIDED READING EXAMPLE 2: INTERMEDIATE READING LEVEL

Once upon a time Mother Goat said to her kids, 'I have to go out. Don't open the door. The wolf could eat you up.' Mother Goat went off. Then the wolf came to the door. 'Open up kids,' he called. 'I am your mother.' The kids looked under the door. They saw his big black feet. 'No, you are not Mother,' they said. 'She has not got black feet.' So the wolf went to the mill.

(continued)

(continued)

He put flour on his feet. 'Now I will go to the house of the little kids,' he said. 'Open up kids,' called the wolf. 'I am your mother.' The kids looked under the door. They saw his white feet. 'It is Mother,' they said. 'I will open the door,' said a little kid. But it was not Mother. It was the wolf. 'Help!' said the little kids and they ran here and there. The wolf looked for the kids.

The teacher would choose a few early literacy skills to focus on during each guided reading session. Below is a list of suggestions for the book mentioned above; we are not suggesting that a teacher attempt to teach all of these aspects in one guided reading session:

- *Phonological awareness*: Clap out the syllables in unfamiliar words (e.g. 'mother', 'kids', 'mill' and 'flour').

- *Phonics*: Explore words containing /ee/, such as 'feet', and /ea/, such as 'eat'.

- *Word study*: Discuss 'ed' endings, such as 'looked'.

- *Comprehension*: Predicting throughout the story. Retelling using the vocabulary of 'character/problem/events/solution'. Discussion on the character of the wolf/mother/kids (inference). The children may need to clarify 'mill' and 'flour'.

- *Sight words*: The words 'saw', 'now' and 'they' can be tricky for children at this stage of reading development, and are found frequently in early readers. The beginning of the story, 'Once upon a time...', should be highlighted before reading if the children have not read it before.

- *Concepts about print*: It may be appropriate to discuss the author's use of speech marks and link this to fluency instruction.

- *Fluency*: The children could take on the roles of the characters and the narrator and read extracts aloud, paying attention to punctuation (especially speech marks).

- *Vocabulary*: The words 'mill' and 'flour' may need to be discussed. The dual meaning of 'kid' may warrant discussion (homonym).

Source: Riordan (1998)

Guided reading using poetry

It is important that children have the opportunity to read different genres at their instructional level. Poetry can work well in guided reading lessons as it can provide an enjoyable context to learn different literacy skills. Poetry is a genre that doesn't tend to be 'levelled' in the same way as fiction or non-fiction texts. However, suitable resources include Chanko (2014) and Yolen and Fusek-Peters (2010), which contain many useful poems for guided reading for emergent and early readers.

'If You Smile at a Crocodile' (Goldish, in Chanko, 2014) is an example of a poem that could be used in a guided reading lesson (see below). This guided reading session might begin by predicting from the title what the poem might be about. The teacher might then discuss some well-known sight words that appear in the poem with capital letters at the beginning, such as 'And', 'Has' and 'Be', as sometimes the different format can cause unnecessary confusion (particularly for early or struggling readers). The teacher could encourage the children to clap the syllables in some of the words that might have been unfamiliar to them, such as 'crocodile', 'toothy' and 'teeth', to counteract potential reading difficulties and to enhance phonological awareness. The teacher might discuss the meaning of 'swamp' and 'chomp' for vocabulary development. Then the children should be encouraged to 'whisper-read' the poem themselves. Having read the poem a few times for fluency, the teacher might lead a discussion about various concepts about print, such as the use of the exclamation mark and bold print, and the impact that these would have on reading expression. The children might echo-read lines from the poem to rehearse reading with expression. The children could then reread the poem to a partner. If the children are already familiar with generating questions, they might be encouraged to create a question about the poem to ask the group. Having answered everyone's questions, the teacher and children could chorally read the poem together to develop fluency.

If You Smile at a Crocodile
The crocodile
Has a toothy smile,
His teeth are sharp and long.
And in the swamp
When he takes a chomp
His bite is quick and strong!
So if you smile at a crocodile,
There's just one thing to say:
If he smiles too,
Be sure that you
Are VERY far away!

Assessing guided reading

Guided reading is generally assessed through the use of running records (see Chapter 4). However, teacher observation should also be used to note student interest in the text's genre or topic, ability to read with expression, participation in group discussion, and overall attitude to reading. The teacher should create a reading record for each student to bring home that includes a comment box for parents. All books read in guided reading should also be read at home. Using the record form, parents can write a note about students' reading performance at home (for an example, see Appendix F).

Children should also be encouraged to participate in oral self-assessment. They should discuss anything they find challenging/easy about the book they are reading and the strategies that they use to overcome any difficulties with the text. This is a good way to close a guided reading session. Alternatively, this self-assessment could be a whole-class discussion at a plenary session (following guided reading).

Benefits and challenges of guided reading

Benefits

- In a guided reading session, all children have the opportunity to be successful in reading as texts are tailored to their personal reading level rather than a 'one-size-fits-all' class basal reader. This reduces the sense of reading failure. It is also much easier for the teacher to use a text that is appropriate for a group of children, as core readers (where all children read the same book) are often too hard or too easy for many children. Individualised instruction promotes reading success and a positive attitudes towards reading in general (Fountas & Pinnell, 1996).

- Better able children can be appropriately challenged, and weaker students receive focused instruction.

- It is reasonably easy to track and report children's progress (Knox & Amador-Watson, 2002).

- The children get to read a large number of books (one or two per week, instead of three or four a year). This helps them to feel like 'readers' from the beginning.

- Students are actively involved in the lesson throughout the session, and all students receive targeted support and feedback.

- The learning is socially mediated as the students have the opportunity to discuss the text with the teacher and their peers during the lesson.

Challenges

- If children are not used to working in small groups in this manner, it may take some time and effort to establish this methodology in your classroom.

- Setting up guided reading can be costly as a full set of levelled texts will need to be purchased. Instead of having 'class readers' on your booklist, include a charge for English classroom materials to help cover the cost of the books.

- Guided reading should be a whole-school approach to teaching reading, so it may be difficult to encourage all members of staff to opt in.

Modifying guided reading for the English language learner

While English language learners will find guided reading sessions beneficial, some modifications to planning and teaching could result in further language learning opportunities (Avalos et al., 2007). When planning a guided reading lesson for ELLs, the teacher should take time to analyse the text so as to identify potential challenges for students who are learning English. First, the cultural relevance of the text should be determined in terms of content (expository) or context (narrative). Does the text contain any themes or topics that may be unfamiliar to the English language learners? Sometimes a brief discussion might be enough to clear up any confusion. However, if you feel that the content or context of the text is unsuitable for your ELLs, it might be wise to choose another text at the same level so as to preserve a positive association with reading. It is recommended that all children read a wide variety of genres in the guided reading context (Fountas & Pinnell, 1996). However, variations in text structure may cause more difficulties for ELLs than for native speakers as sentence syntax and vocabulary can vary enormously across narrative and expository texts. Also, expository texts tend to be written in the present tense, whereas narrative texts tend to be written in the past tense. English language learners might find this confusing and may need additional support to understand the text.

When planning for instruction, it is recommended that a few receptive and productive vocabulary words be chosen for explicit instruction. Receptive vocabulary words are those that are used infrequently in conversation (also referred to as tier 2 and tier 3 words) and are required for the development of cognitive academic language proficiency (CALP), essential for the navigation of academic texts. Productive vocabulary relates to words that are commonly used, but may be confusing to English language learners due to dual meanings (such as homophones and homonyms) or the use of figurative language. The use of complex language or sentence syntax can also cause confusion, as can the use of punctuation when it alters the meaning of the text. Avalos et al. (2007) recommend that teachers spend longer on each guided reading text with ELLs than they might with native speakers, so that the students can develop a clear understanding of the text while also learning explicit skills in a meaningful context. They also suggest that the teacher read the text aloud to the students initially so as to aid pronunciation and prosody.

While the teacher is working with a small group of students in a guided reading session, it is essential that the rest of the pupils are engaged in meaningful, interesting and appropriately levelled independent literacy work. Literacy centres can be an effective way to balance the guided reading section of your literacy block. While it can be quite time-consuming to set up this practice initially, it can be very beneficial to students, both academically and socially.

Literacy centres

A literacy centre is a station that is set up so that small groups of children can work on a literacy activity independently while the teacher works with a small group at a guided reading station.

The children should always be somewhat familiar with the task that they are expected to complete at each centre. The activities should be something that the teacher would have previously demonstrated to the pupils and worked on in a whole-class manner. The literacy centres provide the pupils with the opportunity to master the tasks independently. Generally, the tasks will be assigned according to ability level and will be active in nature. Workbooks or handwriting practice would not be appropriate literacy centre activities!

Organisation of literacy centres

The following approach has been used to effectively establish and facilitate literacy centres in the junior classes:

- Divide your class into reading ability groups. Use running records and teacher-designed tests (on phonics, sight words and so forth) to determine their reading level.

- Each group should be comprised of four to six children (the same as your guided reading group). You may like to collaborate with the class learning support/language support teacher and timetable the literacy centre time as an in-class support session.

- Each group should participate in two centres daily. Have a chart that clearly shows the schedule (see Figure 7.1). The activities should be rotated so that all children participate in guided reading at least twice a week and have an opportunity to try a range of literacy activities each week. Literacy centre tasks should be differentiated according to children's ability. Thus, not every group will participate in the exact same set of activities.

- Put the materials needed for each activity on a particular week in a designated area of the room. If you are short on space, use large labelled boxes that can be brought to the students' desks.

- Create a rota of 'centre helpers'. Within each group, each child is the leader on a particular day. Write this on the back of a neck tag for your own easy reference. The leader can then wear the neck tag during centre time.

- For the first week or two, focus on teaching the children how to work in the centres and establish the rules. During this time, don't take any guided reading groups, so that you are free to work with the children in their centres and can establish appropriate working habits (giving out materials, sharing, tidying up, and so forth).

- Remember that each centre will be allocated the same amount of time as your guided reading group (8 to 15 minutes), so design centre activities with this time frame in mind.

Ideas for literacy centres

Having developed an understanding of how to organise literacy centres in the classroom, we will now turn our attention to the kind of activities that might be

Figure 7.1 Literacy centre chart

appropriate in the early years classroom. There are a few important points to keep in mind. First, since your groups are organised by ability, your activities will vary a little from group to group so that every child can be successful at each activity. Second, always make sure to take time out (perhaps on a Friday afternoon) to demonstrate the coming week's activities. The children should be engaged in an activity that is familiar to them in some way so that they are able to work independently. And finally, each activity station should last for about 8 to 12 minutes, and no longer than 15 minutes, to ensure students stay on task.

- *Fine motor centre*: It is a good idea to include fine motor activities within centres on a regular basis. Blackboards and whiteboards can provide practice for fine motor skills. Play dough can be used to encourage students to create objects/characters from the big book that you are currently reading in shared reading. Simple watercolour paintboxes and blank paper can be provided to encourage students to paint a character or a scene from the book. Many of the activities described in Chapter 8 could be used in this centre.

- *ABC centre*: This could house a host of alphabet puzzles that vary in difficulty level. The most basic alphabet puzzle requires children to place the letter in the corresponding recess. Jigsaws that create the alphabet from A to Z might also be used to help develop an understanding of alphabetical order. A more difficult puzzle might require children to match upper- and lower-case letters, or it might involve matching the letter to a corresponding picture. Links should be made to whole-class reading contexts such as shared reading.

- *Word-building centre*: This centre could contain a variety of spelling puzzles, ranging from simple consontant/vowel/consonant (CVC) words to more complicated spelling patterns. Cards that contain onset and rime patterns that can be matched together could be part of this centre. These could be homemade using sturdy card or laminated paper strips to create simple words. These activities could be done on the floor, on a table or in a large pocket. Pocket charts are a very useful resource for building words using individual phonemes under study. Again, individual phonemes can be laminated onto paper and provide endless opportunities for phonic skill development. Magnetic boards and letters can be used for open-ended activities where students are challenged to make as many words as possible within the centre time. As children's reading skills progress, they might work on building words using cards with root words, prefixes and suffixes (e.g. creating words such as 'unhelpful' using a prefix, a root word and a suffix). Activities that have the children match contractions to their original extended version, such as 'can't' and 'can'/'not', are also useful (see Figure 7.2). The activities in this centre should be related to the phonics and word study work completed during shared reading time.

Figure 7.2 Contraction apples activity

Figure 7.3 Medial vowel match activity

■ *Word games centre*: Word searches based on high-frequency words can be easily created and help pupils focus on letter strings and patterns within words that are difficult to memorise, such as 'they' or 'was'. Simple memory games can be created by creating pairs of cards that contain target sight words. For better able students, consider including activities focused on synonyms, homonyms and antonyms, such a simple games that require students to match words with pictures or words with words that have the same/opposite meaning. Games based on recent phonics instruction can also be included, such as 'bossy "r" game', 'short vowel match' or 'bingo'. In 'bossy "r" game', the children are provided with five phoneme cards containing /ar/, /ir/, /er/, /ur/ and /or/ and a large number of picture cards of words that contain these phonemes, such as 'bird', 'car' and so forth. In 'short vowel match' (see Figure 7.3), the children are provided with phoneme cards containing the five short vowels and picture cards of words that have short vowels in the medial position (CVC) such as 'cat', 'bag' and 'pin', and the children must work together to match the picture to the corresponding phoneme. In 'bingo', one child is the 'caller' and the other take bingo cards (grid of 6 to 10 phonemes on sturdy cardboard). The 'caller' selects ping-pong balls that have the phonemes written on them and 'calls' out the phoneme. If the children have this phoneme on their grid, they cover it with a counter. The first child to cover all phonemes should shout 'bingo', and they are the winner (see Figure 3.4).

■ *Reading centre*: A pocket chart can also be used to order a poem or a big book extract that has been cut into sentence strips to enhance students' comprehension skills. This activity can be completed by beginning readers using pictures, and then, as reading skills develop, it can be completed using sentences.

■ *Writing centre*: This should contain a wide variety of writing materials and paper of different shapes, sizes and colours. Blank postcards and envelopes should also be included. The addition of a simple 'postbox' can encourage children to write notes and letters to each other to enhance their emergent writing skills (see Figure 7.4). Include flash cards with words such as 'to' and 'from', along with a list of names of the children in the class.

■ *Listening centre*: A listening centre can be created using a set of CD players or iPods/iPads, headphones and some books on CD/e-books. As children get older, you can have them complete a worksheet as part of this centre that might record the book title, rating/review and illustration. Interactive storybooks on tablets or laptops could also act as a listening centre. This centre is particularly useful for English language learners as they have an opportunity to hear more stories in a focused manner.

■ *Buddy reading*: Buddy reading is where two children read big books, storybooks or poems together. An area can be set up in the classroom to facilitate this that contains a large box containing the big books that have been read in whole-class lessons, poems and rhymes on large charts attached to an easel (with a pointer to help the students read in unison) that are very familiar to the children, and favourite library books that have been read

Figure 7.4 Class postbox

aloud often by the teacher. Since the texts are well known to the children, much of the 'reading' will be from memory, but it allows them to enjoy the story/rhyme again in a social manner. For English language learners, it allows them to practise 'language chunks' that they recall from the texts in an engaging context.

Assessing literacy centre activities

Literacy centre activities (both the quality of the centre activity and the children's ability to complete the task) are assessed primarily through teacher observation and teacher-designed tasks. Make sure to position yourself (as you work with your guided reading group) so you can view the whole class and monitor participation during station time. If there is a particular child who is not staying on task, consider reviewing that child's running records to see if the child should be moved into another reading group, as misbehaviour is often symptomatic of a task being too easy or too difficult.

At the end of each station, the teacher should ring a bell. This bell signals that the children should 'freeze'. The teacher quickly moves from group to group to examine their work. This enables the teacher to see whether the station task was appropriate for the group. The teacher should take notes in relation to each group's performance on the tasks. If a group is having difficulty, the teacher may need to modify the task or include it in a whole-group literacy lesson in the coming week so that it can be modelled again. If a group demonstrates that the task was too easy, the task may need to be modified or removed from the rotation for that particular group. When the children are expecting the teacher to check their centre activity in this manner, they tend to remain on task so that they have the activity complete or almost complete when the bell rings.

The children should be encouraged to participate in self-assessment in a whole-class plenary session at the end of guided reading/literacy station time. The teacher can lead a discussion on what they learned and what was easy or difficult. They can be encouraged to rate their work ethic during centre time using 'thumbs up' (very focused and on task), 'thumbs in the middle' (on task most of the time) or 'thumbs down' (off task most of the time).

Benefits and challenges of literacy centres

Benefits

- Literacy centres allow each child to be actively engaged in an interesting task while the teacher works with a guided reading group.

- The children learn how to work both independently (without a teacher by their side) and collaboratively (with their small group). Therefore, it has socio-emotional benefits.

- Literacy centres allow children to work at their own level as centres are differentiated according to reading ability.

- Literacy centres allow children to practise literacy skills to mastery in an enjoyable and meaningful manner.

Challenges

- Implementing literacy centres takes a lot of organisation and can be quite time-consuming.

- Materials will need to be bought that can be costly. While most materials could be handmade, this would be very time-consuming if no commercially made materials were bought.

- The children may not be used to working in this manner, so it could take some time to establish this methodology in the classroom.

Key concepts for practice

■ Guided reading involves small groups of children reading texts at their instructional level.

■ Children's instructional level is determined through the use of a running record assessment and teacher observation.

■ Teachers should aim to teach a range of literacy skills within a guided reading lesson.

■ Fiction, non-fiction and poetry can be used as texts. The use of levelled readers would be recommended. Texts should be analysed by the teacher to make sure that they are culturally relevant and accessible to children before using it in a guided reading session.

■ While the teacher works with a guided reading group, the rest of the class should be engaged in literacy centre work. The children will need to be trained how to work effectively in centres.

■ Literacy centres should be varied and encompass activities related to alphabetics, phonics, word study, high-frequency words, fluency, listening, fine motor development and writing.

REFLECTION: THINKING ABOUT YOUR PRACTICE

■ Does your school use class readers (every child with the same text)?

■ Have you considered using levelled texts?

■ If you currently practise guided reading in your school, could it be improved? How?

■ Do you currently use literacy centres as part of your literacy instruction? If you have, what have been the challenges and opportunities that this type of instruction has presented? If not, how would you go about adapting your classroom instruction to accommodate this type of practice?

■ How have you assessed early literacy skills in the past? Is this an area that needs further development?

For further exploration

Diller, D. (2003). *Literacy work stations: Making centers work*. Portland, ME: Stenhouse.
Diller, D. (2003). *Literacy work stations task cards*. San Diego, CA: Teaching Resource Centre.
McLaughlin, M. (2011). *Guided comprehension in the primary grades*. Newark, DE: International Reading Association.

8 Fine motor development and handwriting

GUIDING QUESTIONS FOR THIS CHAPTER

- How would you explore a wide range of fine motor activities and link them with handwriting instruction?

- How would you teach handwriting in a multisensory, systematic and age-appropriate manner?

Introduction

The chapters thus far in this book have focused on developing fine motor skills relating to one's muscular dexterity in one's hands and arms. Recent research has suggested that young children are increasingly lacking fine motor skills on entering school due to decreased time spent outdoors and increased use of screen time (Gruetman, 2017). Therefore, teachers may have to spend more time developing these skills so that their pupils can manage a writing implement with ease. Teachers will need to draw on a wide variety of activities in order to keep children interested and engaged. Fine motor activities should both precede and be completed in tandem with formal letter formation as children require a certain level of muscular control in order to attempt copying letters, but as instruction progresses they will be expected to write with increasing quantity and fluency, especially when introduced to the writers' workshop, where they will be encouraged to draw, and write letters, words, sentences and stories. This chapter will outline a broad range of fine motor tasks and discuss the transition to formal handwriting instruction.

Fine motor development

Fine motor skills are essential for writing, and without them children's ability to form letters in a fluent, legible manner will be severely affected. Fine motor skills involve the ability to control the small muscles of the body, and are usually defined as the ability to coordinate the action of the eyes and the hands together in performing specific manipulations (hand–eye coordination). Motor control is required in order to form various patterns and letter shapes, and perceptual skills are needed for appropriate letter size, spacing and orientation of letters. The list below outlines some activities that encourage the development of fine motor skills (a list of useful resources for fine motor development can be found in Appendix F):

- *Stencils*: Use a wide variety of stencils, including narrow and wide insets. Make sure that children hold the stencil with one hand while tracing with the other hand. Stencils aid bilateral coordination and develop pencil control.

- *Lacing/threading activities*: Children enjoy lacing cards or lacing beads of different shapes and sizes. Dried pasta can also be used for lacing activities and can be dyed different colours using food colouring. Some children might find it difficult to hold the lace steady as they thread the bead or pasta, so pipe cleaners can also be used for threading. Pipe cleaners are easier as they stand erect and allow for easier manipulation of the beads.

- *Ripping and sticking*: As some children might find cutting challenging, ripping can provide a good alternative that will help develop the hand muscles required for cutting. Soft sugar paper in a variety of colours, glue and a blank A4 page can allow for children to develop fine motors skills in a creative manner.

- *Scissor activities*: Children generally require assistance when they first begin to use scissors. It is important that they are shown how to hold the scissors correctly. Initially, you will need to hold the paper for children. After some practice, they can attempt to coordinate holding the page and cutting. Simply snipping around the edge of a blank page can be very satisfying for young children beginning to cut. When they have mastered this, they should be encouraged to cut the page into long strips. These could be glued in a creative manner to another sheet. From here, children can experiment with cutting various different shapes. They could be encouraged to use a stencil to draw a large shape and then cut it out. Cutting should be combined with other classroom activities across the curriculum to ensure that children get adequate meaningful practice in this skill. For example, they might cut out pictures in order to retell the story from their shared reading session.

■ *Block play*: Playing with different shapes and sizes of blocks and other construction materials can help develop both hand–eye coordination and muscle tone in the hand and arm.

■ *Painting*: Finger painting encourages children to stretch and flex their finger and hand muscles. Painting with a brush can help develop the tripod grip needed for handwriting. It is a good idea to provide opportunities for children to paint standing up at an easel as this can develop arm and hand strength. If the children have access to a plain concrete wall during outdoor play, painting with water can encourage further fine motor development (without any mess!).

■ *Junk art*: Junk art involves creating art from a variety of recycled materials (e.g. cardboard boxes, egg cartons, yogurt cartons) and a variety of art supplies (e.g. googly eyes, paint, paper, feathers). It is usually completely open-ended, and children are encouraged to be creative and imaginative. It is a wonderful opportunity to develop children's fine motor skills as they will need to cut, stick, rip, glue, paint and colour their creations. Initially, children will need a good deal of support in using sticky tape, scissors and other materials, but as they progress they will become increasingly independent.

■ *Blackboard/whiteboard activities*: Provide mini-blackboards and mini-whiteboards for the children to experiment on. Depending on development level, they can simply scribble, draw or write words and sentences. While individual boards are very useful, it is also a good idea to have a large blackboard or a whiteboard so that the children can stand while they draw or write while developing their arm muscles as well as their hand muscles.

■ *Tweezers*: Large plastic tweezers designed for children's hands can be used for a variety of activities. It is a good idea to attempt to provide a storyline to make the activity more enjoyable for the children. For example, if you were reading *Walking through the Jungle* (Lacome, 1995) in shared reading, then a crocodile's mouth could be constructed using cardboard. The children could then attempt to 'feed' the crocodile (with pom-poms) using tweezers.

■ *Water play*: Water play encourages children to grasp and manipulate containers of different shapes and sizes. The inclusion of plastic droppers (or turkey basters) and plastic syringes encourages more advanced hand movements. Whisks can be included for mixing and stirring, especially if some soap flakes have been added to the water for the creation of satisfying bubbles. Water play might integrate well with shared reading texts such as *Big Blue Whale* (Davies, 1997).

■ *Play dough*: Play dough encourages children to use their hands to use tools and also to manipulate the dough. Play can be enhanced by creating 'play dough kits'. A 'play dough kit' might contain matchsticks, lollipop sticks, beads, googly eyes, pipe cleaners, dried pasta, buttons, craft feathers, bun cases, shells, and a variety of cutters and extruders. This kit encourages more creative and artistic expression when using play dough and can also extend the play.

- *Weaving*: Children can be introduced to simple weaving activities involving a cardboard shape (e.g. a hollow heart or a triangle) and different colours of yarn. The yarn is taped to the cardboard, and then children can weave the yarn in and out to create a colourful ornament.

- *Gloop*: Gloop is made from mixing corn flour and water together. It creates a semi-solid material that provides an excellent opportunity to strengthen the hand muscles. It is quite messy, so aprons and a protective table cover are essential.

- *Jigsaw puzzles*: Jigsaw puzzles of different shapes and sizes encourage children to use their hands in different ways. They also develop hand–eye coordination and children's attention to detail, as the ability to see the correct location of a puzzle piece requires children to examine detail. This is the same type of 'careful looking' that children will need to differentiate the letters of the alphabet (especially similar letters such as 'b' and 'd').

- *Pencil-and-paper activities*: Dot-to-dot activities, word searches and mazes can help to develop pencil control.

- *Games for fine motor development*: Card games, Jenga, quoits, latches (Melissa and Doug), tangram puzzles, Mr. Potato Head, Rubik's cube, Etch A Sketch, marbles, Operation and dominoes are all useful games for developing fine motor skills and hand–eye coordination.

- *Rhymes for finger plays*: There are many rhymes that involve small finger movements as the 'actions' that can help develop children's fine motor skills in an enjoyable and meaningful manner. Some examples are given in the box below.

FINGER PLAYS

I have ten fingers *(hold up both hands, fingers spread)*
And they all belong to me *(point to self)*
I can make them do things. Would you like to see?
I can shut them up tight *(make fists)*
I can open them wide *(open hands)*
I can put them together place *(palms together)*

(continued)

(continued)

I can make them all hide *(put hands behind back)*
I can make them jump high *(hands over head)*
I can make them jump low *(touch floor)*
I can fold them up quietly *(fold hands in lap)*
And hold them just so.

This is the church *(interlock all fingers, facing inward)*
And this is the steeple, *(point both thumbs upwards)*
Come inside *(make palms face outward, fingers still interlocked)*
And see all the people *(move the interlocked fingers as if to 'wave')*

Round and round the garden *(trace a circle on the palm of the hand)*
Like a teddy bear
One step, two step *(make fingers take steps)*
A tickle under there! *(tickle oneself under the arm)*

Incy Wincy spider *(create a 'spider' using both hands)*
Went up the water spout *(move hands upwards)*
Down came the rain *(wiggle fingers and move downwards)*
And washed the spider out *(use a sweeping motion)*
Out came the sun *(pretend that hands are parting clouds)*
And dried up all the rain. *(use a seeping motion)*
Incy Wincy spider went up the spout again! *(create spider with hands and move upwards)*

Where is thumbkin? Where is thumbkin? *(close all fingers except for your thumbs, make one thumb 'introduce' itself to the other and wiggle as if to talk)*
Here I am, here I am.
How are you today Sir?
Very well thank you,
Run and hide *(hide each hand behind your back)*
Run and hide.
(Continue in the same manner with 'Pointer', 'Middle Man', 'Ring Man' and 'Pinkie')

Fine motor development at home

Parents of young children often ask the teacher how they can help their children at home. Fine motor activities are an ideal recommendation as they often use household objects and everyday tasks, and so can be easily integrated with family life. Some examples of fine motor activities suitable for parents and children at home are: beat/whisk eggs, butter bread, mix flour with hands, peel apples/potatoes with a peeler, make sandwiches, grind coffee beans, clean tabletops, pour liquid from one container to another, roll pastry, squeeze oranges for juice, tear lettuce for a salad, open bags (crisps, raisins, and so forth), crack nuts with nutcracker, squeeze wet sponges.

Handwriting

Fine motor skill development should precede and accompany handwriting instruction. 'Handwriting is producing letters to support writing words, syntax, and text to transform ideas into written language' (Berninger, 2012, p. 16). Handwriting is a very complex skill to master as it involves the coordination of linguistic, cognitive, perceptual and motor components in an integrated manner (Teodorescu & Addy, 2001). In mastering the skill of handwriting, children come to understand that the symbols they are forming are letters that have a particular sound and name associated with them, come in a variety of shapes and sizes, are formed in particular ways, are turned in a particular way, and look differently when formed in upper and lower case. Beery (1992) suggested that formal instruction in handwriting should be postponed until children can draw a vertical line, a horizontal line, a circle, a cross, a right oblique line, a square, a left oblique line and a triangle. Therefore, handwriting patterns can help children learn the movements required for letter formation in an enjoyable and creative manner. In this section, we will explore the use of handwriting patterns as a precursor to formal handwriting instruction. We will also examine how handwriting should be taught in the early years of schooling.

Handwriting patterns

The repetitive nature of patterns encourages the development of the rhythmic movements required for handwriting. Children can be taught how to hold a writing tool and how to maintain correct posture without the anxiety of correct letter formation. The fluid movements should also reduce pencil pressure and increase children's confidence in using writing tools. Patterns can help children learn the directional sequences and movements required for letter formation (e.g. top to bottom, left to right, clockwise and anticlockwise rotation). Patterns do not require the use of workbooks. Instead, children can be encouraged to make the pattern on blank paper, coloured paper, chalkboards or whiteboards using a variety of writing tools (e.g. crayons, felt tips, charcoal, chalk, paintbrushes, finger paint, pens, pencils, whiteboard markers). While the teacher might mandate a particular pattern or patterns, children should be encouraged to be creative and use colour and space to create the pattern. Children's literature or rhymes and poems might be incorporated into handwriting pattern practice. For example, having read *Walking through the Jungle* (Lacome, 1995) in shared reading, children might be invited to draw the crocodile's teeth in various colours and mediums (see Figure 8.1).

Early patterns can include:

■ straight lines, both up and down;

■ vertical, horizontal and diagonal lines;

■ zigzags;

■ simple circles in both directions;

■ concentric circles beginning at the centre or the outer edge;

■ spirals that wind outwards or inwards;

■ upward loops or garlands;

■ downward loops or arcades;

■ cross shapes and square shapes;

■ x shapes; and

■ triangles.

Figure 8.1 Handwriting patterns (crocodile teeth)

Multisensory teaching

When teaching children to form letters, it is important that you use a multisensory approach. Learning to form letters is difficult for young children, but when they learn the movements in different tactile and kinaesthetic ways it makes it easier to hold letter formation in long-term memory. Multisensory learning also takes account of different learning styles, so instruction should accommodate visual, tactile and kinaesthetic learners.

Use these steps when teaching letter formation:

■ *Skywriting*: Have the children trace the letter in the air, on the table, on a partner's back and so forth, while saying an oral mnemonic (e.g. when learning the letter 'a', say 'start at the top, around, up and down'). The use of an oral mnemonic or a verbal pathway is an important teaching tool for handwriting. The use of verbal directions to help with learning the sequence of movements needed to form each letter helps children to understand and recall the directional movement. It also gives the teacher and children a language to use when talking about the formation of the letter and about its features. It also assists the acquisition of automaticity in writing. When the children become fluent writers, they will no longer need these verbal pathways.

■ *Play dough*: Have the children make the letter out of play dough, using a template if necessary (see Figure 8.2). For example, give each child a small piece of paper or card with the target letter in a large font. This will enable children to either copy the letter underneath the template or place the play dough directly on top of the template. Without a template, some children will find the task very difficult.

■ *Trace the letter in sand trays*: Use a bead as a starting point and have an example of the letter beside the tray (see Figure 8.3). The letter can also be traced in shaving cream or finger paint. Poster paint or hair gel can be poured into a ziplock bag and sealed. This can make an interesting surface for writing a letter.

■ *Write the letter*: When children first attempt to write the letter, it can be helpful to mark a starting point and arrows showing directionality. Try to limit tracing over lines and dots as much as possible as it is more beneficial for children to attempt the letter without these supports. Make sure to emphasise the importance of directionality. If children do not learn to form their letters correctly, they will not be able to join their letters for cursive script. When writing a letter, children should be taught the correct posture, paper positioning and pencil grip.

Figure 8.2 Making a letter out of play dough

Figure 8.3 Making a letter in a sand tray

HANDWRITING WARM-UPS

Before attempting handwriting exercises, spend a few minutes on warm-ups for the arm and fingers. It is a good idea to play relaxing classical music while completing these exercises:

- *Shoulder shrugs*: Roll the shoulders forwards and backwards.

- *Crocodile*: Using straight arms, clap the hands together like a crocodile. Complete the exercise on both sides of the body.

- *Finger squeeze*: Place the fingertips together and bend and straighten the fingers while pushing the fingertips against each other.

- *Imaginary piano*: Pretend to play an imaginary piano with your fingers.

- Open and shut the fingers as wide and as tight as possible.

- *Play dough*: Pinch a ball of play dough between the thumb and the tips of the fingers. Squeeze and release 10 to 15 times.

- *Finger sit-ups*: Place the hand flat on the table. Concentrate on lifting each finger individually while the others remain flat on the table.

General teaching points for handwriting: the three P's

- *Posture*: Children should be seated with two feet flat on the floor, chair pulled in with a straight back. Good posture provides trunk stability, which helps the mobility of arms, wrists, hands and fingers. The non-writing hand should be placed on the page to steady the paper and to bear some body weight. Left-handed children should be seated so that they are not obstructing or being obstructed by right-handed children.

- *Paper position*: Right-handed children should position their page wth the right corner of the paper higher than the left, with the reverse being advisable for left-handed writers. The non-writing hand should hold the paper steady.

- *Pencil grip*: It is essential that children be taught the correct pencil grip from the earliest possible juncture. The appropriate grip is known as the 'tripod grip' (sometimes referred to as the 'froggy grip') (see Figure 8.4). This involves holding the pencil with the index finger, thumb and middle finger. Correct pencil grip is critically important in allowing the fine movements necessary for writing. The longer children use an incorrect pencil grip, the more it becomes habitual and difficult to correct. Incorrect pencil grip tends to lead to fatigue and slow or poor letter formation as children get older and the volume of writing required increases. Left-handed children should hold the pencil slightly further up from the point to avoid developing a 'hook'.

Letter directionality

Make sure to emphasise the importance of directionality when teaching handwriting from the very beginning. Teaching children how to form their letters correctly is one of the most important parts of handwriting instruction. Children will then develop the correct movement memory for each letter, which will enable them to become fluent writers. Also, if children do not form their letters correctly, they will not be able to join their letters for cursive script. Letters should be taught in groups according to directionality and formation similarities. For example, the letters 'o', 'c' and 'a' all have the same starting point and the same directionality. Therefore, they should be taught in succession. Teaching letters with similar movements reduces the learning load while also reinforcing movement patterns. A suggested sequence for teaching handwriting is outlined below:

- Anticlockwise: a, d, g, q, c, e, o, s, u, y, f
- Stick: l, i, t, j
- Clockwise: m, n, r, h, b, p
- Diagonal: k, v, w, x, z

However, you may want to align your handwriting teaching with your phonics programme as it can be helpful to learn letter sounds and formation together in a multisensory manner. If this is the case, you may want to consider the recommendations given in Chapter 3.

Figure 8.4 Tripod grip

Terminology

When teaching handwriting, it is essential that consistent terminology is used in class and throughout the school so as to avoid confusion. It is important to determine that all children understand the terms 'up', 'down', 'right' and 'left', particularly your English language learners. Other language choices will also have to be made, as outlined below. Will you say:

■ capital letters and small letters . . . or upper case and lower case;

■ ascenders and descenders . . . or sticks and tails;

■ entry and exit strokes . . . or starting point and finishing point; and

■ cursive . . . or joined up?

Assessment

Handwriting is a complex skill, so there will be children in every classroom who struggle to master it. These difficulties may cause children to become frustrated and upset, which may lead children to avoid writing as much as possible. It may also cause anxiety for the parents and teachers who watch children struggle to put their ideas on paper. Therefore, it is important that children's difficulties be assessed so that steps can be taken to support their learning. Take time to observe children when they are writing. Monitor their pencil grip, posture and paper position. Note their speed and fluency of writing. Pay attention to the formation of letters: are children forming letters in the correct way, with the correct letter shape, ascenders and descenders, and correct starting point? Are their letters of similar size or do they vary, and to what degree? Can children insert spaces between words as appropriate? How legible are the letters? Do to what extent to they need to check letters on alphabet charts, reference charts or from the board?

Any assessment of children should first consider the following factors:

■ the child's age;

■ the length of time the child attended preschool or school;

■ the amount and the breadth of fine motor development opportunities to which the child has been exposed;

■ whether or not the difficulties experienced by the child in relation to handwriting seem out of keeping in relation to other aspects of their development;

■ other areas of concern (e.g. physical, motor, cognitive, language);

■ whether or not the child has received formal instruction in handwriting, and the extent of this instruction;

- the child's achievement in relation to same-age peers;

- the child's emotional state in relation to their handwriting;

- memory/attention skills;

- vision; and

- the classroom environment.

An exploration of the factors outlined above combined with a thorough analysis of writing samples should enable a teacher to plan for instruction for children who are experiencing difficulties. Significant handwriting difficulties should be carefully monitored, as this may signal dysgraphia, which would require diagnosis by an external professional. Persistent and prolonged difficulties may also be one aspect of children's development that might contribute to a diagnosis of other conditions, such as dyslexia, dyspraxia or ADHD.

IN THE CLASSROOM: DIFFICULTIES WITH LETTER FORMATION

Colin is frustrated because despite being intelligent and knowing what he wants to say, he just cannot get it down on paper the way it should look and so others can read it. Colin has difficulties with handwriting, and it is affecting his mood and engagement in classroom activities. His teacher, Declan, has decided to put an action plan in place to tackle the problem. In consultation with the support teacher, Declan carried out a simple assessment of Colin's handwriting by analysing free writing samples from the writers' workshop. He also gave Colin a simple dictation test and compared the letter formation in both samples. It soon became clear that certain letters were causing Colin considerable difficulty. He formed his 'n', 'm', 'h' 'b', 'p' and 'r' in a backwards fashion and the lines were awkwardly drawn. To reduce his anxiety in relation to letter formation, Declan encouraged Colin to experiment with a variety of drawing tools to create art using patterns resembling arches and bridges to assist the formation of 'n', 'm', 'h', 'b', 'p' and 'r'. They used finger paints and felt tips on paper and also created patterns on the whiteboard using markers in different colours. Colin asked to trace the pattern in the sandbox, and Declan filled a shallow tray with rice so that the patterns could be traced in a different medium. From there, they began to trace the letters in the same way, and Colin enjoyed writing the letters on a small chalkboard using chalks. Soon, he was writing the letters on paper with newly acquired confidence.

Key concepts for practice

■ Fine motor skills are the collective skills and activities that involve using the hands and fingers, skills that require the small muscles of the hand to work together to perform precise and refined movements.

■ Children need well-developed fine motor skills in order to write letters and words with controlled, steady, fluent movements. Therefore, children should have ample opportunities to develop their fine motor skills in the junior classes.

■ Teachers will need to draw on a wide variety of activities in order to keep children interested and engaged.

■ Handwriting fluency enhances academic attainment in a number of ways as it is used across the curriculum throughout the school day. Therefore, due attention needs to be taken in developing effective handwriting skills.

■ An assessment of children's fine motor or handwriting difficulties should be treated in a holistic manner.

REFLECTION: THINKING ABOUT YOUR PRACTICE

■ What fine motor development skill activities do you currently use in your classroom? What changes could you make?

■ To what extent does your approach to handwriting instruction reflect what has been discussed in this chapter?

For further exploration

Featherstone, S. (2013). *The little book of fine motor skills*. London: Bloomsbury.

Massey, E. (2014). *The little book of mark making*. London: Bloomsbury.

Teodorescu, I. (1998). *Write from the start: Unique programme to develop fine motor perceptual skills necessary for handwriting*. London: LDA.

9 The writers' workshop

GUIDING QUESTIONS FOR THIS CHAPTER

- What is meant by a 'writers' workshop' in the early years?

- What does a 'writers' workshop' lesson look like in practice?

- How are writing skills and strategies taught within the context of a 'writers' workshop'?

- How would you organise your classroom to enable the implementation of a 'writers' workshop'?

- How would you plan and teach effective and appropriate mini-lessons that aid children's writing development?

- How would you assess children's spelling and writing development?

Introduction

While correct letter formation is an important skill that needs to be developed in the early years of schooling, children also need frequent opportunities to put this skill into practice in a meaningful manner. The writers' workshop is a place where young children have opportunities to talk and interact with peers while placing their ideas on a page in the form of drawings and words (Calkins, 1986; Graves, 1989). Several decades ago, researchers and educators became aware that young children can read and write in an emergent manner prior to or in conjunction with formal instruction (Clay, 1998; Hall, 1987). This growing awareness and a perceived need to harness these emergent literacy skills so as to achieve developmentally appropriate practice led to a growing body of research on young children's reading and writing behaviours (Bissex, 1980; MacNamee, 1987; Teale, 1987). Researchers identified a developmental continuum from scribbles to drawing to writing that was driven by the medium of talk, and thus emphasised the social nature of emergent literacy (Gentry, 2006). Successful emergent writing programmes develop children's phonological awareness, teach important print concepts through play and activity, and demonstrate the purpose and function of reading and writing to children (Burns, Griffin & Snow, 1999). An effective writing programme develops a 'classroom rich with talk, where children are encouraged to tell about events in their own lives' (Lamme, Fu, Johnson & Savage, 2002, p. 74). In this chapter, we will explore the writers' workshop. This is a teaching methodology that is suitable for all class levels in the primary school due to its meaningful, differentiated and social teaching framework. The chapter will begin by defining the concept of a writers' workshop and identifying the principles that underpin this teaching approach. The various aspects relating to lesson structure will be explored, namely mini-lessons, conferencing and sharing. Advice will be given regarding classroom organisation. Finally, assessment practices for children's writing will be discussed.

The principles of the writers' workshop

An effective writers' workshop contains the following components:

Ownership

At the heart of the writers' workshop philosophy is the notion that children ought to be given a 'voice', that they are encouraged to discover and refine their own personal writing style, as they compose stories that matter to them (Calkins, 1986). The writers' workshop is a constructivist approach that asserts that children should generate their own texts, using material from their own lives. Children should always be allowed to choose their own topics and/or genre. The teacher does not provide writing prompts. The writing workshop philosophy emphasises that children's writing should be honest and real, that children have taken control and responsibility for their own learning while the teacher carefully scaffolds their development. Topic choice freedom helps to promote a workshop environment in the writing process classroom, as all students are encouraged to work at their own pace under the guidance of a facilitative teacher. This can serve to heighten children's self-esteem as they attempt to achieve personal goals, acknowledging that the teacher will support and scaffold them in the learning process (Graves, 1994).

Child as member of the writing community

Young children can best appreciate and understand writing when it is embedded in social purpose (Burns et al., 1999). It is important that children develop an awareness of writing as a means of communication as this will serve to motivate and encourage their will to write (NAEYC & IRA, 1998). Writing is more than just learning and using symbols; it should be viewed as a vehicle that promotes social, emotional and cognitive development (Dyson, 1989). The teacher has a very active role to play in the writers' workshop, acting as a mentor author, modelling writing techniques and conferring with students as they move through the writing process. The writers' workshop is firmly based on Vygotsky's (1978) theory of learning, where the learner receives scaffolded instruction within their zone of proximal development (ZPD). Within a writers' workshop, the focus is on the individual needs of the child, and this allows for differentiation within a supportive environment that promotes social interaction among peers (Fletcher & Portalupi, 2001; Routman, 1991).

The writing process

Donald Graves (1994) was one of the first researchers to analyse writing as a series of stages, each of which was associated with a distinctive type of behaviour. These were defined as pre-writing/planning, drafting and editing/revision. It is important to note that these stages are recursive rather than linear. These stages reflect how real writers write and emphasise the clear communication of what one has to say. Teachers who adopt a process approach to writing do not simply assign topics for writing; they teach children the skills and strategies that real authors use. The writing process is child-centred, focusing on children's understanding and engagement in the craft of writing. Children are encouraged to write regularly on topics of their own choosing, and are allowed to operate at their own pace and at different stages of the writing process at any given time (Calkins & Mermelstein, 2010). For young children, planning often takes the form of drawing as they rehearse what they wish to say in their message. Emergent writers will often use the same theme or topic repeatedly in their writing, in an attempt to redraft to mastery. Thus, it is not unusual to encounter a child who has written 13 versions of his Spider-Man story. What is important is that the teacher gently scaffold the development of the drafts to enhance the quality of the child's writing as he moves from draft to draft.

Time to write/opportunity to write regularly

The writers' workshop needs to be conducted at least three to four times a week, every day if possible. Choose a consistent time (e.g. 9 a.m. every morning). This consistency helps children achieve a 'state of constant composition', which means that they are always thinking about their writing (Graves, 1994) and come to the writers' workshop brimming with ideas and enthusiasm for writing. Indeed, according to Lucy Calkins (1986):

> If students are going to become deeply invested in their writing, and if they are going to live towards a piece of writing and let their ideas grow and gather

momentum, if they are going to draft and revise, sharing their texts with one another as they write, they need the luxury of time. If our students are going to have the chance to do their best and then make their best better, they need long blocks of time.

(p. 186)

Therefore, young children need regular blocks of time to immerse themselves in composition.

Skills and strategies taught in context

In the writers' workshop, skills and strategies are always taught in the context of real writing. There are no worksheets in the writers' workshop. Each workshop begins with a mini-lesson where the teacher raises an issue, demonstrates a useful skill or strategy, or focuses attention on an author's technique (Gillet & Lynn, 2001). When the children begin writing, the teacher conferences with the children, helping them to improve their texts in an individualised manner. Conferences provide the ideal opportunity for teachers to scaffold emergent writers through designing instructional opportunities that include clear demonstrations, explicit teaching, guided assistance and independent practice (Dorn & Soffos, 2001). The workshop ends with a sharing session that provides a forum for not only the celebration of the children's achievements and the development of audience awareness (Hayes, 2004), but also acts as a further outlet for teaching specific writing skills and strategies (Freeman, 2003).

Response

The children's energy and enthusiasm for writing is kindled through thoughtful response from the teacher during writing conferences and from both the teacher and peers during share sessions. As children progress, they are taught to use self-assessment tools that allow them to critically respond to their own writing.

The lesson structure of a writers' workshop in an early years classroom

The writers' workshop should always follow this lesson structure:

- *Mini-lesson (5–10 minutes)*: The teacher demonstrates the writing process or a new writing skill or strategy using children's literature.

- *Writing/conferencing (15–20 minutes)*: The children begin to write as the teacher conferences with several children individually.

■ *Share/response (5–10 minutes)*: Some children share their writing and their peers respond.

In the junior classes, the entire lesson should last no longer than 40 minutes. In the beginning, the lesson may only last 20 to 30 minutes with the youngest class level (a writing workshop lesson plan example can be found in Appendix H).

Mini-lessons

A mini-lesson is a short lesson lasting no longer than 5 to 10 minutes that is generally at the beginning of the workshop. It should focus on one skill or strategy. The content of mini-lessons is needs-based as the teacher should use an analysis of the children's writing samples in order to decide what to teach so as to progress the children's writing. Mini-lessons should have a 'gentle tone'. This means that mini-lessons should be an invitation to try a new technique in one's writing as opposed to a mandate whereby all the children are expected to demonstrate a new writing skill. Those who try out the new skill or craft element are congratulated so as to encourage less able students to 'give it a go'. Part of the writers' workshop philosophy is the belief that amidst a very positive writing environment, all students will progress at their own level and use new skills when they are able to. There are two methods of teaching mini-lessons. The first is through the use of children's literature: big books, or regular books copied onto an acetate or scanned onto an interactive whiteboard (IWB). It is helpful if the children are familiar with the story (e.g. having already explored it in shared reading) so that they can focus on the specific teaching point. The second method of teaching a mini-lesson is through teacher modelling. Here, the teacher 'thinks aloud' while composing a text, focusing on a particular aspect of process, procedures, writing skill or craft element.

Types of mini-lessons

There are three main types of mini-lessons: procedures and processes, skills, and craft. Procedures and processes lessons might include:

■ writing the title, author's name and date on writing;

■ establishing workshop rules;

■ using a writing folder;

■ choosing topics;

■ think, draw, write, share;

■ effective planning;

- crossing out, not rubbing out;

- using materials (stapler, paper, pencil sharpener, and so forth); and

- using the 'inbox', understanding the ongoing nature of the workshop (once you finish a piece, place it in the 'inbox' and begin a new piece).

Procedures and processes lessons are essential to the smooth functioning of the writers' workshop as they outline the routines and expectations that are involved. Simple things such as where to sharpen one's pencil or where to find paper should be modelled as part of a mini-lesson. As children progress and their stories grow longer, they will need to know how to use a stapler effectively and how to place completed work in the 'inbox' so that the teacher can read and respond to it. It is important to teach the children to cross out errors in their work with a single line so that the teacher can assess the child's thought process in creating the text. A lesson on adding one's name, date and a title to one's work is very important as it encourages an organised classroom and incomplete stories are less likely to go 'missing' in the classroom. One of the most important 'rules' of the workshop is that 'we are always writing or reading over our writing' ('writing' refers to both drawings and text in this instance). The writers' workshop is cyclical in nature (i.e. when you complete a piece of writing and have read over it – and made any necessary revisions/edits – you begin a new piece of writing). There are no 'early finishers' in the writers' workshop as the writing simply continues throughout the workshop. 'Writing time' is for writing. This understanding should be explicitly taught in a mini-lesson. An important process lesson is 'think, draw, write, share' as it introduces children to the notion of the writing process. For young children, the 'thinking and drawing' is an important part of planning and intentionality in writing. It helps them to remember their ideas and to build on their thoughts through writing. As children progress, they may be able to plan using a simple written grid, such as the examples found in Appendix I.

Writing skills lessons might include:

- using the high-frequency word wall, high-interest word wall and/or environmental print as a writing support;

- using the alphabet frieze or phonics chart as a writing support;

- managing space (size of letters, spaces between words);

- using left-to-right, top-to-bottom progression;

- using upper-case and lower-case letters appropriately;

- using exclamation marks;

- using question marks;

- using commas;

- using full stops;

- using ellipses for tension;

- using speech marks;

- strategies to correct spelling; and

- using 'ing' and 'ed' endings.

Skills mini-lessons teach children how to use the mechanics of writing, such as spelling, spacing and punctuation. For example, a very useful skills mini-lesson might be focused on spelling. In order to promote independence in spelling and fluency in writing, demonstrate how to edit one's writing for spelling in a mini-lesson. While writing a text in front of the children, pause when spelling some tricky words, and model attempting to spell the word and then placing a circle around the word to highlight that it requires the teacher's assistance at a later stage. This should discourage a long line of children asking, 'How do you spell . . .', Towards the end of each writing session, the teacher can check the children's work and assist them with ant words that caused spelling difficulties. This will encourage writing fluency, self-assessment and independence. When you confer with children, you will be able to see spellings that require assistance instantly, and this allows children to continue working independently without being hindered by spelling. However, when it comes to spelling, while invented spelling is encouraged, make sure that the children understand that they are expected to spell sight words that are currently on the class word wall correctly, and should always check to see if the word that they require is already available to them. Young children should have a number of supports available to them in the classroom, such as alphabet friezes and phonics charts to assist invented spelling. They should also have high-frequency word walls and high-interest word walls in the classroom to aid spelling. They will require instruction on how to use these resources effectively. These types of lessons are probably best taught through teacher modelling, whereby the teacher attempts to construct a text in a mini-lesson and 'thinks aloud' about how they will use the various supports to assist them in composing. In a similar manner, the teacher could also model 'finger spaces' between words and the appropriate use of upper- and lower-case letters. Children's literature that is familiar to the children (such as a shared reading text read some time ago) could be used to highlight how an author might use various punctuation, such as exclamation marks to indicate surprise or excitement or question marks to pose a question. Some books might make effective use of ellipses, such as *Dear Zoo* (Campbell, 2009), or speech marks in memorable dialogue, such as *Owl Babies* (Waddell, 1998). Again, anchor charts can be used to summarise learning and support children as they begin to experiment with punctuation (see Figure 9.1).

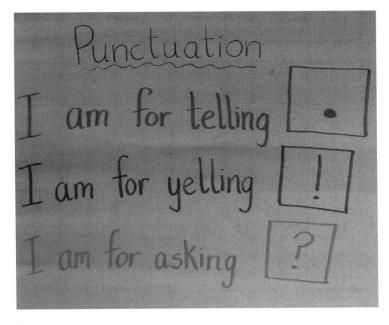

Figure 9.1 Anchor chart for punctuation

Craft mini-lessons might include:

- writing effective leads/endings;

- describing a character;

- describing a setting;

- deleting information for clarity and conciseness;

- using effective adjectives;

- omitting extra 'thens' and 'ands';

- varying sentence beginnings and sentence structure;

- eliminating excessive adjectives (e.g. 'very');

- inserting information by using an asterisk or a caret;

- using strong verbs; and

- how to write in a specific genre.

If you want to enhance the quality of the children's writing, you may choose to do a mini-lesson on effective story leads. This topic could be explored through examining a range of children's literature to see how 'real authors' begin their stories in an exciting or interesting manner. An anchor chart could be created using the examples found. The teacher could then model their attempts to begin a story in an interesting manner, inspired by the techniques found in literature. The same technique can be used in exploring character or setting descriptions. The book *My Mum* (Browne, 2008) is a wonderful text to use in teaching character descriptions to young children. A mini-lesson on adjectives, or 'wow words', could involve return-ing to a story that the children have enjoyed and asking them to identify the wow words that they hear, which can then be added to a class anchor chart. *The Rainbow Fish* (Pfister, 2007) is a useful text for this type of lesson. The use of adjectives could be further explored using teacher modelling. In the example in Figure 9.2, the teacher returned to a story that had been written with the class in the past, and revised it to include adjectives using a caret to make the story more engaging.

The use of strong verbs can enhance children's writing. This topic could be explored using children's literature, searching for words that an author used instead of 'said' or 'went'. Julia Donaldson's books might be useful here. The teacher could then model the process of using that new learning through 'thinking aloud' while composing a text.

If you want your students to try a variety of genres in the writing workshop, you can demonstrate them through teacher modelling and discussion and analysis of books previously enjoyed by the children. Genres that are appropriate for this age group include counting books, alphabet books, rhyming books, concept books, lists and maps, cards for all occasions, letters (you can have a class postbox to encourage writing in this genre), surveys and signs.

Figure 9.2 Teacher modelling the use of adjectives

Writing/conferencing

Following the mini-lesson, the children begin writing. In a writing workshop, all the children work at their own pace and choose their own topics. Therefore, some children will be planning stories, others will be drafting, and some will be editing or revising their work. The classroom should be reasonably quiet to enable the children to concentrate, so encourage children to whisper if they need to talk and always whisper/talk quietly when conferring with children.

While the children are writing, the teacher should be conferencing with individual children about their writing. A conference is a conversation between the teacher and a child about their writing. In an effective conference, the teacher is a responsive listener. The teacher should only talk about 20 per cent of the time and the child should talk about 80 per cent of the time. The aim of the conference is to support and extend the child's thinking through conversation and questioning. The teacher should keep a record of who they conferred with and any issues that arose (for an example of a conferencing record form, see Appendix J). Conferencing can be a form of individualised teaching as it can provide teachers an opportunity to teach each child at their teachable moment. The instruction means a lot to the child as it is taught in the context of its application, and is therefore more memorable. The focus of a conference is the development of a child's skills as a writer, and the child is central to this process, thereby promoting the child's self-confidence, responsibility and ownership of the piece. Conferencing can not only help the teacher to recognise the individual needs of the child, but it can also allow the teacher to appreciate the child's uniqueness and individuality. It allows the teacher and child to work together to discover what is important in the life of that particular pupil.

GIVING FEEDBACK IN A CONFERENCE: TWO STARS AND A WISH

'Two stars and a wish' is a method of giving feedback to a young writer in a conference situation. You begin by telling the child two specific things that you liked about their writing (e.g. 'I really liked how you remembered to add a title to your piece, and there are some great details about that dress you wore, like you said it was "pink" and "sparkly" and "very long"'). Then discuss one aspect that you want the child to improve. Give specific guidance in relation to how they can improve (e.g. 'I noticed that you forgot to put spaces in between your words. If this is difficult to remember, try putting your finger down between each word to help you').

Share/response

At the end of the lesson, a few children should be invited to share their writing with the group. Again, keep a record of who shared and any issues that arose for possible future mini-lesson topics (for an example, see Appendix K). Sharing should always be voluntary. Sharing is important because it gives children an audience and validates their efforts to communicate through writing. If children are writing for real audiences, they will make every effort to ensure that their message is understood. It also encourages critical reading of their work (essential when attempting to edit or revise) as they learn to distance themselves from their writing and see their work through the eyes of another, anticipating their eventual audience. Sharing sessions can support work in progress through helpful feedback as well as celebrate completed drafts. Sometimes you might like to do a 'buddy share' instead of or as well as a whole group share session. Students' work can also be shared with a wider audience by placing it on noticeboards. Children can also be encouraged to write their story in 'book format' and place it in the class library.

MAXIMISE YOUR SHARING!

When children share their work, the rest of the class should be encouraged to be active listeners.

- Begin by expecting the children to be able to summarise the author's story (e.g. 'What do you remember?').

- Model how to ask an author questions about their story (e.g. 'What colour was the bike?').

- Model how to comment on a specific detail (e.g. 'I loved the way you described …', 'Your ending really surprised me because …', 'Your title was good because …', 'The beginning was good because …', 'You used some great adjectives like …').

Getting started with the writers' workshop

It is probably advisable to wait until the children have learned some letter sounds and a few sight words before they are expected to write in a workshop setting. When they have some preliminary work completed in relation to phonics, the writing workshop is an engaging, meaningful way for young children to put their budding phonic knowledge into practice.

When starting the writing workshop in a junior classroom, the teacher should begin by doing a number of lessons on labelling pictures as drawing is how young children plan their writing. The teacher might begin the lesson by saying, 'Hmm, what will I write about today … well, I love my cat very much, so perhaps I'll write about him.' Then the teacher might draw the cat and label it by saying, 'Hmm, cat … what sounds do I hear in 'cat' … /c/ /a/ /t/.' The teacher should write the word as they 'sound it out'. Then they should add their name to the text. The board should then be cleaned and the flip chart turned over so that the story is no longer visible. The children should be encouraged to, 'Put on your thinking caps' and to think, 'What will you write about today?' The teacher should discourage 30 'cat' stories as much as possible and encourage the children to choose topics that interest them. When they complete one topic, they can either add more drawings and labels to their text or begin a new 'story'. Over the next few days, the teacher should add more details to the drawings modelled and begin labelling several things in the picture. When most of the children are confident doing this, the teacher should progress to modelling sentences. Begin with just one sentence. The teacher should model how to use the word walls, alphabet friezes and phonics charts to help construct sentences. As the children progress, the teacher should start adding sentences until they are filling a page or even spreading the story over two pages. When the children become competent in writing sentences, the teacher can begin to diversify the content. For example, if the children are using a lot of dialogue in their stories, then the teacher might decide to model the use of speech marks in their story. This can also be taught by highlighting the speech in a story and having the children take the character roles. The teacher can also add speech bubbles to demonstrate this skill (see Figure 9.3).

Figure 9.3 Teacher models how to use speech marks

Organising your classroom for the writers' workshop

In order to implement the writers' workshop effectively in your classroom, your classroom should contain the following:

■ *A well-stocked classroom library*: Children need to read (or be read to) in order to write. A wide variety of books will support reading aloud to children, and can also be referred to or used by the teacher in mini-lessons.

■ *A print-rich environment*: Such an environment supports and scaffolds children's writing. Displays that include days of the week, months of the year, colours and children's names in a large, clear font can be helpful to get children started. Pick up on ideas and topics that the children might want to write about, such as the weather, the playground, games and local attractions, and then support these ideas with printed and illustrated word displays.

■ *An alphabetised word wall*: It is important that children attempt to spell known sight words correctly from the beginning. Create a large alphabetised word wall with known sight words in a large, clear font. Begin the year with a blank word wall and build it slowly with the children so that it is useful and meaningful (see Figure 4.1). Create an A4 laminated version of your word wall and stick it to the back of their writing folders as a desk reference.

■ *A high-interest word wall*: The content of this word wall will be unique to each class. Monitor children's interests and add keywords to this word wall (see

Figure 9.4 High-interest word wall

Figure 9.4). If a child wants to write about Spider-Man or Batman over and over again, it would not be recommended that they repeatedly spell it incorrectly using invented spelling. You can also create A4 individualised versions of this word wall on stiff coloured card that can be placed in their folders (brightly coloured for easy retrieval). Examples of words found on this wall might include 'Barbie', 'dinosaur', 'princess', 'castle', 'dragon', 'birthday' and 'monster'. Make sure to include an image to accompany these words if possible for easy retrieval.

■ *Writing materials*: Begin by using plain A4 sheets. Gradually introduce a few lines (create your own and photocopy). Add more lines as children progress. Have two folders for each child – one folder for everyday use and the other as a portfolio where writing can be filed month by month. Use heavy-duty plastic folders that are clearly labelled. Keep each group's folders together in a colour-coded file display for easy distribution and collection.

Writing development in the writers' workshop

The most important assessment is formative in nature, as that is what makes one's teaching focused and effective on a daily basis. In the writers' workshop, mini-lessons should be derived from the children's writing samples. Therefore, the teacher needs to continually assess how the children are doing in order to plan instruction. Information gathered from conferences and share sessions will also inform mini-lessons. The teacher may realise that his or her students have not grasped a particular skill or strategy and plan future mini-lessons accordingly. Alternatively, the teacher may realise that most of the children have understood a particular skill except for a small group of struggling pupils. In this situation, the teacher may decide that some small group mini-lessons are the best course of action. Gentry's (1981) spelling stages and Culham's (2005) 6 + 1 traits will help the teacher know what to look for in his or her students' writing development.

Spelling development in the writers' workshop

Richard Gentry (1981) and Uta Frith (1980) were among the first researchers to reveal that children pass through distinct stages of spelling development as they learn to spell. An understanding of these developmental stages allows teachers to notice and adjust their teaching within the writers' workshop. Spelling development is gradual and there often tends to be an overlap between stages. Children will pass through these stages at different rates, so generally these spelling stages tend not to be aligned with particular age groups. Effective assessment informs teaching. In order to ensure that children advance to the next stage of spelling development, their writing samples should be analysed and their spelling stage noted. Then Gentry's indicators (discussed below) should be used as a guide to plan instruction alongside the children's ongoing writing samples.

The first stage is termed 'pre-communicative'. At this stage of development, a child strings letters, numbers and random symbols and scribbles together on paper. The child understands that symbols represent a message and can be read. In Figure 9.5, the child has used random letters to fill the page. However, when he was asked to 'read' this story, he began, 'Once upon a time there was a boy and he had a ball . . .' and continued to create a fictional story, despite the fact that his story was unreadable to others.

The next stage is the semi-phonetic stage. While the children's letter formation is still quite underdeveloped, they know the sounds and names of some of the letters of the alphabet, and are able to use this knowledge to label their drawings and create texts. At this stage, words are often represented with one or more consonants, and vowels are usually absent or incorrect. In Figure 9.6, we can see that the child has labelled the sun 'san', flower is 'flr', butterfly is 'btfi' and 'mammy' is spelled 'mami'.

As children's awareness of letter–sound correspondence increases, they move to the phonetic stage. At this stage, children demonstrate a good knowledge of English phonemes and words are spelled phonetically. Visual patterns are not generally demonstrated, and thus many irregular words will be spelled incorrectly. Children understand left-to-right orientation. Figure 9.7 reads, 'My hamster is [a] girl. I said [I] love my hamster'. We can see that irregular words such as 'said'

Figure 9.5 Pre-communicative spelling in the writers' workshop

Figure 9.6 Semi-phonetic spelling in the writers' workshop

Figure 9.7 Phonetic spelling in the writers' workshop

and 'love' are spelled incorrectly, indicating a lack of visual spelling strategies. When children reach this stage, it is important that they are encouraged to spell high-frequency words (such as those found on the Dolch list) correctly so that

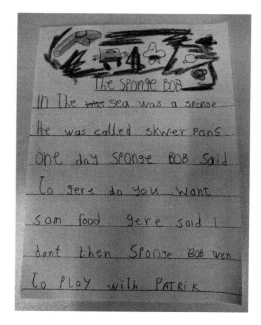

Figure 9.8 Transitional spelling in the writers' workshop

they can progress to the transitional stage. Children have begun to demonstrate an understanding of left-to-right and top-to-bottom orientation. However, there is little attention given to spacing between words, which can make writing samples at this stage challenging to read.

At the transitional stage of development, children tend to move away from a heavy reliance on phonics and present the first evidence of a new visual strategy. Children at this stage may still have some difficulty with letter strings and transpose letters in the middle of words, such as the 'au' in 'because'. In Figure 9.8, we can see that a lot of irregular words are spelled correctly, such as 'was', 'one' and 'said'. The child has also managed to write a reasonably coherent story that stays on topic. Conventions of print, such as punctuation and speech marks, are absent, but the writing is legible and readable by others.

The final stage is the correct or competent stage when children have mastered phoneme/grapheme relationships. Children at this stage are now very aware of word structure/patterns that are characteristic of the English spelling system. Such children have the ability to recognise when a word does not look correct and propose alternative spellings.

6 + 1 traits in the writers' workshop

Initially, one would use Gentry's spelling stages to assess and guide writing instruction. This is because when children are beginning to write, the main concern is that they are able to communicate a message that can be read by others. However, when

Table 9.1 Culham's 6 + 1 traits

Trait	Criteria
Ideas	• Focused, main idea is clear, stays on topic. • Ideas are developed. • Relevant, quality details presented to support the main ideas. • Ideas are connected to each other.
Organisation	• Clear beginning, middle and end. • Interesting introductions and satisfying endings, with some action in the middle. • Good use of transitions. • Sequencing is logical and effective. • The title is original and captures the central theme of the piece.
Voice	• The tone of voice adds interest to the message and is appropriate for the purpose and the audience. • The reader feels a strong interaction with the writer, sensing the person behind the words, the reader feels 'moved'. • Writing feels vibrant and 'full of life'.
Word choice	• Words are specific and accurate. • Striking words and phrases catch the reader's eye and linger in the reader's mind. • Lively verbs add energy. • Precise nouns are used. • The writer has made an effort to use a wide range of vocabulary when appropriate. • Audience has been considered.
Sentence fluency	• Sentences vary in length as well as structure. • Varied sentence beginnings. • Use of creative and appropriate connectives (not just 'and then'). • The piece is easy to read aloud, not choppy, awkward or rambling.
Conventions	• Appropriate punctuation is used. • Capital letters are used appropriately. • Spelling is age-appropriate.
Presentation	• Handwriting is legible. • Letters are formed correctly. • There is appropriate spacing between words.

Source: Cullham (2005)

children's writing samples place them at the phonetic stage, it is time to develop their writing craft (i.e. how you tell your message is as important as your message). Therefore, the teacher requires a more holistic form of assessment to guide teaching, such as Culham's (2005) 6 + 1 traits in writing criteria, which address a variety of writing skills and strategies. The 6 + 1 traits assessment analyses a child's writing in relation to seven different traits that are found in competent writing: ideas, organisation, voice, word choice, sentence fluency, conventions and presentation. Details for each trait can be found in Table 9.1.

Putting it into practice

Examine the writing sample in Figure 9.9. This child is an English language learner (ELL) in her second year at school (term 2). She is a strong writer, but there is plenty of room for further development. How would you rate it using 6 + 1 as a guide?

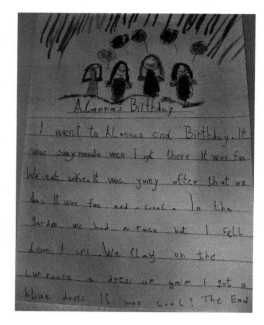

Figure 9.9 Writing sample

- *Ideas*: This piece of writing is not particularly strong in relation to the ideas trait. While it appears to stay on topic somewhat, the story meanders into a play date rather than a birthday party. However, there are some birthday-related details in the first few lines.

- *Organisation*: This piece has a clear beginning, middle and end. The beginning is strong, and there is action in the middle, but the ending is a bit unsatisfying. A variety of transitions would improve the piece. The title captures the central theme of the piece but is not that exciting.

- *Voice*: The piece is relatively easy to understand and we can visualise the writer.

- *Word choice*: Some adjectives are used, but a wider range of vocabulary could be used.

- *Sentence fluency*: Sentences are of varying lengths. Some work could be done on sentence beginnings.

- *Conventions*: Some spellings need attention, but on the whole the spelling is quite good for an ELL child in her second year at school. Some work needs to be done on punctuation.

- *Presentation*: After a shaky start, the handwriting becomes reasonably uniform. Some work may be needed on the letter 'p' and the formation of 'w'.

Since the writer is an ELL, you could also discuss certain issues such as past tense (e.g. 'We eat cake' in line 3).

Self-assessment using 6 + 1 criteria

Assessment criteria should be shared with children as much as possible so that they can take an active role in their own learning. Self-assessment of writing might be encouraged through the effective use of pictorial and text rubrics. Rubrics should always be based on the writing skills and strategies that have already been taught to children in mini-lessons, during conferencing and share sessions. All the children should be able to achieve a reasonably high score on the rubric if they stay on task during the lesson (i.e. it is important that the standard is achievable or children will lose confidence and interest in writing). A rubric should be introduced in a step-by-step manner so that the children fully understand what the criteria are. At the beginning, a visual rubric would be recommended whereby the standard is presented using pictures. Three levels of achievement, represented by 'thumbs up', 'thumbs in the middle' and 'thumbs down', will indicate the expectation. One criterion could be based on 'on-task behaviour' (see Figure 9.10), whereby 'thumbs up' is achieved if children draw a picture that is detailed, write their name and write a few sentences. 'Thumbs in the middle' is achieved if children draw a picture (not very detailed), write their name and write a few words. 'Thumbs down' is achieved if the picture is incomplete and their name and writing is absent. If

Figure 9.10 Pictorial rubric for 'on-task behaviour' and finger spaces

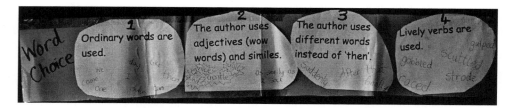

Figure 9.11 Word choice rubric

there has been considerable instruction with regard to spacing between words, this could be part of the rubric, 'thumbs up' being achieved when the spaces are optimal size, 'thumbs in the middle' when some spacing is a little too large or too small, and 'thumbs down' if the spacing is very erratic. Handwriting could be assessed using the visual rubric as well, using textual examples to demonstrate the level of achievement. At the share session, with teacher guidance, children could be encouraged to self-assess their work using the rubric.

As the children progress, the rubrics can grow in complexity and become more text-based with some accompanying visuals. Taking each trait individually, the criteria can be spread from one to four, and described in language that is accessible to young learners. See Figure 9.11 for an example of the word choice rubric (adapted from Culham, 2005). This rubric would only be used as a self-assessment tool when all the learners had engaged in mini-lessons based on this trait and were reasonably confident in the trait's usage in their writing.

Tracking progress

Summative assessment has a role in the writers' workshop. Simple portfolios can be created where students add one piece of writing per month. Children can have a role in choosing the piece of writing, encouraging self-assessment. Depending on children's ability, they can either write a note explaining why this piece was chosen or dictate the reason to the teacher. This note can then be attached to the writing sample. As the months progress, the teacher can chart children's spelling developmental stage (Gentry, 1981) and children's performance in relation to writing traits (Culham, 2005). These results may highlight students who are falling behind or those who require more challenge in the writers' workshop. This will inform the teacher's long-term plans.

The writers' workshop and the English language learner

The writers' workshop is a suitable methodology for English language learners as it differentiates by design and correlates well with second language acquisition theory. Krashen (1985) outlines the need for language to be 'comprehensible' to the learner for successful acquisition to occur. As the instruction in the writers' workshop is often multimodal (uses words and images), needs-based and often individualised (particularly within conferences), the 'messages' can be comprehended by the learner and put into practice. Krashen (1985) also discusses the prominence of the 'affective filter' in language learning. This theory holds that if a learner is not comfortable and at ease in a language learning situation, then he or she is unlikely to benefit from instruction. The writers' workshop is designed so that children can experiment with writing at their own pace, using their own interests as writing fodder, which allows the 'affective filter' to open and language learning to occur. Swain (1996) and Long (1996) emphasise the need for 'output' and interaction to develop language skills. In the writers' workshop, children are encouraged to interact with the teacher and their peers to develop their writing at all stages of the lesson (mini-lesson, conferences and sharing). Pupils who arrive at school already literate in their home language (but not in English) should be encouraged to write in their home language within the workshop, gradually creating bilingual texts and then moving towards writing in English in class, while continuing to write in their home language in other contexts (Cummins & Swain, 2014).

Key concepts for practice

- Young children need regular opportunities to compose texts on topics of their own choosing. The teacher should take care to develop a 'writing community' in the classroom where the children and teacher share their writing regularly.

- The writers' workshop is an appropriate methodology for ELLs as it is meaning-based and is pitched to each child's emerging language competence.

- A writers' workshop lesson is composed of a mini-lesson, writing/conferencing time and a share session.

- Writing skills and strategies should be taught in a meaningful context. Mini-lessons based on children's writing needs may focus on procedures and processes, writing skills, or the craft of writing.

- Individual conferences between a child and the teacher should serve to develop the child's writing in the context of his or her own composition.

- The writers' workshop should always include a sharing session where children are encouraged to give feedback to their peers in a constructive manner.

- Care needs to be taken in creating a classroom environment that supports writing.

- Spelling can be assessed along Gentry's developmental continuum, while Culham's 6 + 1 traits criteria can serve as a helpful guide in developing children's writing in a holistic manner.

REFLECTION: THINKING ABOUT YOUR PRACTICE

- How is writing taught in your school in the junior classes?

- Do you feel that there is a good balance between teaching letter formation and creative writing?

- Do you use many literacy worksheets in the junior classes? Do you feel that the number could be reduced to allow room for a writers' workshop?

- Do you think this chapter may change how you currently approach writing instruction?

For further exploration

Avery, C. (2002). . . . And with a light touch. Portsmouth, NH: Heinemann.
Calkins, L. (1986). The art of teaching writing. Portsmouth, NH: Heinemann.
Culligan, B. (2009). Spelling and handwriting. Dublin: Culligan.
Gentry, J.R. (1981). Learning to spell developmentally. The Reading Teacher, 34(1), 378–381.
Gentry, J.R. (1987). Spel . . . is a four letter word. Lemington Spa: Scholastic.

10 Developing language and literacy through play

```
GUIDING QUESTIONS FOR THIS CHAPTER

■ How can I organise my classroom for play-based learning?

■ How can I encourage effective literacy learning during play in my classroom?

■ How can I assess play-based learning?
```

Introduction

While early literacy skills can be developed using the meaningful methodologies discussed thus far in this book, they can also thrive when educators make time for extended periods of play in their early years classroom. Play has been identified as a crucial aspect of child development, most notably in the early childhood years (Hirsh-Pasek, Golinkoff, Berk & Singer, 2008; Singer, Golinkoff & Hirsh-Pasek, 2006). It has been found to contribute to children's physical, social, emotional, creative and cognitive development, and is understood to be a powerful and empowering form of learning (Singer & Singer, 2009). A play-based curriculum can help to encourage a wide vocabulary, creative thinking, collaborative skills and problem-solving to a much greater extent than a traditional learning environment (Skolnick-Weisberg, Kitteredge, Hirsh-Pasek, Golinkoff & Klahr, 2015). It has also been found to significantly enhance pupil engagement (Walsh et al., 2006). Therefore, it provides a wonderful forum for the development of early literacy skills within a meaningful context (Roskos & Christie, 2012). This chapter considers some of the ways that the classroom environment can be arranged to facilitate literacy development through play.

Play-based learning and literacy development

Play-based learning with a literacy focus involves creating situations where children can interact with each other in a particular play context that encourages reading, writing and oral language as a means of communicating with each other and the class teacher. When children are actively engaged in using language to read, write and explore print in their play, they are learning how written language works.

Teacher participation during play has been found to increase children's cognitive challenge, language and literacy development, and higher-order thinking skills (Walsh et al., 2006). In the early years classroom, it is necessary to recognise that while free play is an effective vehicle for children to explore their social and self-regulatory skills, research suggests that it might not be the best way to achieve specific curricular objectives in relation to literacy learning and development (Fisher, Hirsh-Pasek, Golinkoff, Singer & Berk, 2010). Adult-directed play is controlled by the teacher, but this often does not allow chidlren to develop their creativity or to take control of their own learning. However, guided play (Skolnick-Weisberg et al., 2015) is a combination of adult initiation and child direction. It is important for the teacher to take the lead in some situations (such as modelling language or social skills), while also recognising the need to step back at times so that the children can develop their own initiative and creativity in different ways, which also allows the teacher to observe the children and to take notes on their learning and development. Indeed, according to Skolnick-Weisberg et al. (2015), 'guided play is the best way to incorporate play into early curricula without compromising educational goals, while allowing children to enjoy school' (p. 9). The adult in guided play may initiate the play context but does not direct the play within that scenario. An important aspect of the teacher's role during guided play is scaffolding the children's learning (Fisher et al., 2010) so that the children can reach an optimal level of development. As a result of the adult's role in developing the learning environment and the provision of subtle scaffolding, children are more likely to develop a knowledge of the key concepts or skills than they would through free play, and are more likely to be highly motivated to engage in the play scenario than a more formal methodology because it is enjoyable, social and meaningful (Skolnick-Weisberg et al., 2015).

Guided play provides a very appropriate forum for expanding and developing children's oral vocabulary as play demands communication from players. When planning for each play area, the teacher should carefully consider what new vocabulary could be modelled for the children. Pepper and Weizman (2004) recommend that a teacher should plan for vocabulary development by considering various categories such as nouns, verbs, describing words, questions, location words and feelings, as children need all these language components to develop complex speech patterns. Vygotsky (1978) highlighted the essential role played by the teacher in developing a broader range of vocabulary, a variety of language registers and more complex sentence structure through carefully modelling and scaffolding during play. Indeed, the use of targeted vocabulary, open-ended questions, and expanding and extending on children's utterances during play has been found to increase children's lexical diversity, increase target word frequency and produce longer utterances from children (Combs, 2010).

Generally, most play activities with a literacy focus tend to be a form of 'guided play'. Guided play might include fine motor play, story-based play and sociodramatic play. The organisation of play may be similar to how literacy centres were implemented earlier in this book (using rotas, centres or areas for particular activities, children working in small groups). In this chapter, we will explore how to organise a classroom for guided play that enhances language and literacy skills in an effective manner.

Fine motor play

Fine motor play activities such as play dough, junk art, threading, sand, water, jigsaws and construction develop hand–eye coordination and strengthen the muscles needed to write effortlessly, as outlined in Chapter 8. These activities

Table 10.1 Vocabulary development during fine motor play

Type of fine motor play	Vocabulary possibilities
Play dough	Pinch, squeeze, chop, roll, cut, pull, twist, squash
	Colours
	Numbers/counting
	Shapes
	Names of cutters shaped like objects (e.g. duck, car, cow)
	Can I have a go of...? Can you pass the...?
	First I will... then I...
Junk art	Sizes of materials
	Names of materials
	Descriptions of materials (shiny, rough, smooth, bumpy, flat, straight)
	Cut, paint, tear, draw, make, stick, glue, add, paste, colour, build
	Colours
	Numbers/counting
	Descriptions of objects created
	Can you pass me the... I need to... first I will... then I need to... where is the... how can I?
Sand and water	Splash, drop, cold, wet, dry, gritty, rough, smooth
	Fill, full, half full, empty, half empty
	How many...?
	Counting (how many scoops?)
	Build, make, measure
	Names of additional resources (boat, ship, dolphin, fish, whale, rescue boat, excavator, bulldozers, spades, buckets, droppers, pumps)
Construction	Build, design, create, plan
	Blueprints, sizes and shapes of blocks/brocks (cylinders, cuboids, cubes)
	Colours
	Measure (length, width, height)
	Description of creations

also aid the focus and concentration needed to become literate. Finally, they encourage social communication and the use of specific vocabulary; thus, this type of play can enhance children's oral language ability. Table 10.1 outlines examples of vocabulary that could be modelled and encouraged by a teacher during fine motor play.

Story-based play

This is when children are guided in acting out a scenario from a story or poem that is familiar to them. Specific props relevant to particular narratives are provided, such as bear masks, a golden wig, bowls, chairs and beds in order to facilitate the re-enactment of the story of Goldilocks. This sort of play may be modelled during a whole-class literacy lesson (such as shared reading) and then re-enacted during literacy centre time. Therefore, this type of play tends to have direct links to shared reading (discussed in Chapters 5 and 6) or to books read aloud by the teacher (see Chapter 1). Often this play also emanates from rhymes, poems and other activities within whole-class literacy lessons. This sort of play tends to be particularly effective for English language learners (ELLs) as they have the opportunity to practise new vocabulary that they learned during shared reading in a relaxed, social and meaningful manner. The availability of particular props in a 'storytelling area' during play sessions facilitates this type of play among small groups of children. This type of play offers the teacher the opportunity to model and encourage narrative storytelling scripts (e.g. 'once upon a time'), language chunks (e.g. 'over the hills and far away'), and specific nouns and verbs found in the stories or rhymes – they may be tier 1 or tier 2, depending on the age, ability and native language of the children (see Table 10.2).

Table 10.2 Vocabulary development during story-based play

The Three Billy Goats Gruff	
Narrative structure	**Language chunks**
Once upon a time there was . . .	Trip, trap, the goat walked over the bridge
At first, and then, after that, suddenly, from then on	Sweet, green grass
	It is only me!
	Oh no you're not!
	I'm going to eat you up!
	You don't want to eat me . . .
	Oh, alright.
Tier 1 nouns/verbs	**Tier 2 nouns/verbs**
goat	troll
field	meadow
grass	barren
walked	hoof
jumped	roared
loved	charged

Location words

over, under, on, up, above, across
in the distance

Describing words

Little Billy Goat, Middle Sized Billy Goat and
    Great Big Billy Goat
brown, green
hungry
juicy
bigger
tastier

Questions

Who's that?

IN THE CLASSROOM . . . THE STORYTELLING CENTRE

In Fiona's class, the children have learned a large number of rhymes and songs. As many of the children are learning English as an additional language, Fiona always uses props and visuals when teaching a rhyme, poem or song. For example, she used five toy rubber ducks, a blue blanket (for water) and some 'hills' created from cardboard when she taught 'Five Little Ducks'. When she reads big books, she also tries to use props and visuals to support understanding. For example, when she read 'The Three Little Pigs', she used a selection of character masks so that the children could act out the story during lessons. Fiona gathered a number of small boxes to house the different materials. At the end of every week, she would create a 'story box' for any new poem/rhyme/song or book that the children had learned or read during the week. She would add the relevant props and/or visuals and a book or a laminated poem/rhyme/song to accompany it. She created a 'storytelling corner' in her classroom where the children could come and retell any poem/rhyme/song of their choosing using the props and visuals (see Figure 10.1). This became one of the most popular activities among the children.

Source: Author's experience in practice

Figure 10.1 Props for storytelling

Sociodramatic play

This is a play situation based on a real-life experience such as shopping, dining out or visiting the dentist. Props relevant to the scenario are provided. This type of play enhances literacy skills but also has links across the curriculum. Every few weeks, a new sociodramatic theme might be introduced in the classroom based on the children's interests and/or curricular demands. For each theme/scenario, the teacher has to consider the props/equipment required to inspire a certain type of play, how it might relate to curricular goals, specific language that could be developed within the theme, and the opportunities for reading and writing that might occur during play.

Oral language development in sociodramatic play

Sociodramatic play provides a very appropriate forum for expanding and developing children's vocabulary as it requires the development of joint attention, the ability to give and follow instructions, and also the ability to work collaboratively and interact with others. Table 10.3 gives some examples of the range of vocabulary that might be used in 'The Baby Clinic' sociodramatic play scenario as an insight into the possibilities for language development that play might present within the play session. Sociodramatic play themes offer an opportunity to learn a specific 'language style' or register. For example, in 'The Baby Clinic' scenario, phrases such as 'Do you have an appointment?', 'Please take a seat', 'Have you completed the form?', and so forth are required to communicate effectively and

Table 10.3 Oral language development in sociodramatic play

Key vocabulary: sociodramatic play in 'The Baby Clinic'
Nouns
baby, toddler, newborn, soother, bottle, injection, vaccination, queue, waiting area, doctor, nurse, temperature, vomit, ill, check-up, stethoscope, weighing scales, pounds and ounces, record book
Verbs
waiting, crawling, eating, drinking, vomiting, screaming
Describing words
feverish, upset, worried, scared, terrified, poorly, happy, ordinal number (first, second, third, last)
Questions
Do you have an appointment? Can you sign your name here? What is the matter? How long . . .? How old . . .? Did you bring your vaccination record booklet? Have you completed the form?
Location/chronological words
on, under, between, next to, before, after

appropriately. The ability to answer imagined questions and develop characters and narratives in an imagined reality such as 'The Baby Clinic' (e.g. the 5-year-old playing the role of a new mother discussing her baby's health) requires the child to draw on cognitive, creative and language skills in a holistic and integrated manner. The examples of nouns, verbs and describing words listed are examples of how the play scenario might develop subject-specific vocabulary and the ability to demonstrate understanding of new words in a meaningful context.

Writing development during sociodramatic play

Sociodramatic play provides an effective forum for developing emergent reading and writing language curricular objectives in an informal manner. There should be a 'writing table' available to the children during the play session to use in a variety of ways, stocked with paper of different colours, notepads and sizes, and a choice of writing implements (Excelsa, 2014). Children should be encouraged to make use of these materials to develop their play through the creation of signs and posters, cards and invitations, notes, lists and drawings. Teacher modelling and scaffolding is crucial to enable children to develop their skills in this area, such as the conventions of print, sentence structure and invented spelling. Children may use seemingly random symbols or letters to represent whole words or syllables, or scribbles that may be meaningless to an adult. However, it is often the case that children can read these 'scribbles' to tell about the drawing that was made. Children's attempts to use writing to communicate during play should be celebrated during the review session, which might serve to encourage more reluctant writers to attempt similar tasks. For example, in a restaurant, children might attempt a number of writing tasks, such as writing orders, writing the specials board, signing for a credit card, recording bookings or even writing reviews after a meal. Further examples are given in Table 10.4.

Reading development during sociodramatic play

Emergent reading can also be supported in sociodramatic play by providing various texts for use during play. For example, storybooks might be read before bedtime when playing 'house' or cookbooks might be referred to when playing in the kitchen. In scenarios such as a 'restaurant', menus would have to be consulted. Signs such as 'Waiting Room' may be read in the doctor's office or signs stating 'Sale – 50% Off' in a clothes shop may be used to entice potential 'customers'. In addition, a reading corner stocked with interesting and engaging children's literature should always be available to all children during the play hour. Each play area should be adorned with appropriate environmental print, such as signs and labels, to encourage reading and print awareness to help develop the skills, such as letter recognition and concepts about print.

Table 10.4 Reading and writing opportunities during play

	Reading	Writing	Oral language
The restaurant	Menus, specials board, bills, cookbooks	Writing orders, specials board, signing for a credit card, bookings book, writing reviews after a meal	Nouns: names of food/dishes, knife, fork, spoon, cup, glass, bottle, waiter/waitress, bill, money, cash register, table, chair Verbs: eating, waiting, sitting, enjoying, munching, devouring, drinking, cooking, preparing Describing words: starving, famished, hungry, stuffed, full, satisfied, tasty, delicious, yummy, disgusting, revolting, bitter, sweet, sour Questions: 'Do you have a booking?', 'Table for two, please', 'Can we see the menus?' 'What are today's specials?' 'What would you recommend?', 'Can we get the bill, please' Location/chronological words: time of booking, first, second, third, on, in, before, after, beside
Doctor's office/ hospital	'Waiting Room', 'Toilets', 'No Smoking', magazines in the waiting area	Taking down appointments, prescriptions, filing in charts	Nouns: patient, doctor, nurse, receptionist, examination table, medicine, stethoscope, injection, bandage, wound, crutch Verbs: 'take your temperature', 'check your heartbeat', vomit, cough, fall, 'ambulance', 'emergency' Describing words: 'diseased', 'injured', feverish, poorly, bleeding Questions: 'So you have an appointment?', 'You can see the doctor now', 'Do you need a prescription for your medicine?', 'take your temperature', 'check your heartbeat'
At the bank	Signs – the name of the bank, 'Queue Here', 'Foreign Exchange', 'Bank Manager', name tags for staff, flyers and posters, 'Loans'	Filing in forms, writing down transactions	Nouns: money, credit card, cheque, cashier, ATM Verbs: queuing, waiting, saving, spending, exchanging, withdraw, lodge, need, want Describing words: rich, poor, polite, rude, 'in a hurry', excited Questions: 'Good morning, how can I help you?', 'Would you like to withdraw . . .?', 'Would you like to lodge . . .?', 'Would you like a loan?', 'Would you like some foreign currency?', 'Do you wish to pay your credit card bill?'
The clothes shop	Signs – the name of the shop, 'Sale', '50% Off', 'Mens', 'Ladies', 'Children', 'Babies', 'Shoes', 'Jumpers', 'Trousers', 'Coats', 'Please Queue Here', 'Please Pay Here', 'Exit'	Making signs and flyers for the shop, doing a stocktake of inventory	Nouns: jumper, trousers, jeans, shoes, scarf, hat, socks, dress, coat, gloves, boots Verbs: try, dress, hate, love, adore, want, wish Describing words: big, small, just right, too large, too small, colour words, delightful, gorgeous, disgusting, terrific, horrible, tight, loose Questions: 'Do you have that in a larger/smaller size?', 'Can I help you?', 'Would you like to try that on?'

Other sociodramatic play ideas might include:

- the dentist;
- the hairdresser;
- the garden centre;
- the coffee shop;
- a building site;
- at home;
- a museum;
- a farm;
- a library;
- a campsite;
- Santa's grotto;
- the chip shop;
- a dog groomer;
- the vet;
- on the bus/train;
- the school;
- a pet shop;
- the baker;
- the optician; and
- the paint shop.

Organising the classroom

Quality begins with the classroom layout and organisation (Whitebread & Coltman, 2015). The adult must carefully prepare the environment, known as 'the third teacher' (Edwards & Gandini, 2015), so that the play is well resourced and organised as 'high quality play environments support unity between playing, learning and teaching' (Wood, 2013, p. 80). Resourcing play has been cited as a barrier to implementing a play-based curriculum in the past (e.g. Gray & Ryan, 2016). However, many of the resources used for effective play-based learning are reasonably affordable and relatively easy to source. The HighScope approach recommends the use of 'real materials', such as old kettles (with the power lead removed), old pots and pans, and empty milk cartons (Holt, 2010), which can serve to enhance sociodramatic play themes. Items such as colanders and spoons of various sizes can be used in fine motor play (weave pipe cleaners through a colander or use spoons in sand or water play). The Reggio Emilia approach encourages teachers to incorporate natural materials, such as pine cones, shells, rocks and leaves, into play activities, which are freely available and work well in small world play scenarios and in sand and water play (Thornton & Bruton, 2010). Simple materials such as books, magazines, pens, paper and clipboards can enhance any play situation. Charity shops often have a wealth of materials that can be useful for a variety of themes. When choosing materials for play, it is important that they are open-ended, intelligent resources (Wood, 2013) that provoke creativity, imagination, vocabulary development and problem-solving. A teacher who is knowledgeable of play as a learning medium will carefully choose these types of resources and then guide the children in their use in order to maximise learning during the play hour.

Research has shown that children need time to immerse themselves in the play, and to commit to roles, expand their creativity and deepen their learning (Kernan, 2007). The traditional approach to play, where it is generally situated in the first 20 minutes of the school day for 'settling in' (Gray & Ryan, 2016), needs serious attention as children who routinely arrive late to school may miss play entirely. It also does not allow for the 'plan-do-review' structure (NCCA, 2009) of play-based learning, which is critical in developing 'mature play' (Leong & Bodrova, 2012). If play is to be valued in classrooms, then it should be placed on the time-table accordingly, ideally in the middle of ths chool day, so that its time does not become eroded by the distractions of the school day. Play needs to be of good quality so it can be used as an effective learning tool.

Here are some helpful tips on how to organise play activities that might enhance language and literacy development in your classroom:

- Consider your classroom layout. Try to reserve a corner in your classroom for your main play activity, such as 'The Hospital'. If you don't have room, you can use a carefully labelled box storage system.

- Group the children carefully. Think about the following issues: gender, age, ability in different areas of the curriculum, personality, English language proficiency, friendships and antagonistic relationships. Groups should have a maximum membership of six children. Monitor the group composition carefully and readjust it regularly.

- Create a colour-coded storage system and a play activity grid. It is a good idea to use text and visuals in this display so that all children can 'read' it.

- Decide on a consistent time for play.

- Make sure to model how to play in each play centre. Use role play and discussion to highlight appropriate behaviour.

- Add new play centres one at a time. Perhaps use Friday afternoon to model the next week's centre.

- Plan centres well in advance and ask parents for objects such as old phones, laptops and so forth that would work well in a centre.

- Consider allowing the children to take part in planning their role in the play situation. They can sketch their role and discuss their 'play plan' (what they will do and how they will do it) in advance of the play session.

The teacher's role in play

One of the aims of a play-based curriculum is to aid children to develop 'mature play' (Leong & Bodrova, 2012) as research as shown that this skilful 'playing' is more likely to achieve cognitive, social, emotional and creative developmental goals. A teacher can assist children by using a range of strategies during scaffolding, including extending or sustaining the play, where the teacher builds upon the children's ideas, themes and interests during play (Yang, 2013) in order to develop the play narrative. This can be done as a 'co-player' (Tarman & Tarman, 2011) or as a play director. During play, the teacher might also have to play the role of 'mediator' when conflicts arise, and may have to model appropriate learning dispositions and social skills within and outside of the play scenario (Tarman & Tarman, 2011). While a teacher can have a very positive effect on children's play, Jung and Recchia (2013) warn that inappropriate or poorly planned teacher interactions can have a negative effect on play-based learning and restrict its potential. Therefore, effective planning for language and literacy development, similar to the tables presented in this chapter, is essential.

The teacher should be actively involved in a play centre (see Figure 10.2). An adult's skilful interaction in play helps to focus children's attention on the play situation, set up challenges and extend the possibilities. Therefore, the teacher might point out certain important elements to the children (such as the use of a telephone when an imaginary house is on fire). The teacher might also pose challenges such as, 'What if the restaurant ran out of food?' Play situations can also be extended and improved through careful guidance (e.g. in a simple hospital situation, the teacher

Figure 10.2 The teacher's role in play

might say, 'I think she needs an operation, doctor, is the operating room ready?', which incorporates a new element that the children had not thought about before).

With regard to literacy development, the adult plays an important role in modelling and encouraging children's oral language. When planning a play situation (discussed in the earlier section), the teacher should have certain language objectives in relation to key vocabulary. The teacher might also model the reading and writing objectives for the play scenario (e.g. taking an order in a restaurant) so that the children understand how to act. The teacher can then guide the children in their use of new vocabulary and unfamiliar roles. The teacher might lead a discussion on why reading and writing are used in this scenario.

It is important to remember that although the adult can guide and, to some extent, shape the sociodramatic play, essentially the play and action must belong to the children. The teacher will review the play centre on an ongoing basis as part of assessment practice, which will be discussed in the next section.

IN THE CLASSROOM

This year, Claire is teaching 4- and 5-year-olds who are in their first year at school. She has a large class of 28 pupils. A support teacher called Annie works with Claire in her classroom for two hours a day, providing additional scaffolding for children who have additional needs. Many of the children in Claire's class speak English as an additional language and some are still in the 'silent period' of language acquisition, which can make communication challenging at times. Claire encourages these children to interact using gesture and facial expression. She includes the use of props and visuals in every lesson so that they can respond by pointing at a picture or a symbol. One English language learner called Tehera is a 'selective mute'. She will only speak during play-based learning situations such as sociodramatic play, block play and small world play. She refuses to communicate verbally in any other learning situation. In play, she is quite animated and interacts positively with her peers and the teacher. She clearly feels comfortable in this type of learning situation. In order to overcome Tehera's anxiety about speaking in different learning situations, the teacher and the support teacher are making a special effort to develop their relationship with Tehera. They take turns play-ing with her group and praising her interaction efforts. Each play session begins with a planning session and ends with a review session. Claire and Annie decide that the review session might be a good opportunity to encourage Tehera to speak in front of the class. They begin by asking her to review her play on a one-to-one basis. After a few days, Claire sits with Tehera's group and asks them to discuss their play. Slowly, Tehera volunteers information. Having spent a couple of weeks discussing their play as a small group, Claire encourages the children to tell the whole group about their play. She uses photographs taken during the play session projected onto the interac-tive white board to jog their memories and to help them remember key vocabulary. Tehera simply listens at the first few sessions, but after a few days raises her hand and contributes something to the discussion. This is a turning point, as from then on she begins to talk to her peers and her teachers during lessons.

Source: Author's experience in practice

Assessing play

In order to ensure that the play hour is a high-quality learning experience for children, assessment is a crucial aspect of the teacher's role. Assessment of play should be multifaceted, ranging from teacher reflection of his or her own interac-tions with the children, examining the learning environment and resources and the interactions between children (Moyles, 2004). While the teacher spends most of his or her time interacting with the children during the play hour, it is help-ful to allocate some time for observation, note-taking and photograph-taking. Not only will these tools provide opportunities for self-assessment during the review stage of that day's play; they might also provide fodder for teacher reflection and the discussion in the next day's planning session. Notes, photographs and written reflections could also be placed in individual portfolios for each child that docu-ment their learning journey. Conversations as an assessment method can be very useful in determining whether language goals have been met and if children have understood a particular concept or demonstrated a particular skill that had been planned for that play activity.

Leong and Bodrova (2012) outline a useful approach to assessing children's play. It is based on examining the maturity of children's play through five stages, from the earliest stage, termed 'first scripts', through to complex, multifaceted, language-rich play. Through teacher observation, children can be placed on this play continuum, and plans for developing children's play can be created using the indicators in each category as a guide. This strategy is termed PRoPELS, an acronym that stands for the most critical elements of children's play that can be assessed and scaffolded by the adults. The categories for assessment include: planning, roles, props, extended time frame, language, and scenario.

- **P**lanning – children's ability to think about play in advance of playing.

- **Ro**les children play – including the actions, language and emotional expressions that are associated with a specific role.

- **P**rops – the objects (real, symbolic and imaginary) children use in play.

- **E**xtended time frame – play that lasts for long stretches of time, within one play session for an hour or longer, or extending over several play sessions and over several days.

- **L**anguage – what children say to develop a scenario or coordinate the actions of different players, as well as speech associated with a particular role.

- **S**cenario – what children act out, including the sequence of scripts and interactions between roles.

PRoPELS is a useful tool to assess three dimensions of play that are important for young children's language and literacy development: explication of meaning, reflection on meaning and narrative structure. In assessing children's ability to take on a role and deal with props for an extended time while using appropriate language, the teacher will be able to determine the extent to which children can negotiate meaning among their peers and their ability to build oral and imaginative storylines. From a literacy perspective, the teacher should also have specific objectives in relation to reading and writing, as outlined earlier in this chapter. Teacher observation and note-taking (and also visual and audio recordings, if possible) should be used to assess children's ability to use reading and writing tools during play. The teacher may create specific checklists related to his or her own objectives. If the teacher notes that certain children are struggling, he or she may step in to play alongside this student, modelling the objectives and scaffolding learning. Similarly, if children seem bored by the play situation, the teacher may step in and provide a new challenge for those students to extend and develop their thinking and playing.

Using children's literature to enhance play

While it may be assumed that all children enter school 'able' to play, some may struggle due to poor hand–eye coordination, lack of fine motor dexterity, speech and language issues, or limited creativity and imagination. Many of these difficulties arise from lack of experience playing in a variety of ways on their own or with responsive co-players. Children's literature may provide the 'spark' that encourages enthusiastic engagement in play for those who struggle.

Children's literature can often be used as a stimulus for fine motor play. For example, the children might 'feed' Roald Dahl's *Enormous Crocodile* using tweezers and pom-poms, or create pasta necklaces for Cinderella to wear to the ball. Julia Davies' *Big Blue Whale* might be swimming in the water tray, or the children might dig for treasure in the Neverland sand pit! Story-based play emerges directly from retelling narratives and will require repeated reading of engaging children's literature.

While the theme of sociodramatic play is also often related to children's literature, such as drawing in *Mog and the V.E.T.* (Kerr, 2005) when playing vet, the deeper symbolic nature of mature play may often have to be addressed in order to maximise play's potential. Symbolic play in the form of sociodramatic play has a powerful influence on children's cognitive development as it can enhance metacognition and self-regulation (Whitebread, Colton, Jameson & Lander, 2009). While some children enter school having had a wealth of experience with symbolic play, others struggle to adopt a role in a sociodramatic play area and are unsure as to how to use props and open-ended materials in different ways, skills that are desirable in developing 'mature play' (Leong & Bodrova, 2012). *Not a Box* (Poitis, 2008) and *Not a Stick* (Poitis, 2009) are storybooks that might provide a stimulus for discussion on symbolic play. The young rabbit's insistence that a simple object such as a box or a stick can take the form of a variety of playthings through the use of his imagination may be inspirational to some children and gratifying to others in an infant class. It might also provide teachers with the golden opportunity to begin to include more open-ended materials for use during the play, so as to further develop the children's symbolic play, as a box can be many things – a car, a secret hideout, a house, a castle, a fire engine, a garage, a slide, anything a child's imagination desires!

Mud Pies and Other Recipes (Windslow, 2010) is another book that might serve to enhance socio-dramatic play as it details wonderfully imaginative recipes that could be created in a home corner, a restaurant or even in a witch's cauldron. This book may also be used to encourage new activities in sand play as the addition of a few simple resources (such as plates, spoons, bowls and bun trays) could inspire a kitchen or 'Sand Café' where the main ingredient is sand! A play dough area could provide another forum for imaginative baking, while also developing children's social and emotional skills, creativity, imagination, and fine motor skills (Swartz, 2005).

Fantasy play is another form of symbolic play that is similar to sociodramatic play but differs as it is focused on scenarios that are unrealistic and based in fantasy worlds, such as a fairy forest, a dragon's lair or Gotham City. However, children are often unsure how to develop narratives or plot lines beyond the recognition of being the character or 'chasing bad guys'. Children's literature, such as *Eliott: Midnight Superhero* (Cotringer, 2013), *Superhero* (Tauss, 2005) or *Super Daisy and the Peril of Planet Pea* (Gray, 2009), can provide a forum for discussion on the activities of superheroes and storylines that could be adopted and adapted during play sessions. The development of play narratives is an important pre-literacy skill as what may be enacted orally at this stage will develop the skills needed to construct written stories at a later stage. Here, literature can become a resource in developing 'mature play' (Leong & Bodrova, 2012), while also exposing children to new vocabulary such as 'laboratory', 'investigate', 'concealing one's identity' and 'top secret' (all taken from Tauss, 2005) that could be used meaningfully during play. While these books would work well to inspire fantasy role play, they might also enhance small world play focused on superheroes. Songs, poems and rhymes about superheroes might also further children's learning while still maintaining their interest (Sargent, 2015).

Play-based learning and the English language learner

Play provides an ELL with the 'risk-free' environment essential for the 'affective filter' (Krashen, 1985) to be open to language learning. As children generally play in small groups in nooks and corners around the classroom, the English language learner may feel more comfortable trying out the new vocabulary associated with the play situation in order to interact with peers in a positive manner. As children are interested and engaged in play, they are highly motivated to use any new words/phrases or language registers modelled by the teacher and their peers. Play also allows English language learners to experiment with written language in an accessible manner by creating resources that might complement their play (notes, signs, lists and so forth). Environmental print associated with various different play scenarios (such as signs, forms and authentic literature) will allow English language learners to become familiar with the English alphabet, and may prompt discussion in relation to the symbols used in their home language and how these differ from the English alphabet.

Key concepts for practice

- Play provides an engaging, 'risk-free' context for developing oral language, reading and writing skills for all children.

- Guided play has been found to be the most beneficial to young children in terms of enhancing literacy development.

- When planning for play, the teacher should consider what new vocabulary could be introduced and practised in the play scenario. The teacher should also pay careful attention to the props provided for the children as they can affect the children's depth of engagement and learning. Environmental print, writing materials and other literacy-related props should be modelled and encouraged during play.

- There are a number of roles that the teacher can adopt during play, depending on his or her purpose. Active involvement in some way (be it co-player, mediator or observer for assessment) is essential.

- Play should be assessed in a holistic manner.

- Children's literature can be used to enhance play in a variety of ways.

REFLECTION: THINKING ABOUT YOUR PRACTICE

- Do you currently implement a play-based curriculum? If you have, what have been the challenges and opportunities that this type of instruction has presented? If not, how would you go about adapting your classroom instruction to accommodate this type of practice?

- How would you enhance the development of literacy through play?

- How do you assess play in your school? Is this an area that needs further development?

For further exploration

Featherstone, S. (2001). *The little big book of role play*. London: Featherstone Education.

Moyles, J. (1989). *Just playing? The role and status of play in early childhood*. London: Open University Press.

Roskos, K.A. & Christie, J.F. (2000). *Play and literacy in early childhood*. Mahwah, NJ: Lawrence Erlbaum.

Zigler, E.F., Singer, D.G. & Bishop-Josef, S. (2005). *Children's play: The roots of reading*. Washington, DC: Zero to Three Press.

Bringing it all together . . .

GUIDING QUESTIONS FOR THIS CHAPTER

■ What does it mean to use meaningful contexts for early literacy instruction throughout a typical day in an early years classroom?

■ How can one design a classroom schedule that could incorporate the various approaches to reading, writing and oral language explored in this text?

Introduction

Tara teaches a class of 29 4- and 5-year-olds in a suburban school. A large portion of the class are English language learners. It is the second term, and the children are well settled into school and are very familiar with the classroom's routines. This extended classroom vignette attempts to illustrate how the various methodologies discussed thus far in the book might come together on a typical day in an early years classroom.

A Monday in February . . .

'One, two, three, four, come and sit down on the floor. Five, six, seven, eight, hurry up and don't be late!' the children sing as they assemble on the reading rug for the start of literacy block. The 4- and 5-year-olds transition to another song, 'Hello everybody, it's time to say, it's time to start a brand-new day. So wake it up, shake it up, give me five, give me ten, that's a wrap, let's begin.' Then 29 children are sitting cross-legged on the rug, arms folded with enthusiastic faces. 'Good morning everyone,' greets the teacher. 'Good morning, Tara,' they respond. 'Well, we've had a lot of cold and snowy weather lately, haven't we?' says Tara. 'Yes, I love it!' states Max. 'I don't, it makes my feet cold,' says Anna. 'We had a snowball fight yesterday, it was so much fun!' contributes John. 'Here's a song about the snow, I think you will really like this one, Anna,' smiles Tara, 'say each line after me!'

> The more it snows – tiddley pom,
> The more it goes – tiddley pom,
> On snowing!
> And nobody knows – tiddley pom,
> How cold my toes – tiddley pom,
> How cold my toes – tiddley pom,
> Are growing!

The children echo Tara's enthusiastic voice and laugh at 'tiddley pom'. 'That sounds crazy!' says Ibrahim. They recite it again in the same manner, developing their phonological awareness through the rhythm and rhyme of this amusing poem. 'Well, our big book this week is also about snow,' says Tara. 'It's called *The Snowy Day*.' The children lean towards the text enthusiastically as Tara places it on the easel. 'The author is Ezra Jack Keats; does anyone remember any other book we read by the same author?' Kendra raises her hand, '*Peter's Chair*, I think that was him.' 'Yes, it was,' responds Tara as she picks up *Peter's Chair* and holds it alongside *The Snowy Day* so that the children can see the author's name on both books. 'Hey,' says Max, 'is that Peter in this book too?' 'Let's read the blurb to check,' insists Ola. Tara reads the blurb, only to reveal that Peter is indeed the main character in this book. 'I wonder if Peter is in all his books?' queries Adellina. 'That's a good question,' says Tara. 'I will try to find some more books by this author to see if that's true.'

Greta displays the hand sign for making a prediction. 'Yes, Greta, what is your prediction?' asks Tara. 'I predict that he is gonna spend his whole day running about in the snow because the picture shows loads and loads of snow!' says Greta. 'I predict he will make snowmen and snowballs and snow angels because it says so in the blurb,' says John. 'I predict he'll be sad 'cause it looks like he has nobody to play with,' chimes in Maria. 'Great predictions, everyone,' says Tara. 'Today, we are going to learn a new strategy called making connections. When you read something in a book that reminds you of something from your own life, another book or something you may have seen on television, that is called a connection. When you have made a connection, you can show me by making a 'c' sign with your hand. I will demonstrate a few of my own connections and then you can give it go.' Tara starts reading the text and demonstrates some connections as she reads. For example, she says, 'Oh, I've got a connection! I love making footprints in the snow, especially if no one else has been there and you are the first to step on a garden of snow,' and 'Oh, I have a connection. I usually love snowball fights, except one time someone put a snowball down my neck, and that was horrible!' The children are enthusiastic about this strategy, and before long many are making the 'c' sign with their hands. Tara calls on a few students to share their connections. At one point, when there are a lot of 'c' signs held aloft, she encourages the children to share their thinking with their partner. The room is alive with discussion, and as they near the end of the book many make the 'p' sign to share predictions about the fate of the snowball placed in the pocket, and what the following morning might bring, weather-wise. As they finish reading, they share final connections, and Tara asks them to 'tell their partner' what it means to make connections. Then Ashra and Arvind share their thinking with the class, stating, 'Making connections is about reminders, like the story reminded me of getting wet socks from the snow like Peter did.' 'Thank you, Arvind and Ashra, that's a great way to describe connections,' responds Tara.

Next, Tara draws their attention to a flash card with the phoneme /ow/ on it. 'Now, you might have noticed that this letter sound was in the book quite a lot; it is the sound /ow/,' she says. 'Let's say it together – /ow/. What words in the book contained /ow/?' Ibrahim responds, 'Snow!' 'Yes,' says Tara, 'let's add that to our list,' noting it down on the chart paper. She opens the first page of the book. 'Now, everyone, put on your sound goggles and see if you can find any other words that have /ow/ in them on this page.' They hunt through the book in this manner and locate 'snowman', 'snowsuit', 'snowball' and 'slowly'. Tara adds them all to the list and draws illustrations beside the words to ensure that her English language learners can understand the words that they found. Tara adds some new words containing /ow/ for the children to decode, such as 'bow', 'low', 'bowl' and 'blow'. They read over the list and Tara teaches them a jingle about the sound /ow/, drawing their attention to the phonemes as they sing:

I see the snow,
I see the snow,
/s/, /n/, /ow/
I see the snow (to the tune of 'The Farmer's in the Dell')

Tara then presents the class with a flash card for the word 'he'. 'This is our new word – he,' she says. 'Let's see if we can find it in our book.' Tara uses an A3 acetate page so that the children can underline 'he' when it occurs in the book. They find 'he' numerous times in the book. Then they discuss the letters that 'he' contains and check to see how many syllables are in the word. Tara asks them to tell their partner a sentence that contains 'he', and then a number of children share their sentences with the class. 'Where will it go on the word wall?' asks Tara. 'It starts with /h/, so it has to go under it,' says Anna. Then Tara places it on the word wall. Tara concludes the lesson by asking the class what the new sound is, and they sing the /ow/ jingle again. They also sing

'The More it Snows' again with great enthusiasm. They then spend five minutes reviewing all letter sounds previously learned as individual sounds and blending them to form simple words. Then Tara leads the children in singing 'The Wheels on the Bus' as a transition to the next part of the literacy block – guided reading.

The children then walk to their reading groups, and on checking the chart the group leaders take the relevant activity box for their group. One group heads straight for the guided reading table, their books in tow, having seen 'the tigers' in the 'guided reading' position on the chart for today's first activity. Tara takes a minute to check on each group to ensure they understand their activity while the guided reading group read over their familiar text to themselves. Then she returns to the group and asks them what they thought about the story. 'It was good, I liked the bit where the bird knocks down all the apples,' says James. 'Yeah, me too,' says Adellina. 'I didn't know that birds liked apples,' says Emily. 'Me neither,' says Tara. 'Well, today we are going to read a new book called *Max Wants to Fly*.' 'I have a prediction,' says Adellina. 'I predict the bird will let him hop on his back, then he could fly.' Flora shrugs, 'Nah, I think he will jump on something high and the bird will catch him.' 'I wonder why a mouse would want to fly?' laughs James. 'Yes, it seems strange all right,' says Tara. They flip the book over and read the blurb together: 'Max tries to fly like Pecky. Find out what happens.' 'Hmmm, maybe he dreams that he turns into a bird,' says Emily.

As they take a 'picture walk' though the book, discussing the possible storyline, Tara pre-teaches a few unfamiliar words that might cause the children difficulty, such as 'wings', 'feathers', 'sky' and 'air', to help them read with fluency. She writes them on the board and reads the sentences that contain the words, pausing before each one to see if the children can use phonics, context or picture clues to help them figure out the word. They clap the syllables in the new words to aid memory and to develop phonological awareness. They locate a few examples of their new sight word 'he' to reinforce learning from today's shared reading session. Then the children start to 'whisper-read', turning up the volume when Tara leans in to hear each child. Having read the book, Tara asks the children if they can retell the story. She has a simple chart showing 'characters, setting, problem, solution' as a prompt. Adellina volunteers, stating, 'Max and Pecky were the characters, the setting was the marketplace, the problem was that he wanted to fly, and the solution was that he used feathers and balloons to help him fly.' Tara tells the children, 'I actually have a connection to this book. I always dream about being able to fly. I think it would be amazing but scary.' Daniel laughs, 'Me too, that would be awesome, but maybe not with crow feathers.' Tara points out the use of speech marks in the text and the children take turns being the narrator, the mouse and the crow in extracts that contain the characters speaking to each other. Finally, Tara asks the children if they noticed any words containing the new phoneme that they learned this morning. Emily raises her hand excitedly, 'Crow has /ow/ in it too!' 'We should add that to our chart!' says Daniel. 'Good idea!' agrees Tara.

Tara will take a second guided reading group now, and the same procedure will operate as before as the chart indicates what activity each group will participate in during the second slot today. All materials will be carefully tidied and returned before a second activity is begun. On the chart this week, Tara has a selection of fine motor development activities related to the theme of this week's big book. For example, 'snowball to snowman' is an activity where the children must use the tweezers to transfer cotton balls from a large tray to a template of a large snowman covered in glue. Using tweezers is challenging and will aid finger dexterity and hand–eye coordination. A popular activity is the creation of snowmen of various shapes and sizes using white play dough. A group near the sinks is painting a snow scene with 'Peter' playing in the snow. Another group has been given blackboards and chalk to experiment with. They are encouraged to draw, write or practise handwriting patterns. The 'lions' group is making alphabet puzzles of different shapes and sizes, while the 'pandas' group is engaged in a CVC word/picture matching game. Throughout the week, each group will have an opportunity to engage in most of these activities. While Tara works with two guided reading groups, her support teacher also takes two groups; one is a regular-sized group and the other is composed of children who have difficulty working in a group due to a range of issues, and so read on a one-to-one basis but partake in activities as a group. Having completed her session with both groups, Tara calls the class to attention by requesting that they all place their hands on their heads. As they do so, she circulates the room to inspect their work. She asks the pandas how they rate their engagement in their activities today. Arvind responds, 'Well, we worked pretty hard, though we had a bit of a fight over who got the new puzzle first, but then we figured it out, but we nearly got every puzzle completed.' Tara compliments him by saying, 'I'm glad you managed to work together as a team and concentrated well.' As the children begin to clean up, they all sing the 'Clean-Up Song' together.

When the classroom is tidy, the children gather on the rug again. They sing 'Twinkle Twinkle Little Star' as a transition. Then Tara draws their attention to the easel and begins, 'Good morning writers. Today I am going to write about . . . my dog. I'm going to draw him first. He has long ears and a waggly tail. I'll add labels for his ears and tail. His tongue is always hanging out. I'll label that too. I'll draw his lead because he loves walks. Now, I'll need to write something . . . hmm, I think I'll write "This is my dog" . . . well "this" is on our word wall. Can anyone point it out for me?' Jack offers to help. 'Thanks, Jack, let me write it down . . . now is "is" also on the word wall, Haritha can you point it out as well? And now I need "my," Ibrahim, can you point out "my" for me? . . . I think I can sound out dog, let me stretch it – /d/ . . . /o/ . . . /g/ . . . and a full stop. Now I'll write . . . "He is fun!" . . . Daniel, can you point out "he" for me? I already wrote it a minute ago, so I can copy from that . . . and "fun"? I think I can sound that out – /f/ . . . /u/ . . . /n/ . . . and a full stop. No, I want it to be more exciting than that, so I'll use an exclamation mark because I want it to sound like "He is fun!"' (shows a rising tone of excitement in her voice). 'Now I'll just make sure that my name and the date is on my piece of work before I start colouring in,' and Tara finishes her writing and rereads it to the class. Then she turns the page of the flip chart so that her writing is no longer visible. 'Put on your thinking caps, everyone. What do you think you would like to write about today?' Tara pauses for a minute or two. 'Now turn to your buddy and tell them what you will write about.' As the children chat to their peers, Tara circulates, listening in and commenting on their ideas. A few children share their ideas to the larger group, then they all return to their seats, where their writing folders and pencils are waiting.

The children spend around 15 minutes writing. As they write, Tara and the language support teacher circulate, armed with clipboards. Having settled the class into writing, they conference with four or five target children, taking notes on the children's progress or any difficulties that they might be experiencing. Then the children reassemble on the rug and some children are invited to share their work. Tara keeps a careful record of who shares so that everyone gets a chance to share regularly if they are happy to do so. Before Eddie shares his piece, Tara reminds the children to listen carefully to his writing as they will have to tell him what it is about when he is finished and will also be expected to ask some questions about his piece. Eddie reads his piece about his birthday present: 'It was my birthday on Friday. I got a new bicycle that is really fast. I also had a big cake.' When he finishes reading, he turns to his audience expectantly and hands shoot up. He calls on Greta first: 'It was about your birthday.'' Then Daniel: 'You got a bike, a fast one, like mine.' Then Adellina: 'And cake.' 'Thanks guys, now questions,' says Eddie, enjoying being centre stage. 'Who gave you the bike?' asks Flora. 'My mum and dad,' responds Eddie. 'Where did you ride it?' asks Arvind. 'Oh, just up and down my street,' replies Eddie. 'I have a connection', says Tara, showing the 'c' sign with her hand. 'I got a bike for my birthday too, though it probably isn't as fast as your one, Eddie!' Eddie smiles, 'Probably not, I go turbo speed!' Two other children have opportunities to share in a similar manner. Tara asks them how they rate their writing today: 'Was it "thumbs up/I did my very best work", "thumbs to the side/I was a little distracted" or "thumbs down/I was very distracted"?' She calls on a child who has 'thumbs up'. 'Maria, tell me about your work today.' Maria smiles, 'Use the word . . . made big story.' 'Great job,' says Tara. 'I added lots of detail,' adds Momen. The children quickly put their folders back into their colour-coded boxes and the table leader hands them to Tara. When the classroom is tidy, they leave the classroom to play outside.

Later in the day, after an active maths lesson that began with a read-aloud of *Mouse Shapes* (Stoll Walsh, 2009) and a rhyme about triangles, the children participate in guided play. This session begins by convening the children on the rug. The children's attention is drawn to the guided play chart on the wall to remind them where their designated play space is today. Tara also reminds them of the choice areas available this week (storytelling, reading corner, writing table and puzzle place). She asks the children to huddle in their groups to discuss how they will play today. The children arrange themselves so that their knees are touching, which helps form a tight circle suitable for discussion. Tara and the support teacher circulate to 'listen in' and scaffold their ideas. After a few minutes, Tara asks the groups to share their plans. The red group volunteers first. 'Well, I haven't had a go at being the vet yet, so I am going to have the first go today, and Maria is going to be my assistant,' announces Ashra. Momen chimes in, stating, 'Daniel is going to be the receptionist, and Eddie and Jack have heaps of sick pets, so we'll be very busy.' 'Wonderful,' responds Tara. 'What sort of equipment will you be using, Ashra?' 'Well, I'll need lots of medicines and injections, and maybe a thermometer if the dogs have a fever,' responds Ashra. 'Will you listen to their heartbeat?' asks Tara. 'Yes I'll use that thing.' 'The stethoscope?' says Tara. 'Yes, the stethoscope,' says Ashra. 'That's a hard word to remember,' says Tara. 'Let's clap it out together . . . ste/the/scope.' The green group also share their plans. 'We were thinking that we would make houses for the different animals that we have,' reports John. 'Yes,' says Kendra, 'I'm making a little house for the brown cuddly doggie and Adellina is going to make a hotel for the cats.' 'Great ideas,' says Tara, 'I better let you all get to work!'

The children move towards the different play areas and begin playing. At first, Tara circulates to all the different centres to ensure everyone is content and engaged. Then she focuses on her target groups for the day. She will spend the first 10 minutes interacting with the water play group, discussing the various sea animals that they are playing with in the water. Then she will move to the block area to investigate the building of animal homes. Finally, she will spend some time with the junk art group to discuss their various projects. As she works with the groups, she takes a few photographs for discussion later. The support teacher will work with the children in the sociodramatic play area and the small world area. He will also work with two target children who need additional support with language acquisition. The children play happily for about 45 minutes; some choose to visit the choice stations, while others remain engrossed in one activity. Tara then asks them to pause play and to tidy up. She loads the photos onto the interactive whiteboard (IWB).

They return to the rug when everything is tidy for a review session. 'First of all, let's all turn to our partner and tell a little bit about how we played today,' says Tara. The room is filled with excited conversation. Then Tara displays the first image. 'Who can tell me what sort of play was happening here?' she asks. James raises his hand proudly. 'I was constructing a helicopter from cardboard. It was tricky, so I needed a bit of help, and John gave me a hand.' 'How did you make it?' asks Tara. 'Well, I got a big box and a small box and stuck them together, then I cut up some cardboard to make the things that spin around.' 'The rotors?' asks Tara. 'Yes, the rotors,' says James. 'Then I got a long skinny box for the tail and put another rotor on it.' Tara displays another image. 'What's going on here?' she asks. Oscar raises his hand. 'That's Sea World. We were making a show with all the animals doing tricks. They were jumping through hoops and doing flips. It was cool!' 'Yeah,' says Ibrahim, 'I had the killer whale and he was swimming very deep.' 'Have you been to Sea World?' asks Tara. 'No,' says Oscar, 'but I saw it on TV before.' Then they look at another image. 'Nina, can you tell me about this?' 'Me help Ashra, dog is . . . is . . .' 'Sick?' asks Tara. 'Yes, he sick.' 'Did you make him better?' asks Tara. 'Yes, better . . . medicine better,' says Nina.

Later in the day, Tara reads *Mog and the V.E.T.* (Kerr, 2005), *The ABC's of Snowflakes* (Lee, 2014), *There Was an Old Lady Who Swallowed Some Snow* (Colandro, 2003) and some poems from *The National Geographic Book of Animal Poetry* (Lewis, 2012) aloud. They go to the gym for physical education, where their warm-up involves pretending to throw snowballs, make snowmen and snow angels. They even pretend to be snowflakes in a blizzard. This thematic approach (a dual focus on snowy weather and animals) helps ELLs learn new vocabulary, but also engages all children in its multifaceted approach to learning. The children sing songs during transitions, including their favourite 'Goodbye Song' before they leave for the day.

Key concepts for practice

- A literacy block can contain shared reading, guided reading/literacy centres and a writers' workshop.

- Literacy skills can be developed throughout the day by using rhymes, songs and teacher read-alouds between lessons and during lessons across the curriculum.

- Provide frequent opportunities for children to talk in pairs, individually with the teacher, in small groups, or as part of a whole-class discussion.

- A thematic approach tends to engage children, focuses your teaching and enables ELLs to learn vocabulary in a variety of contexts.

FINAL REFLECTION: THINKING ABOUT YOUR PRACTICE

■ How will your reading of this book influence your future practice?

■ If you are restricted by curriculum or school policies, how might you adapt some of the ideas in this book to suit your context?

For further exploration

Cunningham, P. & Allington, R. (2015). *Classrooms that work: They can all read and write.* New York: Pearson.

Kennedy, E., Dunphy, L., Dwyer, B., Hayes, G., McPhilips, T., Marsh, J., O'Connor, M. & Shiel, G. (2012). *Literacy in early childhood and primary education.* NCCA Research Report, no. 15. Dublin: NCCA.

Routman, R. (2000). *Conversations: Strategies for teaching, learning and evaluating.* Portsmouth, NH: Heinemann.

Appendix A

Recommended read-aloud books

Beaty, A. (2007). *Iggy Peck: Architect*. London: Harry N. Abrams.

Browne, A. (2003). *Things I like*. London, UK: Walker Books.

Browne, A. (2011). *How do you feel?* London, UK: Walker Books.

Burningham, J. (1999). *Oi! Get off our train*. London: Red Fox.

Carle, E. (2010). *The bad-tempered ladybird*. London: Puffin.

Crebbin, J. (1996). *The train ride*. London: Walker Books.

Crews, D. (2010). *Freight train*. New York: HarperCollins.

Donaldson, J. (2016). *Tabby McTat*. London: Alison Greene Books.

Gray, K. (2009). *Daisy and the trouble with kittens*. London: Red Fox.

Hutchins, P. (2007). *Rosie's walk*. London: Random House.

James, S. (2004). *Baby brains*. London: Walker Books.

Jeffers, O. (2012). *Stuck*. London: HarperCollins.

Kalan, R. & Crews, D. (1992). *Blue sea*. New York: Mulberry Books.

Kerr, J. (2018). *The tiger who came to tea*. London: HarperCollins.

Klassen, J. (2014). *This is not my hat*. London: Walker Books.

McKee, D. (2015). *Not now Bernard*. London: Andersen Press.

Novak, B.J. (2014). *The book with no pictures*. London: Random House.

Rosen, M. (2013). *Even my ears are smiling*. London: Bloomsbury.

Smith, M. (2013). *The hundred decker bus*. London: Macmillan.

Stoll Walsh, E. (1989). *Mouse paint*. Orlando, FL: Red Wagon Books.

Stoll Walsh, E. (1991). *Mouse count*. New York: Houghton Mifflin.

Tullet, H. (2010). *Press here*. San Francisco, CA: Chronicle Books.

Tullet, H. (2011). *The game of finger worms*. San Francisco, CA: Chronicle Books.

Willis, J. (2018). *Tadpole's promise*. London: Andersen Press.

Appendix B

Poems and rhymes for the early years classroom

(Tune: 'Frère Jacques')
Hello... (child's name) Hello...
How are you? How are you?
Glad you came to school today. Glad you came to school today.
Please shake my hand. Please shake my hand. (shake child's hand)

Two little hands go clap, clap, clap,
Two little feet go tap, tap, tap,
One little body turns around,
One little child sits quietly down.

Rain, rain go away,
Come again another day.
All the children want to play!

Pat-a-cake, pat-a-cake,
Baker's man!
Bake me a cake as fast
As you can.
Roll it and pat it and mark it
With B.
Put it in the oven for baby and me!

Jack and Jill went up the hill
To fetch a pail of water.
Jack fell down and broke his crown,
And Jill came tumbling after!

I'm a little teapot,
Short and stout.
Here's my handle,
Here's my spout.
When the tea is ready
Then I shout,
Tip me up and pour me out!

1, 2, tie my shoe
3, 4, shut the door
5, 6, pick up sticks
7, 8, lay them straight
9, 10, a big fat hen.
Let's get up and count again!

Five little monkeys jumping on the bed
One fell off and bumped his head
Mama called the doctor
And the doctor said,
'No more monkeys jumping on the bed!'
Four little monkeys jumping on the bed
Three little monkeys jumping on the bed (and so forth).

Here is the beehive, where are the bees?
Hidden away were nobody sees
Watch and you will see them come out of their hives,
One, two, three, four, five,
Buzz, buzz, buzz.

(Tune: Old MacDonald)
Here we are at school today.
Happy as can be!
We are here to work and here to play.
Happy as can be!
With a clap clap here, clap clap there,
Here a clap, there a clap,
Everywhere a clap clap.
Here we are at school today.
Happy as can be!

There were ten in a bed and the little one said,
'Roll over, roll over.'

So they all rolled over and one fell out.
There were nine in the bed and the little one said,
'Roll over, roll over.'
So they all rolled over and one fell out . . .
*(This is repeated until you get to the number one. Each time 'roll over' is said,
the rolling motion is dramatised)*
There was one in the bed and the little one said,
'Good night!'

One, two, three, four, five,
Once I caught a fish alive.
Six, seven, eight, nine, ten,
Then I let it go again.
Why did you let it go?
Because it bit my finger so.
Which finger did it bite?
This little finger on the right.

Once I saw a little bird
Come hop, hop, hop;
So I cried, 'Little bird,
Will you stop, stop, stop?'
I was going to the window
To say, 'How do you do?'
But then he shook his little tail,
And far away he flew.

Right foot, left foot, see me go.
I am grey and big and slow.
I come walking down the street
With my trunk and four big feet.

Five little monkeys
Sitting in a tree
Teasing Mr. Crocodile
'You can't catch me.'
'You can't catch me.'
Along comes Mr. Crocodile
As quiet as can be
SNAP!!!
(Continue until all monkeys are gone)
Away swims Mr. Crocodile
As full as he can be!!!

Miss Polly had a dolly who was sick, sick, sick.
So she called for the doctor to come quick, quick, quick.
The doctor came with his bag and his hat
And he knocked on the door with a rat-a-tat-tat.
He looked at the dolly and he shook his head
And he said, 'Miss Polly, put her straight to bed!'
He wrote on a paper for some pills, pills, pills
'I'll be back in the morning with my bill, bill, bill.'

This old man, he played one
He played knick-knack on my thumb
Knick-knack paddywhack, give your dog a bone
This old man came rolling home
This old man, he played two
He played knick-knack on my shoe
Knick-knack paddywhack, give your dog a bone
This old man came rolling home
This old man, he played three
He played knick-knack on my knee
Knick-knack paddywhack, give your dog a bone
This old man came rolling home
This old man, he played four
He played knick-knack on my door
Knick-knack paddywhack, give your dog a bone
This old man came rolling home
This old man, he played five
He played knick-knack on my hive
Knick-knack paddywhack, give your dog a bone
This old man came rolling home

Pizza on the table,
Pizza on the chair,
Pizza on the ceiling,
Pizza on my hair.
Pizza on my fingers,
Pizza on my toes,
Pizza on my chinny-chin,
Pizza on my nose.
Pizza on the table,
Pizza on the chair,
Pizza on the ceiling,
Pizza everywhere!

Appendix C

Running record and miscue analysis

Running record

Name: _____   Date: _____

Text: _____   Words: _____

Errors: _____   Self-corrections: _____

Accuracy rate: _____%

Level: _____

Self-correction rate: _____

Page number	Errors	SC tally	Error tally

Miscue analysis

Word	Error	Meaning (relying on semantics alone)	Syntax (relying on grammar rules from oral language)	Visual (relying on phonic knowledge)	Is it a sight word?
home	house	x			
they	them				x
read	read			x	
asked	said	x			
was	saw				x
shaft	shop	x			
policeman	police	x			
one	on				x
box	boy	x			

Appendix D

Comprehension hand signs

Figure D.1 Connection

Figure D.2 Prediction

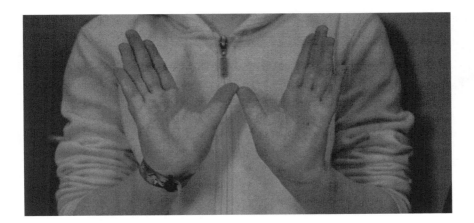

Figure D.3 Wonder (question)

Figure D.4 Clarify

Figure D.5 Visualise

Appendix E

Shared reading lesson plan

Text: We're Going on a Bear Hunt (Rosen, 1996)

Resources: *We're Going on a Bear Hunt* big book, flash card of 'b', flash card of 'to', Post-its of 'to', retelling visuals, letter swatter, play dough, templates, copybooks, pencils

Before reading:

■ Ensure children are sitting comfortably on the rug in a designated spot.

■ Share the learning intentions with the children: 'Today we are going to read a new big book called *We're Going on a Bear Hunt*. We will make predictions and learn how to retell the story. We will talk about some of the words in the book and learn a new sound.'

■ Introduce the book to the children. Read the title and the blurb. Point out the author and the illustrator and discuss their roles. Model a prediction (e.g. 'Where could you hunt for a bear? Hmm, I think I would look in a forest. I predict that maybe they will go to a forest'). Encourage the children to share their ideas with a partner and then with the whole class. Read the book.

Key questions:

■ What does an author/illustrator do?

■ Where could you hunt for a bear? What predictions do you have about this 'hunt'?

During reading:

■ Draw the children's attention to the author's use of exclamation marks and the effect they have on reading.

■ After a few pages, invite the children to participate in 'echo reading' for the refrain (We're going . . . scared) that includes exclamation marks. Encourage the children to do actions for different parts of the book so that they stay actively involved.

■ Discuss the following vocabulary during the reading: 'over', 'under', 'through'; 'thick', 'oozy'; 'stumble', 'trip'; 'narrow', 'gloomy'; 'tiptoe'. Perform actions or examine the pictures to demonstrate understanding.

■ Ask the children, 'Can you remember some of the places that the family went? Tell your partner.' Then a few pairs will share their thinking.

Key questions:

■ What do you think _____ might mean (tier 2 vocabulary)?

■ Can you remember some of the places that the family went? Tell your partner.

After reading (skill development):

■ Focus the children's attention on the sequencing cards. Encourage them to discuss the correct order with a partner. Order them as a whole class. Encourage the children to use the language of retelling (e.g. first they . . . then . . . after that . . . finally).

■ Introduce the new sight word 'to'. Ask the children to find 'to' in the book. Match each 'to' with a Post-it of 'to'. Discuss the word length, syllables and where to place it on the word wall. Ask the children to create oral sentences using 'to'.

■ Show the children a card with the letter 'b' on it. Explain that this letter makes the sound /b/. Ask them if there was any word in the book that started with /b/. Search for words starting with /b/ in the book (e.g. 'bear', 'beautiful, 'big'). The children will highlight the letter 'b' on the page with the letter swatter. Write these words on a chart.

■ Teach the children the Jolly Phonics song for /b/.

■ Skywrite /b/.

■ The children should return to their seats and construct the letter 'b' out of play dough using a template to help them (they will be encouraged to make a few). As they create the letters, circulate and ask the children to trace the letter with their finger while making the sound.

■ Demonstrate how to write the letter on the board.

- The children will open their copybooks and write 'b' and draw a bear.

- Play the /b/ song while they write (monitor their work for correct formation).

Key questions:

- What happened first . . . (then, after that, finally)?

- Can you find 'to' in the story? How many letters are in 'to'? What sounds are in 'to'? 'Where will it go on the word wall? Can you make a sentence with 'to' in it?

- Can you see a word that starts with 'b' in the story?

- What sound does this letter make?

- How do we write it?

Recap and closure:

- Who can tell me something about our story today?'

- What was our new word today?

- Who remembers this sound? Let's all say the sound while we write it in the air.

- Can you tell me any words that start with /b/?

Appendix F

Useful tools for fine motor development

- tweezers or bubble tongs

- hole punch

- clothes pegs

- stickers

- droppers

- plastic syringes

- spoons of various sizes

- play dough

- nuts and bolts

- pegboards and pegs

- glue sticks

- beads and thread

- kinetic sand

- cookie cutters

- pipe cleaners

- colanders

- magnets

- buttons

- theraputty
- jigsaw puzzles
- wooden blocks
- pom-poms
- cotton wool balls
- tongs

Appendix G

Guided reading record form

Reading record: please fill in this log every night.

Title:	Date:	Signed:	Comment:

Appendix H

Writers' workshop lesson plan

Lesson focus: adjectives (craft lesson)

Resources: chart paper with teacher's story, markers, writing folders, pencils, author's chair, date stamp

Introduction (whole-class mini-lesson):

Ensure children are sitting comfortably on the rug (in an assigned spot).

Explain: 'Yesterday we found some great adjectives in *Handa's Surprise*. Can anyone read some of the adjectives that we found from our adjective wall?' . . . 'Why did the author use adjectives in her story?' . . . 'Today I am going to show you how to add adjectives to your writing using my own story and then you can try to use some in your writing today.'

Demonstrate: 'I wrote this story a few weeks ago, you might remember it.' The teacher reads over the text. 'I was reading it again last night and I thought that I really should add some adjectives to make my story more interesting'. The teacher reads the first line. 'Once upon a time a monster lived in a cave' . . . 'I think I can add some adjectives here to make it more interesting, like instead of just monster, I could write "a huge purple monster" (writes the adjectives using a caret to insert the extra information). Since I am adding extra information, I'll use a caret to show were those words go. Now, a cave sounds a little boring, maybe I could write "a dark spooky cave" instead using a caret.' The teacher reads a few more sentences in this manner.

Guided practice: 'Turn and talk to your partner about what adjectives I should use in this sentence.' The teacher gives children time to come up with suggestions and then adds them to the text.

Set expectation: The teacher tells the children to return to their seats and try to add adjectives to their story today.

Key questions: What adjectives can we use to make this sentence more interesting?

Development (writing/conferences)

Independent practice: Children are sitting at their seats, working on their stories. *Children will choose their own topics to write about.*

The teacher settles anyone who needs assistance (one to two minutes). Date stamp all work at the beginning of the session.

Using a conference schedule, the teacher sits with four to six children and conferences with them individually at their seats. (If you have in-class support, the support teacher should also use a conference schedule and conference with four to six other children. You should both try to meet with every child at least once every four to five days.)

Keep a record and note what children are experiencing success and having difficulty with.

Date children's work at the end of the session (this will allow you to assess the quantity of work produced in each session and across sessions).

Key questions/comments:

- Tell me about your story.

- Can you tell me about the adjectives that you used in your story?

- I like the way you . . .

Conclusion (share session, reflect and set goals):

Ask the children to come over and sit in their assigned spot on the rug.

Invite children to share: choose only those who want to share.

Keep a record of who shared their story and any observations.

Set an expectation: 'Today I want to listen carefully to _____'s story and be able to tell them what it was about. I also want you to listen to see if they used any adjectives in their work.'

Celebrate any attempts to use adjectives (relate feedback to mini-lesson taught).

Provide any other appropriate specific praise to the authors for their work today.

Reflect and set goals: What skill were we trying to use today in our writing? Why do authors use adjectives? How will we continue to use this skill?

Key questions:

- What was the story about?

- What adjectives did you notice?

- What skill were we trying to use today in our writing? Why do authors use adjectives? How will we continue to use this skill?

Appendix I

Writers' workshop planning grids

Narrative

Characters	Setting
Problem	**Solution**

Recount

Who?	What?	When?	Where?

Appendix J

Conferencing record form

	Name	Comment/needs
Monday		
Tuesday		
Wednesday		
Thursday		
Friday		

Appendix K

Sharing record form

Date	Name	Title	Comment

Appendix L

Recommended websites

www.readingrockets.org
www.readwritethink.org
http://whattheteacherwants.blogspot.ie
http://lessonplansos.blogspot.ie
www.theottoolbox.com
www.kidsplaysmarter.com
www.handwritingwithkatherine.com
www.theimaginationtree.com
www.storyjumper.com
www.rif.org

References

Adams, M.J. (1990). *Beginning to read: Thinking and learning about print*. Cambridge, MA: MIT Press.

Alanis, I. (2007). Developing literacy through culturally relevant texts. *Social Studies and the Young Learner*, 20(1), 29–32.

Allen, J. (2002). *On the same page: Shared reading beyond the primary grades*. Portland, ME: Stenhouse.

Anderson, R.C., Hiebert, E.H., Scott, J.A. & Wilkinson, I.A.G. (1985). *Becoming a nation of readers: The report of the Commission on Reading*. Washington, DC: National Institute of Education.

Armbruster, B.B., Lehr, F. & Osbourne, J. (2001). *Put reading first: The research building blocks for teaching children to read – kindergarten through grade 3*. Washington, DC: Partnership for Reading.

Au, K.H. (1997). A sociocultural model of reading instruction: The Kamehameha elementary education program. In S.A. Stahl (Ed.), *Instructional models in reading* (pp. 181–202). Hillsdale, NJ: Erlbaum.

Avalos, A.M., Plasencia, A., Chavez, C. & Rascón, J. (2007). Modified guided reading: Gateway to English as a second language and literacy learning. *The Reading Teacher*, 61(4), 318–329.

Bear, D.R., Invernizzi, M., Templeton, S. & Johnston, F. (2012). *Words their way: Word study for phonics, vocabulary and spelling instruction* (5th ed.). Boston, MA: Pearson.

Beck, I. (2006). *Making sense of phonics: The hows and the whys*. New York: Guilford Press.

Beck, I. & Juel, C. (1995). The role of decoding in learning to read. *American Educator*, 19(2), 21–25.

Beck, I., McKeown, M. & Kucan, L. (2002). *Bringing words to life: Robust vocabulary instruction*. New York: Guilford Press.

Beery, K. (1992). *Visual motor abilities*. Cleveland, OH: Modern Curriculum Press.

Bell, N. (1997). *Visualising and verbalising: For language comprehension and thinking*. Avila Beach, CA: NanciBell.

Benjamin, R. & Schwanenflugel, P.J. (2010). Text complexity and oral reading prosody of young readers. *Reading Research Quarterly*, 45(4), 388–404.

Berninger, V. (2012). *Evidence-based, developmentally appropriate writing skills K–5: Teaching the orthographic loop of working memory to write letters so developing writers can spell words and express ideas.* Presented at Handwriting in the 21st Century? An Educational Summit, Washington, DC, 23 January 2012. Available at: www.hw21summit.com/researchberninger.

Bialystok, E. (2001). *Bilingualism in development: Language, literacy and cognition.* Cambridge: Cambridge University Press.

Bialystok, E., Mujumder, S. & Martin, M. (2003). Developing phonological awareness: Is there a bilingual advantage? *Applied Psycholinguistics,* 24, 27–44.

Bissex, G. (1980). *Gnys at Wrk: A child learns to read and write.* Cambridge, MA: Harvard University Press.

Blevins, W. (2006). *Phonics from A to Z.* New York: Scholastic.

Block, C.C. & Pressley, M. (2002). *Comprehension instruction: Research-based best practices.* New York: Guilford Press.

Bryant, P. (1993). Phonological aspects of learning to read. In R. Beard (Ed.), *Teaching literacy, balancing perspectives* (pp. 83–94). London: Hodder & Stoughton.

Byrnes, J. & Wasik, B. (2009). *Language and literacy development.* New York: Guilford Press.

Burns, M.S., Griffin, P. & Snow, C.E. (1999). *Starting out right: A guide to promoting children's reading success.* Washington, DC: National Academy Press.

Calkins, L. (1986). *The art of teaching writing.* Portsmouth, NH: Heinemann.

Calkins, L. & Mermelstein, L. (2010). Launching the writing workshop. Portsmouth, NH: Heinemann.

Chall, J. (1967). *Learning to read: The great debate.* New York: McGraw-Hill.

Chall, J. (1996). *Stages of reading development.* New York: McGraw-Hill.

Chall, J.S., Jacobs, V.A. & Baldwin, L.E. (1990). *The reading crisis: Why poor children fall behind.* Cambridge, MA: Harvard University Press.

Chamot, A.U. & O'Malley, J.M. (1994). *The CALLA handbook: How to implement the Cognitive Academic Language Learning Approach.* Reading, MA: Addison-Wesley.

Chanko, P. (2014). *Levelled poems for small group reading lessons.* New York: Scholastic.

Chomsky, C. (1972). Stages in language development and reading exposure. *Harvard Educational Review,* 42, 1–33.

Clay, M. (1993). *Reading recovery: A guidebook for teachers in training.* Portsmouth, NH: Heinemann.

Clay, M. (1998). *By different paths to common outcomes.* York, ME: Stenhouse.

Clay, M. (2006). *An observation survey of early literacy achievement* (2nd ed.). Portsmouth, NH: Heinemann.

Combs, S.G.P. (2010). The effects of information sharing and modelling on teacher talk and children's language during dramatic play. *Dissertation Abstracts International Section B: The Sciences and Engineering,* 70, 2010-99040-016.

Culham, R. (2005). *6 + 1 traits in writing: The complete guide for the primary grades.* New York: Scholastic.

Cummins, J. (2003). Reading and the bilingual student: Fact and friction. In G.G. Garcia (Ed.), *English learners: Reaching the highest level of English literacy* (pp. 2–33). Newark, DE: International Reading Association.

Cummins, J. & Swain, M. (2014). *Bilingualism in education.* London: Routledge.

Cunningham, P. (1990). The names test: A quick assessment of decoding ability. *The Reading Teacher,* 44, 124–129.

Cunningham, P. (1998). *Making words.* Portsmouth, NH: Heinemann.

Cunningham, P. (2004). *Phonics they use: Words for reading and writing.* Upper Saddle River, NJ: Pearson.

Cunningham, P. & Cunningham, J. (2002). What we know about how to teach phonics. In A. Farstrup & S. Samuels (Eds.), *What research has to say about reading instruction* (pp. 87–109). Newark, DE: International Reading Association.

Dole, J.A. (2003). Professional development in reading comprehension instruction. In A. Sweet & C. Snow (Eds.), *Rethinking reading comprehension* (pp. 176–191). New York: Guilford Press.

Dole, J.A., Duffy, G.G., Roehler, L.R. & Pearson, D.D. (1991). Moving from the old to the new: Research on reading comprehension instruction. *Review of Educational Research*, 61(2), 239–264.

Dorn, L. & Soffos, C. (2001). *Scaffolding young writers: A writers' workshop approach.* Portland, ME: Stenhouse.

Duffy, G. (2002). The case for the direct explanation of strategies. In C.C. Block & M. Pressley (Eds.), *Comprehension instruction: Research-based best practices* (pp. 28–41). New York: Guilford Press.

Duke, N.K. & Pearson, P.D. (2002). Effective practices for developing reading comprehension. In A.E. Farstrup & S.J. Samuels (Eds.), *What research has to say about reading instruction* (pp. 40–65). Newark, DE: International Reading Association.

Dyson, A. (1989). *Multiple worlds of child writers: Friends learning to write.* New York: Teachers College Press.

Edwards, C.P. & Gandini, L. (2015). Teacher research in Reggio Emilia: Essence of a dynamic, evolving role. *Voices of Practitioners: Teacher Research in Early Childhood Education*, 10, 89–103.

Ehri, L. (1992). Reconceptualising the development of sight word reading and its relationship to recoding. In P.B. Gough, L.C. Erhi & R. Treiman (Eds.), *Reading acquisition* (pp. 133–147). Hillsdale, NJ: Erlbaum.

Ehri, L. & Nunes, S. (2002). The role of phonemic awareness in learning to read. In A. Farstrup & S. Samuels (Eds.), *What the research has to say about reading instruction* (3rd ed., pp. 110–139). Newark, DE: International Reading Association.

Ellis, R. (2005). Principles of instructed language learning. *System*, 33(2), 209–224.

Elster, C.A. & Hanauer, D.I. (2002). Voicing texts, voices around texts: Reading poems in elementary school classrooms. *Research in the Teaching of English*, 37(1), 89–134.

Excelsa, C.T. (2014). Teacher's interaction styles during sociodramatic play that promote reading and writing among pre-schoolers. *Social Science Diliman*, 10(2), 56–99.

Fisher, D., Frey, N. & Lapp, D. (2011). Shared readings: Modelling comprehension, vocabulary, text structures, and text features for older readers. *The Reading Teacher*, 61(7), 548–556.

Fisher, K.R., Hirsh-Pasek, K., Golinkoff, R.M., Singer, D.G. & Berk, L.E. (2010). Playing around in school: Implications for learning and educational policy. In A.D. Pellegrini (Ed.), *The Oxford handbook of the development of play* (pp. 341–360). New York: Oxford University Press.

Fletcher, R. & Portalupi, J. (2001). *Craft lessons: Teaching writing K–8.* Portland, ME: Stenhouse.

Fountas, I. & Pinnell, G.S. (1996). *Guiding readers and writers: Grades 3–6.* Portsmouth, NH: Heinnemann.

Fox, M. (2008). *Reading magic: Why reading aloud to our children will change their lives forever.* New York: Mariner Books.

Freeman, M. (2003). *Teaching the youngest writers: A practical guide.* Gainesville, FL: Maupin House.

Frith, U. (1980). Unexpected spelling problems. In U. Frith (Ed.), *Cognitive processes in spelling* (pp. 495–515). London: Academic Press.

Fung, I., Wilkinson, I. & Moore, D. (2003). L1-assisted reciprocal teaching to improve ESL students' comprehension of English expository text. *Learning and Instruction*, 13, 1–31.

Gambrell, L.B. & Bales, R. (1986). Mental imagery and the comprehension performance of fourth and fifth grade poor readers. *Reading Research Quarterly*, 11(1), 454–464.

Gambrell, L.B. & Koskinen, P.S. (2001). Imagery: A strategy for enhancing comprehension. In C.C. Block & M. Pressley (Eds.), *Comprehension instruction: Research-based best practices* (pp. 305–318). New York: Guilford Press.

Gentry, R. (1981). Learning to spell developmentally. *The Reading Teacher*, 34(1), 378–381.

Gentry, R. (2006). *Breaking the code: The new science of reading and writing*. Portsmouth, NH: Heinemann.

Gillet, J. & Lynn, B. (2001). *Directing the writing workshop: An elementary teacher's handbook*. New York: Guilford Press.

Graves, D. (1989). *Writing: Teachers and children at work*. Portsmouth, NH: Heinemann.

Graves, D. (1994). *A fresh look at writing*. Portsmouth, NH: Heinemann.

Gray, C. & Ryan, A. (2016). Aistear vis-à-vis the primary school curriculum: the experiences of early years teachers in Ireland. *International Journal of Early Years Education*, 24(2), 188–205.

Gruetman, H. (2017). *The basics of fine motor skills: Developmental activities for kids*. London: CreateSpace Independent Publishing.

Hall, N. (1987). *The emergence of literacy*. Portsmouth, NH: Heinemann.

Harris, A.J. & Sipay, E.R. (1990). *How to increase reading ability* (8th ed.) New York: Longman.

Harris, T.H. & Hodges, R.E. (1981). *A dictionary of reading and related terms*. Newark, DE: International Reading Association.

Harrison, C. (2004). *Understanding reading development*. London: Sage.

Hayes, J. (2004). A new framework for understanding cognition and affect in writing. In R. Ruddell & N.J. Unrau (Eds.), *Theoretical models and processes of reading* (5th ed., pp. 1399–1430). Newark, DE: International Reading Association.

Helman, L. (2004). Building on the sound system of Spanish. *The Reading Teacher*, 57(1), 452–460.

Hirsh-Pasek, K., Golinkoff, R.M., Berk, L.E. & Singer, D.G. (2008). *A mandate for playful learning in preschool: Applying the scientific evidence*. New York: Oxford University Press.

Holdaway, D. (1979). *The foundations of literacy*. Toronto: Aston Scholastic.

Holt, N. (2010). *Bringing the HighScope approach to your early years practice*. New York: Routledge.

Invernizzi, M. & Tortorelli, L.S. (2013). Phonological awareness and alphabetic knowledge, the foundations of early reading. In D. Barone & M. Malette (Eds.), *Best practices in early literacy instruction* (pp. 15–174). New York: Guilford Press.

Juel, C. (1988). Learning to read and write: A longitudinal study of children in first and second grade. *Journal of Educational Psychology*, 78, 243–255.

Jung, J. & Recchia, S. (2013). Scaffolding infants play through empowering and individualising teaching practices. *Early Education & Development*, 24(6), 829–850.

Kennedy, E., Dunphy, L., Dwyer, B., Hayes, G., McPhilips, T., Marsh, J., O'Connor, M. & Shiel, G. (2012). *Literacy in early childhood and primary education*. NCCA Research Report, no. 15. Dublin: NCCA.

Kernan, M. (2007). *Play as a context for early learning and development*. Dublin: NCCA.

Kintsch, W. (1994). The construction-integration model of text comprehension and its implications for instruction. In R.B. Ruddell & N.J. Unrau (Eds.), *Theoretical models and processes of reading* (5th ed., pp. 1270–1328). Newark, DE: International Reading Association.

Knox, C. & Amador-Watson, C. (2002). *Responsive instruction for success in English (RISE): Building literacy and content knowledge with English language learners – participant's resource notebook and reading booklet*. Barrington, IL: Rigby Professional Development.

Koskinen, P.S., Blum, I.H., Bisson, S.A., Phillips, S.M., Creamer, T.S. & Baker, T.K. (1999). Shared reading, books, and audiotapes: Supporting diverse students in school and at home. *The Reading Teacher*, 52(1), 430–444.

Krashen, S. (1985). The input hypothesis. In *The Input Hypothesis: Issue and Implications* (pp. 1–35). London: Longman.

LaBerge, D. & Samuels, S.J. (1974). Towards a theory of automatic information processing in reading. *Cognitive Psychology*, 6(2), 293–323.

Lamme, L.L., Fu, D., Johnson, J. & Savage, D. (2002). Helping kindergarten writers move toward independence. *Early Childhood Education Journal*, 30(2), 73–79.

Lantolf, J.P. & Beckett, T.G. (2009). Sociocultural theory and second language acquisition. *Language Teaching*, 42(4), 459–475.

Leong, D.J. & Bodrova, E. (2012). Assessing and scaffolding make-believe play. *Young Children*, 67(1), 28–34.

Lewis, M. & Ellis, S. (2006). *Phonics: Practice, research and policy*. London: Paul Chapman.

Lloyd, S. & Jolly, C. (1995). *Jolly phonics*. Chigwell: Jolly Learning.

Long, M.H. (1996). The role of the linguistic environment in second language acquisition. In W.C. Ritchie & T.K. Bhatia (Eds.), *Handbook of second language acquisition* (pp. 413–468). San Diego, CA: Academic Press.

Lundberg, I. (1984). *Learning to read: School research newsletter*. Sweden: National Board of Education (August).

MacNamee, G.D. (1987). The social origins of narrative skills. In M. Hickmann (Ed.), *Social and functional approaches to language and thought* (pp. 287–304). Orlando: Academic Press.

McConkie, G.W. & Zola, D. (1987). Two examples of computer-based research on reading: Eye movement monitoring and computer-aided reading. In D. Reinking (Ed.), *Reading and computers: Issues for theory and practice* (pp. 144–158). New York: Teachers College Press.

McEwan, E.K. (2004). *7 strategies of highly effective readers*. Thousand Oaks, CA: Corwin Press.

Meier, T. (2003). "Why can't she remember that?" The importance of storybook reading in multilingual, multicultural classrooms. *The Reading Teacher*, 57, 242–252.

Moats, L.C. (1995). The missing foundation in teacher education. *American Educator* (Special Issue: Learning to Read: Schooling's First Mission), 19(2), 9, 43–51.

Moll, L.C. (2000). Inspired by Vygotsky: Ethnographic experiments in education. In C.D. Lee & P. Smagorinsky (Eds.), *Vygotskian perspectives on literacy research* (pp. 256–268). Cambridge: Cambridge University Press.

Monobe, G., Bintz, W. & McTeer, J. (2017). Developing English language learners' reading confidence with whole-class repeated reading. *The Reading Teacher*, 71(3), 347–350.

Morrow, L.M. & Gambrell, L.B. (2002). Literature-based instruction in the early years. In S.B. Neuman & D.K. Dickinson (Eds.), *Handbook of early literacy research* (pp. 348–360). New York: Guilford.

Moyles, J. (2004). *Just playing? The role and status of play in early childhood education.* Philadelphia, PA: Open University Press.

Muniz-Swicegood, M. (1994). The effects of metacognitive reading strategy training on the reading performance and student reading analysis strategies of third grade bilingual students. *Bilingual Research Journal,* 18(1–2), 83–97.

NAEYC & IRA (International Reading Association) (1998). *Learning to read and write: Developmentally appropriate practices for young children. Joint position statement.* Washington, DC: NAEYC.

National Early Literacy Panel (2008). *Developing early literacy: The report of the National Early Literacy Panel.* Washington, DC: National Institute for Literacy.

NRP (National Reading Panel) (2000). *Teaching children to read: An evidence-based assessment of the scientific research literature on reading and its implications for reading instruction – reports of the sub-groups (National Institute of Health Pub. No. 00-4754).* Washington, DC: National Institute of Child Health and Human Development.

NCCA (National Council for Curriculum and Assessment). (2009). *Aistear: The Early Childhood Curriculum Framework.* Dublin: National Council for Curriculum and Assessment.

Neuman, S. & Roskos, K. (1990). The influence of literacy-enriched play settings on preschoolers' engagement with written language. In S. McCormick & J. Zutell (Eds.), *Literacy theory and research: Analyses from multiple perspectives* (pp. 179–187). Chicago, IL: National Reading Conference.

Nichols, W.D., Rupley, W.H. & Rickleman, R.J. (2004). Examining phonemic awareness and concepts of print patterns of kindergarten students. *Reading Research and Instruction,* 43(3), 61–67.

Oakhill, J., Cain, K. & Yuill, N. (1998). Individual differences in children's comprehension skill: Toward an integrated model. In C. Hulme & R.M. Joshi (Eds.), *Reading and spelling: Development and disorders* (pp. 343–367). London: Erlbaum.

Padak, N. & Rasinski, T (2008). *Evidence-based instruction in reading: A professional development guide to fluency.* Boston, MA: Allyn & Bacon.

Paivio, A. (1971). *Imagery and verbal processes.* New York: Holt, Rinehart & Winston.

Paris, S.G. (2005). Reinterpreting the development of reading skills. *Reading Research Quarterly,* 40(2), 184–202.

Pearson, D. (2001). *Comprehension strategy instruction: An idea whose time has come again.* Paper presented at the annual meeting of the Colorado Council of the International Reading Association, Denver, CO.

Pearson, P.D. (1985). Changing the face of reading comprehension instruction. *The Reading Teacher,* 38(8), 724–738.

Pearson, P.D. & Gallagher, M. (1983). The instruction of reading comprehension. *Contemporary Educational Psychology,* 68, 317–344.

Pena, E.D. & Halle, T.G. (2011). Assessing preschool dual language learners: Travelling a multi-forked road. *Child Development Perspectives,* 5(1), 28–32.

Pepper, J. & Weizman, E. (2004). *It takes two to talk: A practical guide for parents with children with language delays.* Toronto: The Hanen Centre.

Piaget, J. (1962). *Play, dreams and imitation in childhood.* London: Norton & Company.

Pufpaff, L. (2009). A developmental continuum of phonological sensitivity skills. *Psychology in the Schools,* 47(7), 679–691.

Raphael, T.E., Highfield, K. & Au, K. (2006). *QAR now.* New York: Scholastic.

Rasinski, T. (2003). *The fluent reader.* New York: Scholastic.

Rose, J. (2006). *Independent review of the teaching of early reading: Final report*. Available at: www.standards.dfes.gov.uk/rosereview.

Rosenblatt, L.M. (1994). The transactional theory of reading and writing. In R.B. Ruddell, M.R. Ruddell & H. Singer (Eds.), *Theoretical models and processes of reading* (pp. 1363–1398). Newark, DE: International Reading Association.

Roskos, C. & Christie, J. (2012). *Play and literacy in early childhood: Research from multiple perspectives*. London: Routledge.

Routman, R. (1991). *Invitations: Changing as teachers and learners, K–12*. Portsmouth, NH: Heinemann.

Routman, R. (2000). *Conversations: Strategies for teaching, learning and evaluating*. Portsmouth, NH: Heinemann.

Routman, R. (2002). *Reading essentials: The specifics you need to teach reading well*. Portsmouth, NH: Heinemann.

Rumelhart, D.E. (1994). Toward an interactive model of reading. In R.B. Ruddell, M.L. Ruddell & H. Singer (Eds.), *Theoretical models and processes of reading* (4th ed., pp. 1057–1192). Newark, DE: International Reading Association.

Sargent, M. (2015). Let's explore bad guys. *Nursery World*, 5, 18–31.

Singer, D.G., Golinkoff, R.M. & Hirsh-Pasek, K. (Eds.) (2006). *Play = learning: How play motivates and enhances children's cognitive and social-emotional growth*. New York: Oxford University Press.

Singer, D.G. & Singer, J.L. (2009). *Imagination and play in the electronic age*. Cambridge, MA: Harvard University Press.

Sipe, L.R. (2001). Picturebooks as aesthetic objects. *Literacy Teaching and Learning*, 6(1), 23–42.

Skolnick-Weisberg, D., Kitteredge, A.K., Hirsh-Pasek, K., Golinkoff, R.M. & Klahr, D. (2015). Making play work for education. *Phi Delta Kappan*, 96, 8–13.

Snow, C., Burns, S. & Griffin, P. (Eds.) (1998). *Preventing reading difficulties in young children*. Washington, DC: National Academy Press.

Stahl, K.A.D., Stahl, S. & McKenna, M.C. (1999). The development of phonological awareness and orthographic processing in reading recovery. *Literacy teaching and learning: An international journal of early reading and writing*, 4(1), 27–42.

Stahl, S.A. (2003). What do we expect storybook reading to do? How storybook reading impacts word recognition. In A. van Kleeck, S.A. Stahl & E.B. Bauer (Eds.), *On reading books to children: Parents and teachers* (pp. 363–383). Mahwah, NJ: Erlbaum.

Stanovich, K. (1980). Toward an interactive compensatory model of individual differences in the development of reading fluency. *Reading Research Quarterly*, 21, 32–71.

Stanovich, K.E. (1986). Matthew effects in reading: Some consequences of individual differences in the acquisition of literacy. *Reading Research Quarterly*, 21(4), 360–407.

Stanovich, K.E. (1992). Speculations on the causes and consequences of individual differences in early reading acquisition. In P.B. Gough, L.C. Erhi & R. Treiman (Eds.), *Reading acquisition* (pp. 307–342). Hillsdale, NJ: Erlbaum.

Stanovich, K.E. (1993). Romance and reality. *The Reading Teacher*, 47(4), 280–291.

Strickland, D.S. & Morrow, L. (Eds.) (2000). *Beginning reading and writing (language and literacy)*. New York: Teachers College Press.

Swain, M. (1996). Discovering successful second language teaching strategies and practices: From program evaluation to classroom experimentation. *Journal of Multilingual and Multicultural Development*, 17(2–4), 89–113.

Swartz, M. (2005). Playdough: What's standard? *Young Children*, March, pp. 100–109.

Sweet, A.P. & Snow, C. (2002). Reconceptualising reading comprehension. In C.C. Block, L.B. Gambrell & M. Pressley (Eds.), *Improving comprehension instruction: Rethinking research, theory and classroom practice* (pp. 19–53). San Francisco, CA: Wiley & Sons.

Tarman, B. & Tarman, I. (2011). Teachers' involvement in children's play and social interactin. *Ilkogretim Online*, 10(1), 325–337.

Teale, W.H. (1987). Emergent literacy: Reading and writing development in early childhood. In J. Readence & R. Baldwin (Eds.), *Research literacy: Merging perspectives* (pp. 45–74). Rochester, NY: National Reading Conference.

Teale, W.H. (2003). Reading aloud to young children as a classroom instructional activity: Insight from research and practice. In A. van Kleeck, S.A. Stahl & E.B. Bauer (Eds.), *On reading books to children: Parents and teachers* (pp. 114–139). Mahwah, NJ: Erlbaum.

Teodorescu, I. & Addy, L.M. (2001). *Write from the start, book 2: Developing fine motor and perceptual skills for effective handwriting.* London: LDA.

Thornton, L. & Bruton, P. (2010). *Bringing the Reggio approach to your early years practice* (2nd ed.) London: Routledge.

Trabasso, T. & Bouchard, E. (2002). Teaching readers how to comprehend text strategically. In C.C. Block & M. Pressley (Eds.), *Comprehension instruction: Research-based best practices* (pp. 176–200). New York: Guilford Press.

UKLA (United Kingdom Literacy Association) (2005). *Submission to the review of best practice in the early teaching of reading.* Royston: UKLA.

Ur, P. (1996). *A course in language teaching.* Cambridge: Cambridge University Press.

Vygotsky, L.S. (1978). *Mind in society: The development of higher psychological processes.* Cambridge, MA: Harvard University Press.

Walsh, G., Sproule, L., McGuinness, C., Trew, K., Rafferty, H. & Sheey, N. (2006). An appropriate curriculum for 4–5-year-olds in Northern Ireland: Comparing play-based and formal approaches. *Early Years*, 26(2), 201–221.

Waterland, L. (1985). *Read with me: An apprenticeship approach to reading.* Stroud: Thimble Press.

Whitebread, D. & Coltman, P. (2015). *Teaching and learning in the early years* (3rd ed.). London: Routledge.

Whitebread, D., Colton, P., Jameson, H. & Lander, R. (2009). Play, cognition and self-regulation: What exactly are children learning when they learn through play? *Education and Child Psychology*, 26(2), 40–52.

Wilhelm, J. (2001). *Improving comprehension with think-aloud strategies.* Jefferson City, MO: Scholastic.

Wood, E. (2013). Free choice and free play in early childhood education: Troubling the discourse. *International Journal of Early Years Education.* Published online, 2 September. doi:10.1080/09669760.2013.8305623.

Yang, Y. (2013). A qualitative study of teacher's involvement in children's play. *Literacy Information and Computer Education Journal*, 4(4), 1244–1251.

Yeh, S. & Connell, D. (2008). Effects of rhyming, vocabulary and phonemic awareness instruction on phonemic awareness. *Journal of Research in Reading*, 31(2), 243–256.

Yolen, J. & Fusek-Peters, A. (2010). *Here's a little poem.* London: Walker Books.

Yopp, H. (1995). A test for assessing phonemic awareness in young children. *The Reading Teacher*, 49(1), 20–29.

Zimmerman, S. & Hutchins, C. (2003). *7 keys to comprehension: How to help your kids read it and get it!* New York: Random House.

Children's literature cited

Andreae, G. (2010). *ABC: Alphabet rhymes for you and me*. London: Orchard Books.

Anholt, L. (2016). *Leonardo and the flying boy*. London: Frances Lincoln Children's Books.

Blume, J. (2014). *The pain and the great one*. New York: Atheneum.

Browne, A. (2000). *Gorilla*. London: Walker Books.

Browne, A. (2008). *My mum*. London: Walker Books.

Browne, E. (2003). *Handa's hen*. London: Walker Books.

Campbell, R. (2009). *Dear zoo*. London: Macmillan.

Clay, M. (2000). *No shoes*. Portsmouth, NH: Heinemann.

Clay, M. (2015). *Follow me moon*. New York: Scholastic.

Colandro, L. (2003). *There was an old lady who swallowed some snow*. New York: Cartwheel Books.

Cookson, P. (1998). *Unzip your lips: 100 poems to read aloud*. London: Macmillan.

Cookson, P. (2000). *The works: Every poem you'll ever need for the literacy hour*. London: Macmillan.

Cotringer, A. (2013). *Elliot: Midnight superhero*. London: Scholastic.

Dahl, R. (1978). *The enormous crocodile*. London: Puffin Books.

Davies, N. (1997). *Big blue whale*. London: Walker Books.

Donaldson, J. (2003). *The Smartest Giant in Town*. London: Macmillan.

Donaldson, J. (2003). *Room on the broom*. London: Macmillan.

Donaldson, J. (2016). *A squash and a squeeze*. London: Macmillan.

Donaldson, J. & Scheffler, A. (2002). *Monkey puzzle*. London: Macmillan.

Gravett, E. (2007). *Little mouse's big book of fears*. London: Macmillan.

Gray, K. (2009). *Super Daisy and the Peril of Planet Pea*. London: Red Fox Picture Books.

Hayes, S. (2003). *This is the bear*. London: Walker Books.

Hoberman, M. (2007). *You read to me, I'll read to you: Very short stories to read together*. New York: Little, Brown & Company.

Hutchins, P. (2007). *Rosie's walk*. London: Random House.

Ironside, V. (2011). *The huge big bag of worries*. London: Hodder Children's Books.

Kerr, J. (2005). *Mog and the V.E.T.* London: HarperCollins.

Lacome, J. (1995). *Walking through the jungle*. London: Walker Books.

Lee, A.K. (2014). *The ABC's of snowflakes*. Scotts Valley, SC: CreateSpace.

Lewis, J.P. (2012). *The National Geographic book of animal poetry*. San Diego, CA: National Geographic.

MacCaughrean, T. (2007). *The great chase*. London: Rigby Star.

Martin, B. & Archambauld, J. (1995). *Chicka chicka boom boom*. New York: Scholastic.

Mitton, T. & Doyle, M. (1998). *Mr Marvel and the car*. London: Pearson.

Onyefulu, I. (1996). *One big family: Sharing life in an African village*. London: Frances Lincoln Children's Books.

Pfister, M. (2007). *The rainbow fish*. London: North South Books.

Poitis, A. (2008). *Not a box*. London: HarperCollins.

Poitis, A. (2009). *Not a stick*. London: HarperCollins.

Riordan, J. (1998). *The wolf and the kids*. London: Pearson.

Rosen, M. (1996). *We're going on a bear hunt*. London: Walker Books.

Seuss, D. (1996). *There's a wocket in my pocket*. New York: HarperCollins.

Slepian, J. & Seider, A. (2001). *The hungry thing*. New York: Scholastic.

Stoll Walsh, E. (2009). *Mouse shapes*. New York: Houghton Mifflin.

Tauss, M. (2005). *Superhero*. London: Scholastic.

Voce, L. (2000). *Over in the meadow*. London: Candlewick Press.

Waddell, M. (1996). *Farmer duck*. London: Walker Books.

Waddell, M. (1998). *Owl babies*. London: Walker Books.

Waddell, M. (2006). *The pig in the pond*. London: Walker Books.

Windslow, M. (2010). *Mud pies and other recipes*. London: NYRB Children's Collection.

Woody (2000). *I want my mum!* London: Pearson.

Index